# COMMUNICATIONS FLOWS
A Census in the United States and Japan

# INFORMATION RESEARCH AND RESOURCE REPORTS

VOLUME 3

*Editors-in-Chief:*

N. SZYPERSKI

and

F. WINKELHAGE

*Gesellschaft für Mathematik
und Datenverarbeitung mbH Bonn*

NORTH-HOLLAND AMSTERDAM · NEW YORK · OXFORD
UNIVERSITY OF TOKYO PRESS

# COMMUNICATIONS FLOWS
## A Census in the United States and Japan

Ithiel De SOLA POOL
Massachusetts Institute of Technology,
Cambridge, Massachusetts, U.S.A.

Hiroshi INOSE
University of Tokyo, Tokyo, Japan

Nozumo TAKASAKI
Research Institute of Telecommunications
and Economics, Tokyo, Japan

Roger HURWITZ
Massachusetts Institute of Technology,
Cambridge, Massachusetts, U.S.A.

1984

NORTH-HOLLAND AMSTERDAM · NEW YORK · OXFORD
UNIVERSITY OF TOKYO PRESS

© UNIVERSITY OF TOKYO PRESS,
  Tokyo, Japan, 1984

All rights reserved. No part of this publication may be reproduced, stored in a retrieval system, or transmitted, in any form or by any means, electronic, mechanical, photocopying, recording or otherwise, without the prior permission of the copyright owner.

Published jointly by
UNIVERSITY OF TOKYO PRESS

and

ELSEVIER SCIENCE PUBLISHERS B.V.

ISBN: 0 444 87521 2

*Sole distributors for Japan and Asia:*
University of Tokyo Press
7-3-1 Hongo
Bunkyo-ku
Tokyo 113
Japan

*Sole distributors for the U.S.A. and Canada:*
Elsevier Science Publishing Company, Inc.
52 Vanderbilt Avenue
New York, N.Y. 10017
U.S.A.

*Sole distributors for the rest of the world:*
ELSEVIER SCIENCE PUBLISHERS B.V.
P.O. Box 1991
1000 BZ Amsterdam
The Netherlands

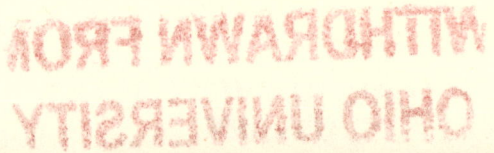

# CONTENTS

List of Tables——*vii*
List of Figures——*viii*
Preface——*xi*

Chapter 1  Introduction——*1*
  1.1  Communications Indicators——*2*
  1.2  Five Indices——*4*
    1.2.1  Measures of Information Flow——*5*
    1.2.2  Measures of Cost——*7*
  1.3  Sources of Data and Data Problems——*8*
    1.3.1  Data Sources——*8*
    1.3.2  Data Problems——*9*
    1.3.3  Some Summary Concerns——*10*

Chapter 2  Some Major Conclusions——*15*
  2.1  The Information Explosion——*16*
  2.2  Demand Is a Function of Cost——*17*
  2.3  Information Overload and the Ratio of Words Supplied to Words Consumed——*20*
  2.4  Arrested Growth of Print Media——*24*
  2.5  The Emergence of Data Communication——*27*

Chapter 3  Some Aggregate Trends——*35*
  3.1  Japanese–American Comparisons——*36*
  3.2  Media Groupings——*41*
    3.2.1  Grand Totals——*42*
    3.2.2  Mass Media Compared to Point-to-Point Media——*50*
    3.2.3  Determinants of Point-to-Point Flows——*52*
    3.2.4  Print vs. Electronic Media——*58*
    3.2.5  Subgroups of Media——*65*
    3.2.6  Office Communications——*67*
    3.2.7  Functions of Communication——*72*

Chapter 4   The Individual Media—*77*
   4. 1   Radio Broadcasting—*78*
   4. 2   Television—*83*
   4. 3   CATV—*85*
   4. 4   Records and Tapes—*89*
   4. 5   Movies—*91*
   4. 6   Education—*93*
   4. 7   Newpapers—*96*
   4. 8   Magazines—*101*
   4. 9   Books—*102*
   4. 10  Direct Mail Advertising—*105*
   4. 11  First Class Mail—*107*
   4. 12  Telephone—*109*
   4. 13  Telex, Telegrams and Mailgrams—*112*
   4. 14  Facsimile—*116*
   4. 15  Data Communication—*118*

Appendix I   American Data Sets—*121*

Appendix II  Information for Work, Living, and Entertainment—*185*

Index—*195*

# List of Tables

2.1 Average Annual Growth Rates in Communication Flows—*16*
2.2 U.S. Costs (in [1972] cents) of Transmitting One Thousand Words—*19*
2.3 Words Consumed as Percent of Words Supplied—*21*
2.4 Change in Balance of Print and Electronic Media—*26*
3.1 Annual Growth Rate in Per Capita Supply and Consumption—*42*
3.2 Japanese per Capita Annual Flow as Percentage of Comparable U.S. Figures—*47*
3.3 Some "Hard" Indicators—*48*
3.4 Composition of the Aggregate Flows by Media—*49*
3.5 American and Japanese Growth Rates for Mass and Point-to-Point Media—*52*
3.6 Point-to-Point Transmission as Percent of Total Flow—*52*
3.7 Growth Rates in 1970s Compared to Full Period—*52*
3.8 Changes in the Composition of the Aggregate Flows for Mass and Point-to-Point Media—*60*
3.9 Growth Rates of Print and Electronic Media since 1960—*63*
3.10 Most Recent Data on Growth Rates of Print and Electronic Media—*63*
3.11 Mail among the Print Media—*66*
3.12 Point-to-Point Media among Electronic Media—*66*
4.1 Volume of Production of Words by Medium in Japan—*79*
4.2 Volume Consumption of Words by Medium in Japan—*79*
4.3 TV Growth Rates—*84*
4.4 TV Viewing Time—*84*
4.5 Per Annum Growth Rates in Words Supplied by Magazines—*102*
4.6 Annual Growth Rates in Book Use—*103*

# List of Figures

2.1  Volume and Costs of Communication by Media——*18*
2.2  Supply and Consumption per Capita of All Media——*19*
2.3  Costs of Production and Consumption of Media: Japan, 1975 ——*20*
2.4  Growth Rates in Words Consumed——*23*
2.5  Growth Rates of Print Media in Japan——*25*
3.1  Volume Supplied, All Media——*44*
3.2  Volume Consumed, All Media——*44*
3.3  Supply per Capita, All Media——*45*
3.4  Consumption per Capita, All Media——*45*
3.5  Supply per Capita——*51*
3.6  Consumption of Mass Media——*51*
3.7  Supply of Point-to-Point Media——*53*
3.8  Domestic Information Flow and GDP: Japan——*54*
3.9  Domestic Information Flow and GDP: U.S.A.——*55*
3.10 Japan–U.S. Information Flow——*56*
3.11 U.S.–Japan Information Flows and Foreign Trade——*57*
3.12 Share of Communication Media in U.S.–Japan Communication ——*59*
3.13 Share of Media, Excluding Mail, in U.S.–Japan Communication ——*59*
3.14 Electronic and Print Supply, U.S.A.——*64*
3.15 Electronic and Print Supply, Japan——*64*
3.16 Electronic and Print Media Consumed per Capita——*65*
3.17 Growth Rates: Mail vs. Electronic Point-to-Point Media——*67*
3.18 Per Capita Supply of Information by Function, U.S.A.——*75*
4.1  Words Supplied by Each Mass Medium: Japan——*80*
4.2  Words Consumed from Each Mass Medium: Japan——*80*
4.3  Words Supplied by Point-to-Point Media: Japan——*81*
4.4  Broadcasting Trends, U.S.A.——*86*
4.5  Broadcasting per Capita, Japan and U.S.A.——*86*
4.6  Broadcasting Costs, U.S.A.——*87*
4.7  TV Costs, U.S.A.——*87*
4.8  Trends in Movies and Records & Tapes, U.S.A.——*90*
4.9  Movies per Capita, U.S.A. and Japan——*92*
4.10 Movie, Record & Tape Costs, U.S.A.——*92*

LIST OF FIGURES ix

4.11 Trends in Education——*95*
4.12 Education Costs, U.S.A.——*95*
4.13 Newspaper Trends, U.S.A.——*98*
4.14 Newspapers per Capita, Japan and U.S.A.——*98*
4.15 Newspaper Costs, U.S.A.——*99*
4.16 Newsprint Price Index 1970–1977——*99*
4.17 Other Print Mass Media, U.S.A.——*104*
4.18 Other Print Mass Media per Capita——*104*
4.19 Magazine, Book, Direct Mail Costs, U.S.A.——*106*
4.20 First Class Mail and Telephone, U.S.A.——*110*
4.21 Mail and Phone per Capita, U.S.A. and Japan——*110*
4.22 Mail and Phone Production Costs, U.S.A.——*111*
4.23 Mail and Phone Transmission Costs, U.S.A.——*111*
4.24 Trends in Telegraphic Media, U.S.A.——*114*
4.25 Per Capita Telegraphic Trends——*114*
4.26 Telegraphic Costs, U.S.A.——*115*
4.27 Facsimile and Data Costs, U.S.A.——*115*
4.28 Per Capita Facsimile Trends, Japan and U.S.A.——*117*
4.29 Facsimile and Data Communications, U.S.A.——*117*

# PREFACE

We are living in an age of information explosion on the one hand and information dearth on the other. In the developed part of the free world, concerns have been voiced about generation of information in a volume which is far greater than can possibly be consumed. In other areas, including the developing part of the world, the concept known as the "new world information order" has emerged that urges strengthening of local information resources and balancing transborder flow of information. Quantitative evaluation on the amount of information being generated and consumed, however, has never been carried out on a global scale covering various forms of electronic and non-electronic media. Without knowing the quantity of information supply and consumption, the notion of information-rich or information-poor can be no more than a naive emotional feeling.

In particular, the understanding of an information explosion based upon quantitative evaluation seems to be crucial for the United States and Japan, which are major information suppliers and consumers in the world. Such studies may also influence other countries to conduct similar research, and through a concerted global effort the information flow census may be recognized as an important social indicator for information-oriented societies. This was the motivation behind a U.S.–Japan collaborative study that brought the present volume into existence.

More specifically, the first author of this book, while on sabbatical at the Research Institute of Telecommunications and Economics in Japan, found an earlier study of communications flows by the Japanese Ministry of Posts and Telecommunications. He proposed an improved methodology and suggested that another attempt be made in the United States and Japan, as a part of a collaborative study program of the Massachusetts Institute of Technology and the University of Tokyo.

The present study could not have been completed without the

dedicated efforts of the participants who collected and analyzed an enormous amount of data. It would likewise have been impossible without the generous cooperation of many institutions which provided us a large amount of their own data. In particular, the authors wish to express their heartiest gratitude to Ms. Sophia Wang, Mr. Richard Fryling, Ms. Anne Fryling, Mr. Gavan Duffy, Professor Tadao Saito and Mr. Takahiro Ozawa for their significant contributions. The authors likewise wish to acknowledge the cooperation of many communications research institutes and scholars that tabulated the basic data for the different media and answered our many and often difficult questions. These include Messrs. Joseph Alterman of the National Association of Theatre Owners; Howard Anderson and David Mack of the Yankee Group; A. C. Barry of the New England Telephone Co.; Leo Bogart, Ted Knecht and Joseph Wallis of the Newspaper Advertising Bureau; Herbert Dordick of the University of Southern California; David Forney and Robert Stearns of the Codex Corp.; F. Gerald Kline of the University of Michigan; Delbert Staley of NYNEX; Sanborn Associates; Evelyn Woods Reading Dynamics; Kenneth Costa of the Radio Advertising Bureau; Roger Carman of Western Union, Michihiko Ito of the Nippon Telegraph and Telephone Public Corporation and Sei Kageyama of the Kokusai Denshin Denwa Co.

The financial support provided by the John and Mary Markle Foundation, the Xerox Corporation, the Japan Society for the Promotion of Science and the Nippon Telegraph and Telephone Public Corporation are gratefully acknowledged. The authors also wish to acknowledge with thanks the support through the Grant-in-Aid for Scientific Research of the Japanese Ministry of Education, Science and Culture for the publication of this volume. Last but not least, the authors wish to thank Suzanne Wethered and Nancy Wilson for their preparation of the manuscript, and Susan Schmidt and Megumi Shimizu of the University of Tokyo Press for their editorial assistance.

January 31, 1984

Ithiel de Sola Pool
Hiroshi Inose
Nozomu Takasaki
Roger Hurwitz

# Chapter 1
# INTRODUCTION

## 1.1 Communications Indicators

Everyone talks about an "information explosion" and "information overload." Such phrases imply measures of communications. Yet until recently the only figures that could be cited about these were non-comparable statistics about individual media. In the U.S., Nielsen, and in Japan, Video Research report TV audiences; while newspaper circulation figures are compiled in the U.S. by Ayers and the Publishers' Annual and by the Japan Newspaper Editors and Publishers' Association. Hundreds of commercial services and reference manuals estimate the annual size and growth of particular media. But can one add up such apples and oranges to make a statement about the flow of information in a society?

This is a special case of the classic problem of index number formation. We are asking for a social indicator that combines a viewer watching TV, a student in a classroom, a reader of Dostoyevsky, and a clerk at an airline computer terminal. We are asking for an index that sums these up and provides a number that measures the common thing that they all are doing: consuming information.

Such index numbers are always faulty, but they are often useful. The unemployment index counts equally a head of a family who was just fired and a youth who files for a possible job while still attending high school, but it may not count a discouraged incompetent who has not worked for ten years and has given up actively looking. The cost of living index measures the price of a market basket, but whose market basket? In the U.S. it was criticized for including the cost of purchasing a house (which very few people do in any given year), but it could be equally criticized if it did not include housing. We have no illusions that we can avoid such problems with a comunications measure. Still, if we design an index number for the flow of information with some care and skill, it may tell us something.

What are the apples and oranges that we must combine to make up an indicator of communication? They are the different media through which people communicate, e.g. books, telephone calls, radio, magazines, etc. In this study we have collected data on:

Radio
TV
CATV
Records and tapes (U.S. only)
Movies
Education in the classroom
Newspapers
Magazines
Books
Phone books (Japan only)
Direct mail
First class mail
Telephone
Telex
Telegrams
Mailgrams (U.S. only)
Facsimile
Data communication

How can we put them together? What common denominator do they have? They all transmit words, so words may provide an obvious index. The very thought may seem ludicrous. Every word is certainly not of equal merit. Barely audible words crooned as background music from the radio are not equivalent to "In the beginning was the word" on the first page of a great book.

An index number may nonetheless be defended against such a phenomenological critique. First of all, an index number reports mass phenomena: the law of large numbers washes out many individual differences. The index creator must still be ware of systematic differences that make for differences in averages. Such differences require that one complicate the index. Price indices and unemployment indices are not the same things they were 50 years ago. They have been refined and re-refined. Tens of millions of dollars have been spent on their improvement—showing both that they are considered useful and that there is much to be done toward their improvement. Lifelong careers have been devoted to the task. Not only have the indices been improved; they have also been multiplied. There is not just one unemployment index in the United States; there are eight, so as to measure separately the different concepts of who is genuinely

4 INTRODUCTION

unemployed. Similarly, there are different measures of the cost of living in the city and on the farm, of industrial workers and of the middle class, of people who live alone and of large families, and so on.

The indices that we will be presenting are new and therefore crude ones. They are not, however, totally new. A pioneer attempt at a total census of communications flows was made in Japan under the guidance of Tetsuro Tomita at the Ministry of Posts and Telecommunications.[1] That work was our inspiration. Yet that census, as its own creators recognized, had flaws. The originators did it a second time, improving the methodology. At that point the first author of the present study happened to be on sabbatical at the Research Institute of Telecommunications and Economics in Japan and suggested that a third attempt be made, this time in both the United States and Japan.

The methodology was thus revised once more. The earlier efforts had attempted to include pictures and music in the index, assigning them values in numbers of words. We felt such conversions to be beyond the state of the art; indeed it strains the limits of audacity to throw all explicit words together. We do lose much in excluding non-verbal communications, but we do not know how to include them in a meaningful way.

## 1.2  Five Indices

The earlier efforts of Mr. Tomita and his team produced not one index but several, designed for different purposes. We follow their lead. The reader will find below separate indices for the volume of information supplied and for the volume of information consumed. He will also find separate indices of the cost of production, transmission, and consumption of information. Clear-

---

1) Summaries in English are "The Volume of Information Flow and the Quantum Evaluation of Media," *Telecommunication Journal*, Vol. 42, No. 6, 1975, pp. 339–349; "Volume of Information Flow; Quantum Evaluation of Media," Dentsu's *Japan Marketing Advertising*, 1972–3, pp. 100–107. The full report, "Information Census Flow," was published by the Ministry of Posts and Telecommunications, Japan, 1975. The M.P.T. studies implemented an approach developed at the Keizai Kikaku Kyokai (Association for Economic Planning) around 1969. Cf. Yoichi Ito, "The 'Johoka Shakai' Approach to the Study of Communication in Japan," in G. Cleveland Wilhoit and Harold de Bock, eds., *Mass Communication Review Yearbook*, Vol. 2, Beverly Hills, Calif.: Sage, 1981, p. 680.

ly, there is no one index that can serve all purposes.

Measures of the flow of words can be made at four levels. First, there is the act of authoring: each word in a newly composed statement would be counted once if we were measuring that. Second, there is the act of publishing. In a count of words published, the same words would be counted twice if they were published twice, as in different newspapers or different reprints, but the count would not include the number of exemplars that reached individuals. A third level is what we have called words supplied: not only is the number of times a word has been published counted, but also the number of individuals to whom each exemplar has been made available. And the fourth level is words consumed—namely, how many words individuals choose to absorb. Our study deals only with the third and fourth levels: words supplied and consumed.

### 1.2.1 Measures of Information Flow

The concept of volume of words *consumed* focuses on the reader, or viewer, or listener, and asks what he or she takes in. A newspaper may be at hand, but if it is unread, its words are not consumed. Thus the basic data on words consumed come from measures of the behavior of the audience members: how much time they spend using a medium and how much they absorb per unit of time.

The concept of volume of words *supplied* starts with the publisher, or producer, or letter-writer, and asks how much he puts out that is available to the audience, whether or not the audience members choose to attend to it. Thus if the publisher of a newspaper has delivered a paper to a home with four residents (over 10 years old), we count every word in that paper, times four, as having been supplied. The words are there if the residents wish to attend to them.

The same distinction can be made for television. In counting TV words consumed, we take account of the fact that attention by a viewer during the daily three hours or so that the average viewer watches is limited to one TV station at a time. On the other hand, we count as volume supplied all those words that were broadcast in the reception area of each set during the whole 24 hours. So if there was one station before, and a second is added (broadcasting just as many hours), the volume supplied is doubled, though the habits of the viewer, and thus his consumption of TV, probably remain unchanged.

The data on words supplied and words consumed derive from quite independent sets of observations. The data on words consumed come from time budgets and other studies of the behavior of the audience. Data on words supplied derive from circulation figures or other such data on publishing. Very different trends are observed in the resulting data.

The distinction between words supplied and words consumed is central to the notion of information overload. There are physiological and psychological limits to the words a person is able to consume. There are no such limits to the words that communications technology can supply. The existence of the word "overload" implies something about the ratio of words supplied to words consumed.

The distinction between words consumed and supplied cannot be applied in practice to all media. For example, we have no data that enable us to distinguish the number of words spoken by one party from the number of words heard by the other during a phone call. There is undoubtedly some loss due to inattention and noise, but we know of no existing measure for it. Nor is the loss great enough to have motivated us try to measure it ourselves. For the telephone we take the words produced and the words consumed as identical numbers.

In this study we have followed that practice for all "point-to-point" media. The distinction between consumption and supply is made only for mass media. In a point-to-point medium, be it a letter or telegram or phone call, the motivation of the parties at each end to pay attention is sufficient that deliberate inattention is relatively small (and in any case unmeasured), and the sender does not normally have the time or resources to send vast amounts of material that will not be read or heard. A mass medium, on the other hand does exactly that. It pours words out to the audience in the hope that they will deign to pay attention to some of them. In fact they pay attention to only a small part, and so for mass media it is essential to make the distinction between volume consumed and volume supplied.

The mass media on our list were:

> Radio
> TV
> CATV
> Records and tapes (U.S. only)
> Movies
> Education in the classroom
> Newspapers
> Magazines
> Books
> Direct mail
> Phone books (Japan only)

The point-to-point media on our list were:

> First class mail
> Telephone calls
> Telex
> Telegrams
> Mailgrams (U.S. only)
> Facsimile
> Data communication

### 1.2.2 Measures of Cost

We distinguish (a) production costs, (b) transmission costs, and (c) consumption costs. Production costs are the costs of producing messages, up to the point at which they are ready to be sent. Such costs do not depend on whether or not the messages get sent. Production costs include the costs of writing a book or a letter, the costs of producing a TV program, the costs of assembling and editing the news for a newspaper.

Transmission costs, in our definition, are costs of distributing messages, once they have been composed. Typically, but not always, these are variable costs, depending on the size of the audience reached. They include the costs of printing newspapers and the costs of the ink and newsprint as well as the delivery costs. They include the capital costs of a TV transmitter as well as its operating costs. They include the costs of telephone calls or of postage or of telegrams.[2]

Consumption costs we define as investments that the receiver

---

2) In the Japanese study only transmission costs were tabulated.

has to make to put himself in the position to receive messages, but not including the variable costs of paying for individual messages. Consumption costs include the purchase and repair of radio or TV sets and the cost of a computer terminal, but not the subscription to a magazine or newspaper, which is covered in the transmission costs.

Distinguishing these three types of costs is important because different industries are organized in different ways and put the burden of costs in different places. Statistics are usually compiled for organizations which pay for them, so the records kept for different industries are likely to report different parts of the total cost, according to the clients' needs. The post office, for example, keeps financial records on what it spends in delivering letters, but it is not concerned with what it costs for someone to type the letter in the first place. On the other hand, a newspaper considers composition a part of its budget. Unless one distinguishes carefully and compares media in parallel fashion, comparative assertions about costs across media may be nonsense.

For each medium we compiled separate time series for

- volume of words consumed in millions per annum
- volume of words produced in millions per annum
- cost of production per annum
- cost of transmission per annum
- cost of consumption per annum

The Japanese data were compiled for 1960, 1965, 1970, and 1975. The U.S. data were compiled for each year from 1960 through 1980.

## 1.3 Sources of Data and Data Problems

### 1.3.1 Data Sources

The data that we use in this census derive mostly from published sources. We used ratings reports for broadcasts, circulation figures for publications, annual reports of postal administrations and carriers, census data on underlying population figures, etc. Much of the data that we would like to have had did not exist. The earlier Japanese study done by the Ministry of Posts and Telecommunications could sometimes solve that problem by asking for data, with the authority of government. The U.S.

effort had no such power, and we also lacked the resources to do sample surveys in the field.

In some instances, we did collect raw data for critical constants that, as far as we could tell, did not previously exist. Usually, when data had not previously been collected, there was no way in 1979 to go back and reconstruct a time series since 1960. But sometimes the figure we needed was one that was not likely to change very much over a couple of decades, and could be estimated as a constant by using a reasonable sample. For example, how many pages does the average American book have? Not finding any authoritative estimate of that, we turned to sampling the Boston Public Library. Similarly, we found no estimate of the number of words spoken per radio minute (whether on talk shows or in music). So we taped random minutes off the air for a full day, moving from station to station, and then counted. In similar fashion we made a count of spoken words for TV and another one for written words on the screen, of which there were surprisingly many. Commercials, of course, were included. Our sample revealed 131 oral and 22 written words a minute on the TV screen.

In a few instances corporations, trade associations, or institutions helped us by making informed estimates of such matters as relative reliability of different estimates of computer data flows. Wherever we rely on informed estimates, that is indicated in the footnotes, along with all data sources used.

## 1.3.2 Data Problems

None of our data are totally reliable, and, what is more troublesome, the quality of the data varies from item to item. We are deeply conscious of the inadequacy of some of the source data. There are gaps in information on some of the largest and most studied media. Perhaps the most troubling one is the lack of good estimates of trends in the time people spend reading. The electronic media, because they have no proof of the delivery of a copy, have developed elaborate systems of diaries and ratings to show would-be advertisers what attention they are getting. The print media generally rely on statistics of delivered copies, and rarely do research on the actual reading done by the receivers of the copies. Sporadic studies report reading time and attention, but there are hardly any time series.

*10* INTRODUCTION

Another problem concerns the newest and most rapidly growing medium of communication, data communication over networks of computers. Time series for data communication could not be generated for this study in quite the same way as were the series for the other media. For one thing, the medium is so new that adequate reporting of traffic does not yet exist. No one has created a measurement system. A second problem in estimating the volume of data communications is that while data on a network flows "point-to-point," it does not necessarily flow "person-to-person" in the same way that all the other "point-to-point" media do. It may flow between machines and no person may be involved. Who is the consumer?

A third kind of data problem is illustrated by radio ratings, namely the problem of time series discontinuity in the U.S. When TV took most of the national advertising away from radio, and radio network broadcasting largely disappeared, the money available for radio rating research shriveled. Only a few firms continued to do that work, and the methods they could afford to use were limited. From 1960 to 1963 the most useful data in the U.S. were collected by A.C. Nielsen, but it stopped its radio ratings in 1965. In that year the Arbitron Company began surveys of the radio audience, but since 1974 the Radio Advertising Bureau has been the most important data collector. The methodologies used by these researchers were not identical, nor did the resulting figures overlap. Such discontinuities in methods of data collection arise all too frequently.

### 1.3.3 Some Summary Concerns

While there are data problems for every single medium, the trends that we find are likely to be more robust in most cases than the absolute figures. This is so because the same methodology and therefore the same biases are usually present in successive years even though there are occasional points of discontinuity. But what are these consistent biases; do we have some evidence of them?

If we add together the minutes of consumption of each medium by an average American individual in 1977, we come to a little over eight hours a day (489 minutes), and to slightly less than eight hours for average daily mass media consumption (473 minutes). That is up from nearly six and a half hours (384 minutes) in 1965 for mass media consumption. These seem surprisingly high numbers in comparison both to the available hours in the day and to other studies. A 1965 time budget study using diaries found only four hours and six minutes a day of use of all media; a repeat study found that had risen by 1975 to four hours and 39 minutes.[3] This latter estimate is somewhat on the low side of most current studies. Virtually all studies of TV viewing report that the average American spends something like three hours per day with the TV set (Robinson reported two hours and 46 minutes in 1975). The radio tends to be on, at least in the background, for a couple of hours (Robinson claims only just over one hour), and newspaper reading takes something on the order of a half hour. These total five and one-half hours. But there are also other media, for example the classroom included in our data, that most studies do not count. Nevertheless, one wonders whether the average person can find seven or eight hours a day to spend with the media. Five, even six hours a day would not surprise us, but seven or eight hours is puzzling.

To resolve this puzzle one must realize that much of the time that one medium is in use, another may also be in use. People report in their time-budget diaries that they read with the radio or TV on; they phone with these on; they even have the radio and TV on at the same time. So our figures for each medium are not truly additive. There are no good estimates of simultaneous media use, though a reanalysis of the raw Robinson Michigan data could produce some. The published figures divide media usage into primary use and secondary use; the latter was 46% in 1965 and 41% in 1975. But these secondary uses could themselves be secondary to such other diary entries as eating, commuting, or dressing. If we guess that 20 or 25% of media use occurs during the concurrent use of two media, then total time spent on media would be 10 or 12% less than the eight hours a day which results from adding up all figures for an individual.

It is also possible that there are biases toward overestimation in most of the major reporting series. First, despite all the care

---

3) John P. Robinson, *How Americans Used Time in 1965*, Ann Arbor: Univ. of Michigan, Institute of Social Research, 1977. For the comparative international study see Alexander Szalai, *et. al.*, *Use of Time*, The Hague: Mouton, 1972. Robinson's 1975 figures are reported in *Changes in Americans' Use of Time: 1965–1975*, Cleveland: Cleveland State University Communications Research Center, 1976.

which social science researchers take to control against wishful results and other errors, there is no doubt that more often than not research results, when they err, are biased in a direction that pleases the sponsor. For all the care taken, public opinion pollsters working for political parties are more likely to err in overstimating their clients' vote than in underestimating it. Market researchers are more likely to be overly optimistic than overly pessimistic. This systematic bias is generally not due to malignancy or fraud. It is the product of many subtle pressures. Even when attempts are made to hide the identity of the client from the field data collectors and respondents, those persons in the field often know or suspect the nature of the client. Second, there is the fact that the very subject of a study may enhance its seeming importance: a study of magazines, for example, makes one think more about magazine reading. Finally, there is a process of selective reporting. If there is more than one plausible index that comes out of the data, the one selected for publication may be the one that is more useful to the client. Furthermore, if complex indices are compounded from other indices, the error in the original index may grow.

For all these reasons, it would not be surprising if the sum of what each medium reports in data series on its audience turns out to be a high estimate. Perhaps the cautious reader of this report who happens to be interested in absolute levels of media use, rather than trends, should discount the figures he finds by 10% or even 20%. It may be that we do not spend quite as much time with the media as the media claim. But even if that is true, the general order of magnitude of media use is impressive, and so is the rate of growth.

Subtracting perhaps an hour or so from the eight that our separate series add up to because of simultaneous use of two media, and subtracting another hour or so for possible reporting bias, brings us down toward a range of use of media that seems plausible for the population as a whole. The 36 million people (20% of the over-10 population) who do clerical, professional, or managerial work in offices spend on average an additional 33 minutes a day reading and another hour and 13 minutes a day meeting and phoning.[4] We lack adequate bases to estimate

---

4) Xerox Office Profile (unpublished).

comparable figures for the millions of teachers, blue collar and service workers who read and discuss on the job.[5] For the population as whole Robinson has an estimate of 55 minutes a day in conversation and visiting as a primary activity in 1965, and 49 minutes in 1975; it is cited as a secondary activity for 236 minutes in 1965 and 140 minutes in 1975. If we add in all these items—which are not in our reported data—then (allowing still for simultaneous uses of media of communication) it does seem that the average American may spend 9 or 10 hours a day communicating in one way or another.

We have digressed into these rough estimates of time spent communicating because the thoughtful reader of what follows is bound to ask for them. Our objective, however, is not to make such estimates of totals; it is to compare trends in different kinds of media. Since an inquisitive reader, however, will want to use the data to come up with such overall estimates, we present what may help him or her in thinking through the implications of our data and warn against traps in simple additions of our reported time series.

---

5) Cf. also A. Sharon, *Reading Activities of American Adults* (Princeton: Educational Testing Service, 1972), on reading at work for blue collar and service workers in the early 1970s.

# Chapter 2
# SOME MAJOR CONCLUSIONS

## 16 SOME MAJOR CONCLUSIONS

While differences exist, a common picture of the new information society emerges from the Japanese and American data. We find in both an information explosion, a growing overload of messages for humans to absorb, and an evolution of traffic that is largely shaped by costs. Therefore growth is mainly in electronic media, while media produced by conventional printing processes tend to stagnate.

### 2.1 The Information Explosion

An explosive growth in communications supplied is the first thing one notes in the data.

Words supplied by all media combined grew in the U.S. at a rate substantially higher than the Gross Domestic Product and in Japan at a rate parallel with the remarkable growth of that country's whole economy.[1] As a result, the words made available to the average American by the media which we tabulated added up in 1980 to nearly 11 million a day. Of these about 48,000 were absorbed. (In the U.S. in 1975 words supplied were 8.7 million a day, of which 45,000 were actually taken in.) In Japan in 1975, about 1.5 million words were supplied per individual per day, while average daily consumption approximated 23,000 words.

In the United States during the latter part of the two decades the rate of growth slowed down, something which had not yet happened by 1975 in Japan. In the U.S. words supplied grew

**Table 2.1**
AVERAGE ANNUAL GROWTH RATES IN COMMUNICATION FLOWS

|  | U.S.A. 1960–1980 | Japan 1960–1975 |
|---|---|---|
| Words supplied | 8.4% | 9.7% |
| Words consumed | 3.2 | 3.8 |
| Real GDP (US), GNP (Japan) | 3.7 | 9.9 |

1) The observant reader will note repeated discrepancies between the figures reported for U.S.-Japanese comparisons in the earlier chapters and those presented in Chapter 4, which deal directly with the Japanese results. The reason is that the methodologies used by the research teams in the two countries could not be quite identical. For the comparative discussions we usually adjust the Japanese figures for consistency with the American team's methodology. In Chapter 4 and in other places (where noted), the Japanese results are presented as originally reported.

at only 5.9% from 1975 to 1980 compared to a GDP growth rate of 3.4%. The key explanatory factor was trends in broadcasting, both for the rapid growth in words supplied earlier and for the slowdown of growth in the U.S. in the most recent years. During the past two decades, radio and TV have overwhelmingly dominated the flow of words. In America in 1960 they supplied 92% of all the mediated words available to the public and in 1980, almost 98%. For those two media the 1960–1980 growth rate was 8.7% and the 1975–1980 growth rate was 6.0%. The other 15 media tabulated, taken all together, grew only at a rate of 3.2% from 1960 to 1980, but at a rate of 5.2% in the last five years.

In Japan, broadcasting, which diffused just a few years later than in the U.S., supplied 84% of the mediated words in 1960 and 91% in 1975. The non-broadcast media grew only slightly over half as fast as did radio and TV.

Such facts caution us about dealing with aggregate figures alone. For the 1950s, 1960s, and early 1970s the information explosion was largely the growth of broadcasting. The number of American radio and TV broadcasting stations grew from 4,865 in 1960 to 9,426 in 1977. That, multiplied by such other factors as the growth in sets, was the key to the growing supply of broadcast material.

## 2.2 Demand Is a Function of Cost

Broadcasting in recent years has not only been the medium of maximum absolute growth and maximum volume, but also the medium of most profligate distribution. Broadcast words are cheap. Transmission costs for TV and radio in the U.S. in 1980 were two thousandths and two ten-thousandths of a cent, respectively, per thousand words. Compared to television, transmission costs for newspapers were 30 times higher and for books, 400 times more. Mailed and telephoned words were 10,000 times as expensive to transmit. Figures 2.1 to 2.3 and Table 2.2 illustrate the extent to which cheapness contributes to the growth of a medium. Those media, such as telegraphy, which are costly per word have grown little in use or have even declined, while those media in which it is inexpensive to supply additional words

18  SOME MAJOR CONCLUSIONS

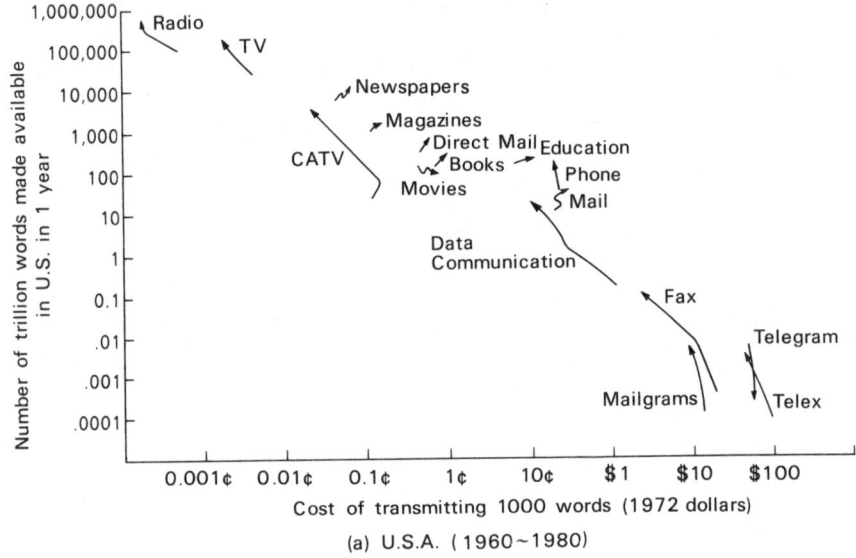

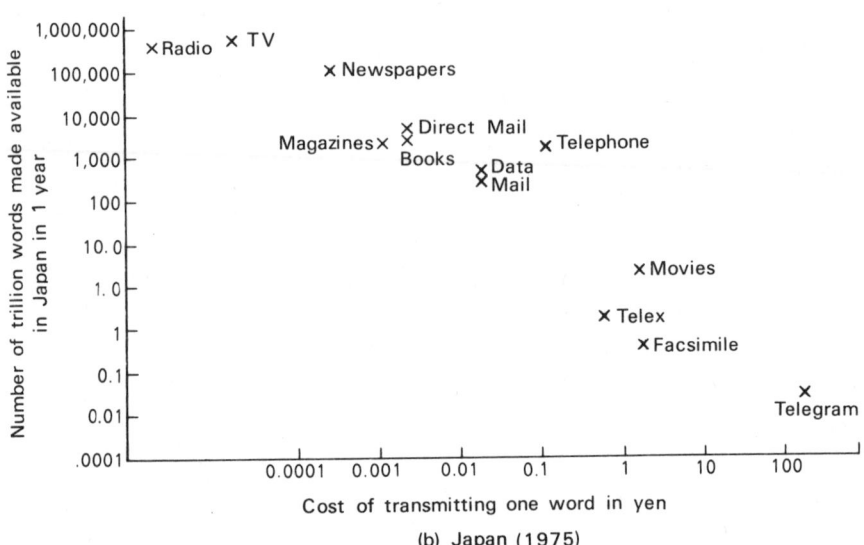

**Figure 2.1**
VOLUME AND COSTS OF COMMUNICATION BY MEDIA
(Plotted on log by log scales)

**Table 2.2**
U.S. COSTS (IN [1972] CENTS) OF TRANSMITTING
ONE THOUSAND WORDS

|  | 1960 | 1980 |
|---|---|---|
| Radio | 0.0005 | 0.0002 |
| TV | 0.005 | 0.002 |
| CATV | 0.13 | 0.025 |
| Records & tapes | NA | 74.8 |
| Movies | 0.48 | 0.57 |
| Education | 6.5 | 14.5 |
| Newspapers | 0.053 | 0.058 |
| Magazines | 0.16 | 0.18 |
| Books | 0.74 | 1.0 |
| Direct mail | 0.51 | 0.59 |
| First class mail | 19.0 | 24.6 |
| Telephone | 23.1 | 19.0 |
| Telex | 9,354 | 4,095* |
| Telegrams | 5,008 | 5,515* |
| Mailgrams | nonexistent | 1,033* |
| Facsimile | 1,914 | 221 |
| Data | 129 | 10 |

* For 1979.

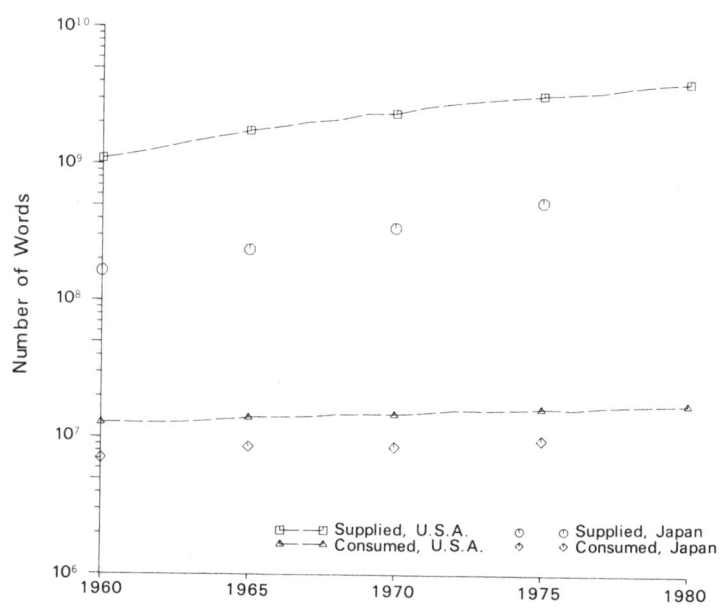

**Figure 2.2**
SUPPLY AND CONSUMPTION PER CAPITA OF ALL MEDIA

## 20 SOME MAJOR CONCLUSIONS

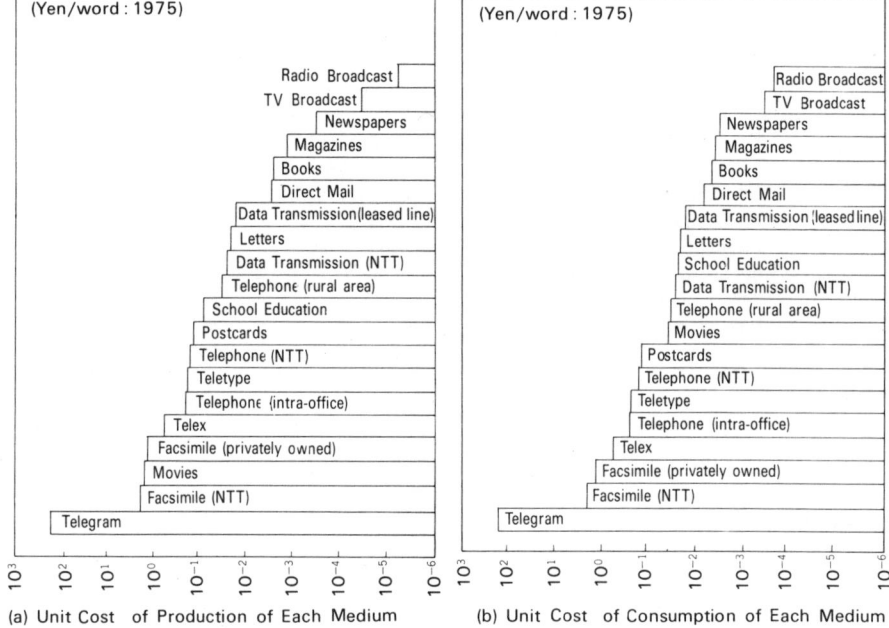

(a) Unit Cost of Production of Each Medium
(Original data with no household factor applied)

(b) Unit Cost of Consumption of Each Medium

**Figure 2.3**
COSTS OF PRODUCTION AND CONSUMPTION OF
MEDIA: JAPAN, 1975

have exploded in volume of words supplied.[2]

Media in which words are expensive to deliver, such as point-to-point media, tend to be paid for by the users and delivered only in the volume actually consumed. As cheaper media come along, some expensive media like telegraphy are displaced. As with other commodities, the cost of words controls their use.

## 2.3 Information Overload and the Ratio of Words Supplied to Words Consumed

There has been no explosion in words consumed. The growth

---

2) Since Japanese costs of transmission were calculated on a different basis and were not time series, they should not be directly compared to the U.S. data, but they show the same relationships in intermedia comparisons.

**Table 2.3**
WORDS CONSUMED AS PERCENT OF WORDS SUPPLIED

|  | U.S.A. | | Japan | |
| --- | --- | --- | --- | --- |
|  | 1960 | 1980 | 1960 | 1975 |
| Radio | 0.3% | 0.1% | 1.5% | 0.2% |
| TV | 2.5 | 0.9 | 3.2 | 1.4 |
| CATV | 0.2 | 0.7 | 2.6 | 3.8 |
| Movies | 9.1 | 11.0 | 11.2 | 5.9 |
| Education | 91.0 | 93.0 | NA | NA |
| Newspapers | 3.8 | 2.0 | 6.9 | 4.0 |
| Magazines | 5.2 | 5.0 | 12.2 | 8.4 |
| Books | 45.6 | 34.8 | 48.6 | 22.7 |
| Direct mail | 0.5 | 0.5* | 14.9 | 19.3 |

* Volume consumed estimated as a constant of words supplied.

in consumption has been far less than the growth in supply. For the whole period from 1960, the overall rate of increase in words consumed via all media grew only 3.2% per annum in the U.S.A. and 3.8% in Japan, just over one-third the rate of growth in words supplied. Furthermore, part of the growth in consumption is accounted for by growth in the consuming population. The American population during the period of our measurements grew by 1.6% per annum, leaving growth in per capita consumption of words at 1.6%. The number of Japanese grew by 1.3% per annum, so their per capita consumption of words grew by 2.5% per annum.

It is noteworthy that any per capita growth in consumption of words exists at all, particularly since a steady growth *rate* would indicate that people are devoting increasingly larger amounts of their time to such consumption. Given the physiological limits on human performance and the physical limit of 24 hours in a day, one might have anticipated constancy in the words people consume. How can we account for the rather robust if modest continuing growth in the communications that people actually take in?

Five explanations may be suggested, though our data do not help us choose among them. First of all, growing leisure allows more time for media use. Second, increased levels of education may raise the average interest of the population in media and also raise their efficiency in media use: presumably educated

## 22 SOME MAJOR CONCLUSIONS

persons consume more words in a day than less educated ones.[3] In the third place, the growth rate may reflect a shift of communication from face-to-face conversation, which we do not measure in this study, to communication that comes through measured media.[4] Fourth, as discussed previously, people use some media concurrently; the growth in consumption may reflect the increase in such usage. Finally, up to some limit, which may well lie in the future, it may be possible for the pace of life to intensify and for people to do more in the same few hours a day.

Whatever the reasons may be, consumption of communications is growing, albeit slowly. This trend is less overwhelmingly accounted for by broadcasting than is the trend noted above in supply. However the consumption of radio and television did grow faster overall than the aggregate of other media. While consumption for all media in the U.S. grew at an average annual rate of 3.2% from 1960 to 1980, that for TV grew by 4.9% per annum and for radio, by 3.7% per annum. Consumption of non-broadcast media, in contrast, grew at just 1.1% per annum. There was consequently an increase in the share of total consumption constituted by broadcast words. In 1960, 56% of the words consumed came over the air; by 1980 the share of these two media was 71%. In Japan from 1960 to 1975, the pattern was similar: radio and TV consumption grew at 4.6% per annum, while the rate for all other media was 2.4% per annum. In consequence, the share of broadcast in total Japanese consumption expanded from 44% in 1960 to 53% in 1975. These are impressive (or perhaps depressing) numbers, but they are far below the 91% or 98% for words supplied.

The growth in words consumed, as in words supplied, slowed in the U.S. during the 1970s. The bend in the aggregate consumption curve seems to come around 1972. From an annual rate of 3.7% (1960–1972), growth fell then to a rate of 2.7%. That drop was indeed largely due to the end of the surge in

---

3) In regard to television and radio, the correlation may be reversed. That is, the less educated presumably consume more television and radio words than do educated persons.

4) Note that Robinson, *op. cit.*, reports a remarkable drop from 1965 to 1975 from 291 to 189 minutes a day in conversation and visiting in the U.S.A. However, the Japanese time budget studies from 1970 to 1980 show no such decline in social intercourse.

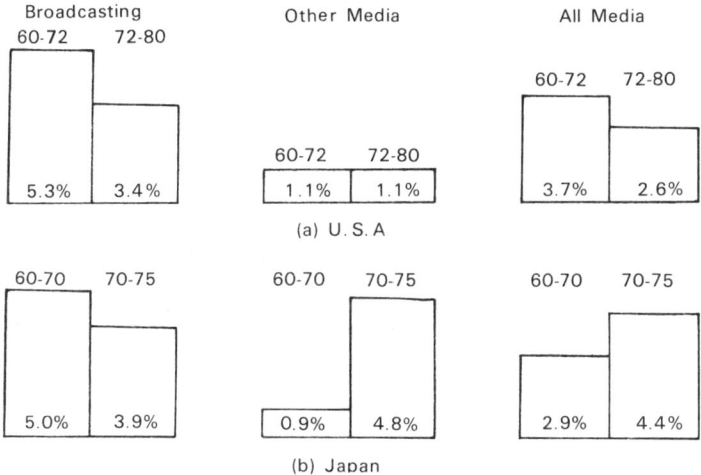

**Figure 2.4**
GROWTH RATES IN WORDS CONSUMED

consuming broadcasting. From 1972 to 1980 consumption of the two broadcast media grew only at 3.4% per annum compared to 5.3% per annum from 1960 to 1972. For all the other media combined the growth rate in consumption was 1.1% from 1960 to 1972 and again 1.1% from 1972 to 1980. In Japan there was a parallel trend in broadcast saturation. In the five years from 1970 to 1975 radio and TV consumption continued growing at 3.9% per annum, but consumption of all other media grew even faster. And the NHK time budget study for 1980 actually shows a small decline from 1975 (the last year of our Japanese data) in time spent on TV watching.[5]

Thus we find that a strong but not absolute physiological constraint limiting the growth of human consumption of information. There may be bursts of growth in consumption of new media, but not of all media at once. As supply grows, selectivity must be increasingly applied in choosing what to listen to or read.

The facilitating of such selectivity is indeed likely to be a major role of new communications technologies. As the overload in the number of words available keeps growing, information seekers

---

5) Kenzo Yamada, "Leisure Time Activities of the Japanese," NHK, Radio and TV Cultural Research Institute, *Studies of Broadcasting*, Tokyo, 1983, p. 98.

will turn increasingly to computer searches, abstracts, and other improved reference devices, so as to encompass their needs within the finite time that humans have.[6] Information overload is a fact and a growing problem; it is not a problem beyond the wit of man.

Selectivity, however, implies a fragmentation of the audience. Jokingly we can picture the struggle of an ever growing number of words to win the attention of audiences. Inevitably the average word must win an ever smaller audience. The implications of such fragmentation are many and both good and bad, but without tools which allow people to search the media and to select what is important and meaningful for them, many of the consequences would surely be disturbing.

## 2.4 Arrested Growth of Print Media

Though *consumption* of broadcasting began in the 1970s to enter the saturation phase of an S-shaped curve, the *supply* of broadcasting (with the coming of cable) and of other electronic media, such as computer data, have not. The supply side for such electronic words is still exploding; growth in the output of the conventional printing press has, however, slowed. Several print media have exhibited sharp declines in growth rates since the late 1960s, and in some instances even absolute declines. That is true for supply and even more for consumption, though it must be recognized that consumption of information for print media is our weakest data.

In Japan electronic words supplied grew at 10.2% per annum from 1960 to 1975 and at 12.1% from 1970 to 1975, while print media grew at 5.4% per annum from 1960 to 1975 but at only one percent per annum from 1970 to 1975.

Words supplied by American electronic media grew at 8.7% per annum from 1960 to 1980. Electronic media other than broadcasting (CATV, records and tapes, telephone, telegrams, telex, mailgrams, facsimile and data) as a group grew fastest—22.6% per annum for the whole period and 19.9% per annum since 1975.

---

6) Ithiel de Sola Pool, *Technologies of Freedom*, Cambridge: Harvard University Press, 1983, ch. 8; Hiroshi Inose and John R. Pierce, *Information Technology and Civilization*, New York: W.H. Freeman, 1984, ch. 7.

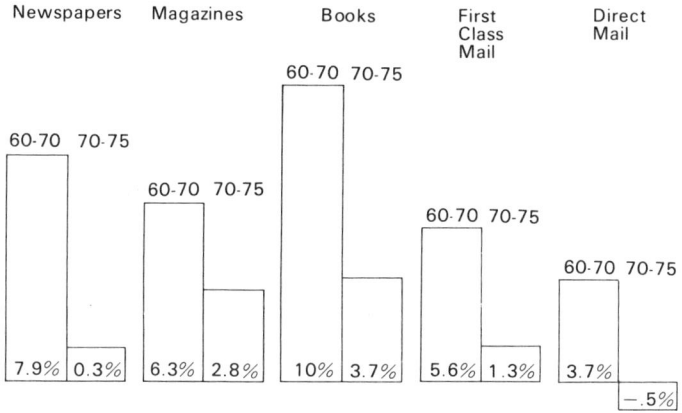

**Figure 2.5**
GROWTH RATES OF PRINT MEDIA IN JAPAN*
* Adjusted for comparison to U.S. data.

In contrast, American print media as a whole grew by only 2.2% per annum for the whole period from 1960 to 1980, and registered almost no growth from 1967 to 1977. In the most recent years, there has been a striking resumption of growth (5.7% per annum for 1977–1980), which seems, however, due primarily to an increasing number of pages in newspapers, rather than to increasing circulation in this medium or the other print media (see Figure 3.14).

These figures do not mean that people have stopped reading. Written words can be delivered electronically or from copying machines as well as off of printing presses. Telex, facsimile, data communication, and even television supply written words to be read. Future media such as videotex and on-line laser printing accelerate the trend toward supplying text electronically, rather than by sheets of paper collated at a printing plant. It is the technology of printing, not literacy, for which our data indicate an arrest.

Not all print media, however, show the same trend. Of the print media we have tabulated—newspapers, magazines, books, and direct and first class mail—the largest volume of material, by far, is supplied by newspapers. Their words comprised 82% of the volume supplied by these media in the U.S. So the general trend we have reported necessarily parallels a newspaper trend.

## Table 2.4
### CHANGE IN BALANCE OF PRINT AND ELECTRONIC MEDIA

| Percent of | U.S.A. | | | |
|---|---|---|---|---|
| | Volume Supplied | | Volume Consumed | |
| | 1960 | 1980 | 1960 | 1980 |
| Print media | 7.6% | 2.3 | 31.4 | 17.0 |
| Electronic media | 92.2 | 97.6 | 58.3 | 76.2 |
| Other media* | 0.2 | 0.1 | 10.3 | 6.8 |
| | 100% | 100% | 100% | 100% |
| | Japan | | | |
| | Volume Supplied | | Volume Consumed | |
| | 1960 | 1975 | 1960 | 1975 |
| Print media | 14.1% | 7.8 | 28.9 | 24.6 |
| Electronic media | 84.6 | 91.9 | 57.4 | 68.4 |
| Other media* | 1.3 | 0.3 | 13.7 | 7.0 |
| | 100% | 100% | 100% | 100% |

\* Movies and education were not classifiable as either print or electronic media, as such.

The annual growth rate in words supplied in the U.S. by this medium was 2.2% from 1960 to 1980 and 1.2% from 1973 through 1980. For magazines the pattern was similar, though with somewhat less growth. For the whole period from 1960 to 1980 the rate of magazine growth was 1.8% per annum, but from 1970 on it was only 1.0% per annum. Similarly, first class mail grew at 2.8% per annum for the entire period, but only at 1.9% per annum since 1970. Direct mail displays a much less regular trend. For the whole period since 1960 the growth rate was 2.4% per annum, but with enough fluctuation so that no conclusions can be drawn about recent trends. On the other hand, the growth rate for books is higher than for the other print media, 2.9% per annum since 1960, and it moreover shows no sign of slowing. Thus three of the five American print media on which we have data demonstrate a common pattern of moderate growth through the 1960s, being arrested in the 1970s. In Japan each of those same five print media showed less rapid growth in supply from 1970 to 1975 than before. So the trend is clearly towards increasing dominance of electronic media. A larger and larger proportion of the communications sent to people is being delivered electronically.

Electronic communications at nearly 98% of total volume in 1980 have already come to dominate the American flow of words supplied (as shown in Table 2.4) and are rapidly coming to dominate the flow of words consumed. The same trend is evident in Japan. The growth of the electronic media has thus both swelled the total information flow and curtailed the potential for expansion of conventional print media. New electronically based information delivery systems like videotex may grow not only relatively but absolutely at the expense of mass printing on paper. The trend toward electronic delivery of written as well as oral words is already conspicuous.

## 2.5 The Emergence of Data Communication

Late in the decade for which we collected data, computer communication began an explosive growth. Starting at close to zero, and becoming a significant medium only in the 1970s, data communication (which is what computer communication is called) has been growing in the U.S.A. at about 28% per annum. What is more, there is reason to expect that extraordinary growth to continue for some time to come.

While in general electronic communication grew more rapidly than other modes during the whole period since 1960 for the first decade and a half of that time, the low-cost electronic mass media, radio, television, and cable, rather than the electronic point-to-point media, grew the most. But point-to-point media, as a group, were also growing substantially. This can be seen by comparing the data on their flows with the two very different sets of mass media figures, words supplied and consumed. In the first case, words supplied, we find that the point-to-point media, while growing faster than the non-electronic mass media, were growing less fast than the electronic mass media. In the case of words consumed, the point-to-point media were growing faster than both the electronic and the non-electronic mass media. Their annual rate of growth was 5.7% from 1960 to 1980 and even accelerated in the last few years to 7.0%, although as we have seen there was a slowing in various other American media. (We shall deal with the Japanese picture separately because there are problems in divergent measurement methods for data communication in the two countries.)

The strong and accelerating growth was not due to the one hard-copy point-to-point medium, namely mail, which as already noted grew only 2.8% per annum for the whole period and only 1.8% per annum since 1970. It was due to other point-to-point media, all of which were electronic, and it was mostly due to the telephone.

Not all the electronic point-to-point media grew, and some did so slowly. As Figure 2.1 shows, cost was the determining factor. Telegrams, a very expensive medium, were displaced by telex and mailgrams. Telephone use, however, continued to expand steadily at 5.7% per annum. Since the telephone was the dominant point-to-point medium, accounting for almost 80% of such traffic throughout the period, the point-to-point data reflect that telephone trend.

Buried in that trend, invisible at first but amounting to 10% of the point-to-point flows by 1980, was a new medium, data communication.[7] A glance at Figure 2.1 reveals that the cost of data communication falls into what was previously an unfilled gap between the costs of point-to-point and mass communications.

The cost of point-to-point communication has in the past been so much greater than the cost of mass communication that the former had to be used with more care and frugality than the latter. The words transmitted via point-to-point media in 1980 were only one-four-thousandths of mass media words supplied and one eighteenth of the mass media words consumed.

We do not for a moment suggest that the respective influence of mass and point-to-point media or even the attention given to them are anything like those ratios. A simple *gedanken* experiment is to consider how people report to their families or friends the letters or phone calls they receive compared to how they report what they have read in the papers, have heard on radio, or have seen on TV. All such reports are ingredients of daily conversation, but a letter or phone call is often reported in remarkable detail, sometimes with relatively precise recall of the

---

7) The estimate of growth in data communication in Japan was made by calculating the capacity of leased telecommunications lines and making an engineering estimate that they are used at about 9% capacity. This method produces a figure equivalent to 24% of of Japanese point-to-point traffic in 1975, and it is not directly comparable to the American estimate, but the conclusions about the shape of the trends which result from these two approaches are not very different.

actual words used. Even untrained people will report a conversation saying, "he said" this, and "she said" that. Much more rarely will an article or a TV show be reported as competently. Comments will be made about how good or bad it was. Particularly notable incidents or characters will be identified, and the general point or subject matter will be reported; but few readers or viewers are able to report any significant amount of what they saw, heard, or read on mass media, word for word.[8]

That difference between recall of point-to-point and mass media reflects the attention typically paid to each. The attention, in turn, is a reflection of the appositeness and saliency of the communication to the receiver. A phone call or a letter may be from someone near and dear; it may deal with one's own problems; and the subject matter of a conversation is actively controlled by the interaction of the receiver with the sender. So an exchange of very few words in a point-to-point message, and especially in a conversation, can have far greater effect than do many words of a mass medium.

One measure of this fact is that people are willing to pay many times as much per word for point-to-point messages as they do for mass media. But because of the higher price of point-to-point media, people use them in different ways. They spend hours on end with TV or radio on. Typically they spend only minutes at a time in phone calls.

Until now point-to-point and mass media have been sharply divided both by technology and by their price. Telephone lines have always been too expensive to be used for broadcast messages.[9] Telegraph, telex, and facsimile have also been too expensive to use as substitutes for newspapers or magazines. Electronic mail, while it has been technically feasible for more

---

[8] For a few people television programs acquire as much salience as conversations with acquaintances or relatives, but the failure to distinguish between the media incident and the latter and the equal investment of mental energy in both constitute rather bizarre behavior.

[9] In the early years of the telephone many attempts were made to provide entertainment services (much like those later carried by radio broadcasts) by phone, but these efforts all failed financially. The longest-lived service was in Budapest, where it lasted about 20 years. Cf. Asa Briggs, "The Pleasure Telephone," in Ithiel de Sola Pool, *The Social Impact of the Telephone*, Cambridge, Mass.: MIT Press, 1977; cf. also Ithiel de Sola Pool, *Forecasting the Telephone*, Norwood, N.J.: Ablex Publishing Co., 1983, pp. 81–82, 121–122.

than a century and a half, is still in gestation.

But with data communications that is changing; computer networks bring the cost of point-to-point electronic communication down to the point at which messages can be delivered at prices close to those of mass media, and yet be addressed to individual receivers. Data communication for the first time bridges the uses of mass media and point-to-point media, competing with both.

The above statements are not entirely forecasts. Data communication has been growing explosively for a decade already. Firms are establishing electronic networks among their offices not only to speed communication, but also because the costs of such message systems are considerably lower than the mail.[10] Banks have introduced electronic transfers of funds not only to eliminate float, but also because such messages are cheaper than the handling of physical checks.

The low cost per word of electronic transmission, coupled with the technological capabilities of computers, has another consequence which we noted in the previous chapter, namely that much of the traffic in data communications consists of messages sent back and forth among computers in order to create, format, validate, store, route, and keep accounts on those messages which are finally delivered to a human receiver.

That is a unique feature of computer communications. From the invention of postal service in the ancient world to the invention of telex, each point-to-point device has conveyed a message from a human originator to a human receiver, without manipulating the message. A letter mailed, a printed newspaper or book, a telegram or phone call may be damaged and degraded in transmission, but the most it can deliver is what the sender has put in it. A computer network, on the other hand, not only transmits the message between the points of input and output but also operates on the data in various logical ways, and often, therefore, delivers something much different than the original message. A computer-mediated transfer of funds, for example, does not just move a check the way the mails do; it uses many of the bits that are sent to establish the validity of the transfer, to protect its security, to debit and credit accounts affected by the transaction, and so on.

---

10) About 10 cents vs. 23.5 cents per 1,000 words in the U.S.A. in 1980.

Likewise, the text displayed at an airline reservation desk, in response to a command by the clerk, is a small part of the traffic he causes as he instructs the system to cancel one seat on a routing and substitute another.

Most of the traffic is never seen by a human being, and only a small part of such communication comes to the attention of the persons it serves. Even today, in the early 1980s, few persons receive messages off of a computer terminal directly, but most are unknowingly engaged in much computer communication. An electricity bill which the ordinary citizen receives in the mail usually starts as a data transmission from the computer where the usage records are compiled via wires to the printer that spews forth the bills. That is genuine data communication. Since the customer in 1980 typically does not yet have a terminal, the bill is forwarded to him by the postal service, and the data communication portion of the flow to the customer remains invisible.

Such facts create problems for our analysis, and indeed for the whole concept of a census of communications flows. Data communication is a very different thing from the other point-to-point media. The others are person-to-person media. For them we can measure, even if crudely, the volume of flow as it impinges on the person at the "terminal" of the system. For data communication, measurement at the person interface is no longer a good measure of the flow.

Our measure of data communication is the bits (translated into words at 50 bits per word) flowing over the transmission system. The figure for that bit flow is not well estimated (though the growth rate probably is), and, more importantly, the meaning of that figure is something different from the meaning of bits reaching a human being. This revolution in the nature of communication from being a purely human act to one that can be machine-generated suggests that the remarkable 28% growth rate in data communication could continue for decades, thus raising the total volume of communication in society by orders of magnitude, as printing did at an earlier time and as radio and television did more recently.[11] If much of the communication of the future is

---

11) At this growth rate and with the volume of all other media held constant, a change of one order of magnitude of total words supplied would occur in approximately 40 years.

*32* SOME MAJOR CONCLUSIONS

among computers, and if only a filtered portion of that communication is delivered to humans, then the growth in the volume of communication need not run into the barriers of human absorptive capability. If words flowing via broadband networks among intelligent machines cost little enough, the volume of words transmitted may come to be several times as great as they are today, without an intolerable information overload for the humans involved.

As we have noted, computers offer additional solutions to the information overload. Computers are extraordinarily efficient devices for searching, sorting, and managing information. They can therefore serve like a card catalogue in a million-book library, headlines and subject-matter sections in a 100-page newspaper, or other guides which make information resources usable. Thus if computer communications create data bases an order of magnitude larger, then computer devices will have to filter that material much faster and with more intelligence.

Ironically, every device for reducing information overload itself creates additional information, since we need more information about the available stock of information in order to handle its overload. So data communication may serve to hold down the messages that human receivers have to attend to, while allowing them to extract those important items from an ever-larger information base. It does this by generating the growing overhead of computer-to-computer messages which the human user never sees. Consequently, the volume of words flowing in the message stream may continue to expand (both in the information base and also in the overhead of messages for information processing) while the volume of words ultimately consumed remains confined to the capacity of the human receivers.

It may well be, therefore, that the slowdown we noted in growth rates of words supplied in the 1970s will prove a temporary phenomenon. It may be the familiar saturation phase of an S-shaped growth curve appearing in one set of media, namely broadcasting, while a new S curve in data communication is just getting under way. This is a pattern familiar to students of historical growth processes. Writers such as Pitrim Sorokin or Derek de Solla Price, who treat the growth of technology or of the economy, note that continuing growth processes are frequently composed of a sequence of such superimposed S-shaped growth processes, each of a particular new technology or institution.[12]

One could argue that computer communication is one of the perhaps four most fundamental changes in the history of communications technology. Any such list is, of course, judgmental, but the case can be made that writing 5,000 years ago, printing 500 years ago, telegraphy 150 years ago, and now computer communication were the four truly revolutionary changes, and that most of the thousands of other changes in communication technology have been but perfecting adaptions of these four.

Before writing, virtually all communications were oral and face-to-face, whether in one-to-one conversation or in mass communication by public oratory. There was, however, no way of separating a message from its human speaker, preserving it over time, or transmitting it over space.[13] Writing freed communications from that constraint. For the first time a disembodied message could be preserved to be read years, decades, or centuries later, and carried to a place distant from its author.

Until printing, however, that revolutionary change did not affect mass communication. The only mass communication remained the oral kind. Preachers or orators in temples or forums could address hundreds of listeners at once, but written communications could be copied only laboriously, one copy at a time. The printing press changed that. It made mass communication possible in written form too. Pamphlets, books, and newspapers became mass media, having the advantages of geographic range and preservability that writing had over voice. As writing had freed single communications from the limits of face-to-face contact, so printing freed mass communication from the same constraints.

Printed or written messages, however, could be transmitted to remote places only as fast as the pieces of paper on which they had been impressed could be carried. It did not have the instantaneousness of face-to-face oral communication. A century and a half ago the discovery that messages could be represented by manipulation of electro-magnetic forces, instead of by ink on

---

12) Pitrim Sorokin, *Social and Cultural Dynamics*, New York: American, 1937–1941. Derek de Solla Price, *Little Science, Big Science*, New York: Columbia Univerisity Press, 1963.

13) Cf. Harold Innis, *The Bias of Communications*, Toronto: University of Toronto Press, 1951; *Empire and Communications*, Toronto: University of Toronto Press, 1972.

paper, freed communication from that physical constraint of slow transportability. For the first time a message could be received at any distance instantaneously.

Electromagnetic signals were more flexible than print in a number of other ways too. It was found that they could be used to reproduce voice and graphics as well as text, something that writing could not do. The telephone and TV were major adaptations of the basic invention of electromagnetic message reproduction, which started with telegraphy. However, all these earlier inventions were "dumb" means of transmission. They simply carried the message that the sender provided. Computer communication is revolutionary in that it frees the communication process from that fundamental constraint. Now, artificial intelligence can, for the first time, create, modify, send, and receive messages, as only human beings have in the past.

Just as each of the three previous revolutionary developments—writing, printing, and electronic communication—have fundamentally changed the communication process and also vastly increased the volume of communication, so data communication seems in our time to have begun doing the same.

# Chapter 3
# SOME AGGREGATE TRENDS

## 36 SOME AGGREGATE TRENDS

This chapter reports time series data from Japan and the United States for various types of media. The subsequent chapter contains time series for individual media. The overall impression is of remarkably similar trends in media use in Japan and the United States. These trends are similar, we believe, because they reflect the course of modern information societies, not just coincidences in two countries. Yet there are national differences.

In general, growth rates are higher in Japan than in the United States, but the level of communications flow is higher in the United States than in Japan. In part these differences can be viewed as a phenomenon of catching up. While there are variations from medium to medium, the per capita flow of words supplied in the U.S.A. has been six times as great as in Japan, and the per capita consumption greater too. However, the gap is narrowing as Japanese growth proceeds at about a point faster per annum than American growth.

### 3.1 Japanese-American Comparisons

In presenting time series from the United States and Japan, every effort has been made to make the two national studies comparable, but some incompatibilities were unavoidable. Before presenting the data, we should evaluate the degree of comparability of our two national data sets. How far can we take the differences in numbers to indicate real differences in phenomena?

(1) For one thing, the research teams in the two countries started at different stages of prior experience. The idea of a communications flow census had come from with Tetsuro Tomita and his colleagues at the Ministry of Posts and Telecommunications in Japan. The present cooperative study between MIT and the Research Institute of Telecommunications and Economics in Tokyo represents in Japan an effort at methodological refinement of the approach, but constitutes for the U.S.A. a first application. In the U.S. the major research effort was to organize and compile data, while in Japan, where the organization and compilation problems had already been handled in previous versions, the present study consisted largely of attempts by a number of scholars to interpret and apply the communications flow data.

(2) Differences in trends and rates can be trusted much more than absolute differences in figures for levels of flow. In this respect

the situation for our communications indices resembles that for other social indicators such as unemployment rates. Anyone who works with such statistics knows that unemployment is defined differently in different countries. In the absence of other knowledge, finding that the unemployment index in country A is 7% and in country B, 6% would hardly justify saying that there is more unemployment in country A. It could be the other way around.

On the other hand, if each keeps its national statistics consistently over time, a change in the index within a country is probably meaningful. If unemployment, as defined and measured in country A, rises by 10%, and by 5% as defined and measured in country B, we are probably justified in concluding that the difference is real. It is still hypothetically possible, although improbable, that the difference in rate of change was entirely within those categories in which the definition differed.

The same point applies to communications flow comparisons between Japan and the United States. We tried to make our category definitions and data treatments similar, but differences in methodology arose. Since direct comparisons of levels of flow are consequently tricky, one should not, without careful scrutiny, take something like a 10% or 25% difference between levels in the two countries as necessarily real. But a change in the direction or rate of change within either country should probably be taken seriously.

(3) One obvious respect in which comparisons between the two countries must be normalized is that of sheer size of population. By virtue of that factor alone we would expect about twice as many words to flow in the U.S. as in Japan. To allow for the population difference, counts of words supplied or consumed are often represented in this chapter on a per capita basis.

(4) The two studies had different operational definitions of the volume delivered by the mass media, this being reflected in the Japanese use of the term "volume produced" in contrast to the American use of the term "volume supplied." The Japanese team counted the number of words delivered to information devices, e.g. radio receivers, or at consumption centers, e.g. movie theatres. They did not multiply this volume by the number of potential consumers at such centers or devices, as did the American team. For example, a word spoken by a teacher in a class-

room was counted in Japan as one word produced and was counted in the U.S.A. as $x$ words supplied, where $x$ is the number of pupils regularly assigned to that class. For movies the American team multiplied the words produced in a film showing by seats in the theatre. In the U.S., the words normally supplied to a household were multiplied by the number of persons over 10 years old in the household. The media we treated as received by households are radio, TV, CATV, records and tapes, books, magazines, newspapers, and direct mail.

In order to permit comparisons of the Japanese and American data on supply of words, we have applied conversion factors to the Japanese figures as originally reported, using Japanese demographic data on the number of persons over 10 per household in 1960, 1965, 1970, and 1975.[1] No adjustments were needed for point-to-point volume, since for those media our study assumes no potential multiple consumption of words produced.

In tabulating consumption, the Japanese study did not reduce broadcast figures for inattention rates. The raw figures for radio and CATV consumption in the United States were reduced by 35% to allow for such inattention. In making comparisons we have applied this American inattention rate to the Japanese data. No adjustments were made, however, for the rather substantial differences in estimates of words read or spoken per minute in the two languages.

Thus differences that the reader notes between the raw Japanese figures and those in the U.S.-Japanese comparisons are due to adjustments which were made for the purpose of aligning the figures from the two studies.

(5) The concept of a "word" is not the same in English and Japanese. For any language, what we mean by a "word" is a philosophical concept for linguists to explore. In written English a word is fairly well defined by the space between groups of letters. The fact that in oral speech we often slur these spaces is a minor difficulty; when we count oral words we generally pretend that a word is what we would define as a word if it were in writing.

---

1) In the absence of other data, we used the U.S. figure on seats per movie theatre for both countries. For education, we based the restated Japanese volume supplied on data for volume consumed, making the fictive assumption that the latter was based on 100% attendance in Japanese schools. This might result in an understatement of educational volume supplied of perhaps 10%.

In Japanese manuscripts there are no spaces between words. The manuscript is written on a sheet with 400 squares, one character in each square. A word is written in one or several characters which may be in different forms of script.

In some comparisons between languages it is rather easy to say that one language tends to express ideas with fewer or more words than another. For example, a translation from English to Hebrew will end up with fewer words since many of the ideas that in English are expressed by particles, auxiliary verbs, or personal pronouns will be incorporated into the declinations and conjugations of the main words. No such easy generalization about relative length can be made about English–Japanese comparisons. Publishers often find that a translation from English to Japanese may take as much as one-third more pages, but a translation the other way is not necessarily shorter and may also be longer than the original. A rule of thumb used by some publishers is that a 400-character manuscript page will accomodate the translation of 137 English words. The Japanese research team counted a word as averaging 3.5 phonetic characters. In digital form an average word could thus be represented by 8-bit bytes in 28 bits. In English the average word is about six alphabetic characters. Given the usual 8-bit byte representation, 50 bits was treated as a word in American counts of electronic media. A Japanese bit flow therefore translates to more words by the conventions used, and that is a point which greatly affects the comparative figures on data communication.

Otherwise, there seems to be no clear difference in the two languages as either written or spoken in the significance of the numbers in a word count. A small ambiguity sometimes exists in Japanese word counts as to whether the particles are counted as separate words or not. Japanese does not use the many articles, "a" and "the," which appear in English. Nor does it contain the many personal pronouns, "he," "she," "it," etc. Japanese, however, uses large numbers of particles, such as "de," "ga," "wa," "ka," which identify a noun as subject or predicate, or a sentence as declarative or interrogatory. If there is any general correction to be made in word-count comparisons between English and Japanese, it is not of such magnitude that we are able to put a number on it.

(6) While both censuses were secondary analyses, utilizing

*40* SOME AGGREGATE TRENDS

time series that were collected and published for other purposes, the American data are based more heavily than the Japanese on market research data. The Japanese data rely more heavily than the American on governmentally compiled statistics. Partly because the original Japanese studies were Ministerial, partly because public statistics are so well collected in Japan and American market research is so highly developed, there may be a small difference of bias in the data sources in the two countries. In the Introduction we voiced a suspicion that the U.S. data have some unintended inflation because of ways in which commercial motivation may creep in. There is reason to speculate that this bias may be less in Japan.

(7) Aside from any consistent pattern of bias, operating procedures in counting which various original data compilers follow will differ from medium to medium, from country to country. Take statistics on radio broadcasting for example. Among the variables are number of broadcasting stations, number of sets, and number of households. A broadcasting station is what the country's authorities consider to be a broadcasting station. How the authorities differentiate it from repeaters, communications radios, and very low power transmitters may vary. The number of sets in use is a market research datum collected by possibly variable surveys or else by extrapolation from sales of sets with some assumptions about their working life. A household is a census datum, with each census organization making rules as to how to handle students, institutional residents, extended families, communal groups, etc. Since we were second-hand recipients of data, we had to accept the data with whatever varying operational definitions the original compilers used.

Among the different media, one for which the methodology differed substantially was data communications. The Japanese team calculated the capacity of leased lines and assumed a usage of 9% of capacity. The U.S. figures were based on surveys of usage.

Use of textbooks was included in the Japanese education data, but in the U.S. textbook use was included in book reading, not in education.

(8) Japanese data were collected for four points in time: 1960, 1965, 1970, and 1975. U.S. data were collected, when available, for all years from 1960 through 1980, and, when data

were missing, interpolations or extrapolations were made, using known data points.

The last Japanese data point was 1975, the last U.S. point 1980. Since most of the series have growth trends, and since the Japanese figures are lower but growing more rapidly than the U.S. figures, using 1975 data for comparisons exaggerates current differences between countries in levels of activity.

With data for only four years, dates of particular turning points in trends cannot be well identified in the Japanese data.

(9) The list of media is not identical in the two studies. There is no mailgram service in Japan. CATV in Japan has virtually no local origination or subscription services, which was what was included in the U.S. count. Japanese CATV was defined to include the broadcast material sent over CATV—which was instead counted as TV in the U.S.A. The following table shows the match between media covered.

| Medium | U.S. Census | Japanese Census |
|---|---|---|
| Radio | X | X |
| TV | X | X |
| CATV | X | Differently defined |
| Records & tapes | X | Not included |
| Movies | X | X |
| Education | X | Textbooks included |
| Newspapers | X | X |
| Magazines | X | X |
| Books | X | Textbooks counted under education |
| Phone books | Not included | X |
| Direct mail | X | X |
| First class mail | X | X |
| Telephone | X | X |
| Telex | X | X |
| Telegrams | X | X |
| Mailgrams | X | Not present |
| Facsimile | X | X |
| Data | X | X |

The divergences of coverage mostly concern media which are either non-existent in one country or small relative to the totals. The divergences should not affect any major conclusion.

## 3.2 Media Groupings

We turn now to examine the growth trends since 1960 for the

flows of communications as a whole and for various specific groups of media.[2]

### 3. 2. 1 Grand Totals

As we have already noted, the volume of words supplied to the American and Japanese public has been growing about two and a half times as fast as the volume consumed. As a result, the volume of words consumed, which in 1960 in the U.S. had been 1.3% of the total words supplied, by 1975 amounted to only 0.5% of those words supplied and by 1980, just 0.4%. In Japan the volume consumed was 3.8% of the volume supplied in 1960 and 1.6% in 1975. Table 3.1 shows overall growth for the two countries, and Table 3.2 compares the two countries' growth rates for individual media.

Though similar in most respects, the Japanese trend differs from the U.S. trend portrayed in Figures 3.1 through 3.4 in revealing a later start and somewhat faster growth rates. So the slowdown in growth rates that appears in the U.S. in the 1970s was not generally apparent in the Japanese data as of 1975. We suspect, however, that if our Japanese figures continued for another five years, we would note the tapering off of the TV boom in supply as well as consumption, and thus see a lagged parallelism with the U.S. data.

**Table 3. 1**
ANNUAL GROWTH RATE IN PER CAPITA SUPPLY AND CONSUMPTION

|  | Supply | | Consumption | |
| --- | --- | --- | --- | --- |
|  | U.S.A. | Japan | U.S.A. | Japan |
| 1960–65 | 9.9% | 7.4% | 1.8% | 3.1% |
| 1965–70 | 6.1 | 8.0 | 1.2 | 0.7 |
| 1970–75 | 6.3 | 9.4 | 2.1 | 3.0 |
| 1975–80 | 4.6 | NA | 1.5 | NA |

In general, the most surprising difference in the two sets of national results is the much higher level in the United States than in Japan in supply of words. One medium, radio, accounts for much of this difference. In 1960 (before television saturation

---

2) In all the following data, unless otherwise stated, volumes supplied and consumed are reported in millions of words per annum for the entire country. Production, transmission and consumption are reported in millions of dollars per annum.

had occurred in either country) radio broadcasting played a somewhat similar role in Japan and the United States. It accounted for 64% of the total words supplied in Japan and 75% in the United States. But in Japan television impacted radio broadcasting far more drastically than in the United States. The underlying reason is probably indicated by the difference in listening minutes, which by 1960 were typically almost six times as great in the United States as in Japan. Whatever the reason, by 1975 radio accounted for only 41% of the words supplied in Japan in that year, but 75% in the U.S.A. That medium, which produces words so cheaply, clearly has a large effect on the totals, and is one important factor in explaining the magnitude of the U.S./Japanese differences.

On the other hand, a few media, particularly telex and facsimile, are more heavily used in Japan than in the U.S.A. Facsimile is particularly well suited to Japanese needs since non-alphabetic kanji characters cannot be typed at inexpensive typewriters or terminals. Japanese offices work extensively with handwritten documents, so the capability for graphic reproduction and transmission is a great convenience. While facsimile use has also been growing rapidly in the United States, the number of words transmitted per capita by facsimile was greater in Japan by about four to one.

The Japanese lead in telex use is even greater, although this is not explainable by the linguistic difference. U.S. telex use is very low compared to that in other advanced industrialized countries in Europe as well as Japan. Since both the telephone system and computer networking in the U.S. are excellent and cheap, telex as an alternative never took hold there. With few offices on the telex network, there is little incentive to subscribe: a network is only attractive if others are reachable on it. Thus for telex it is the U.S. figures, not the Japanese figures, which are the outliers by global standards.

By 1975 Japan also led the U.S. in per capita telegraph use. The telegraph system is declining and losing money in both countries. In Japan, however, where it is part of the government postal service, the service is being maintained at a loss, by political decision. The volume transmitted per capita has remained stable. In the U.S., telegraphy is a private commercial service and is dying. The words transmitted per capita were by 1980

44 SOME AGGREGATE TRENDS

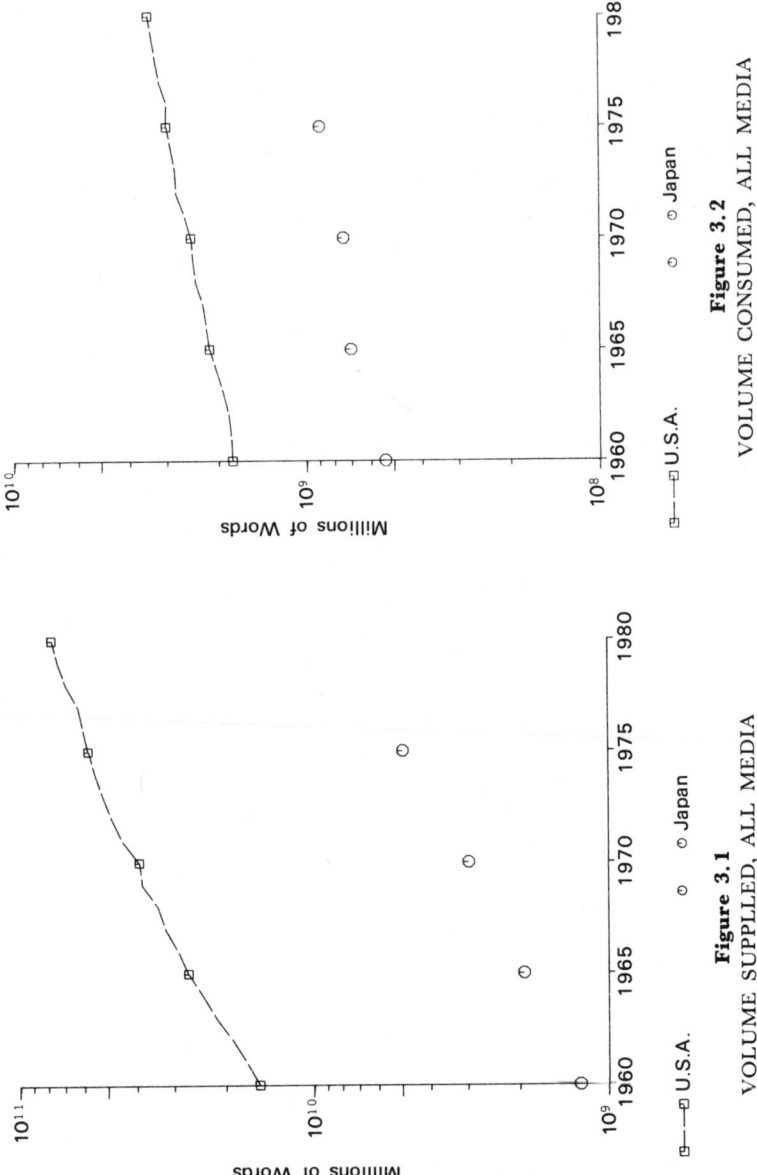

Figure 3.1
VOLUME SUPPLIED, ALL MEDIA

Figure 3.2
VOLUME CONSUMED, ALL MEDIA

MEDIA GROUPINGS 45

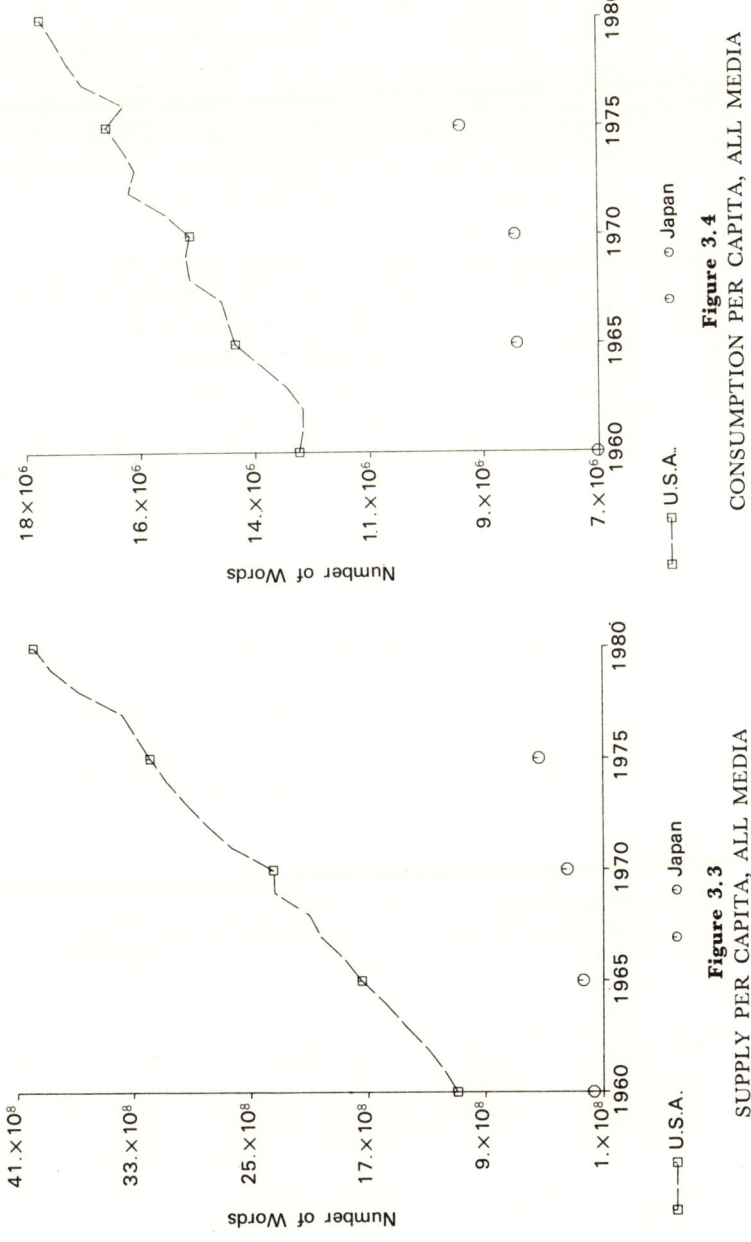

**Figure 3.3**
SUPPLY PER CAPITA, ALL MEDIA

**Figure 3.4**
CONSUMPTION PER CAPITA, ALL MEDIA

but one-eighteenth of what they had been in 1960. By 1975 about twice as many words per capita were transmitted by telegram in Japan as in the U.S.A. However, mailgrams, which do not exist in Japan, were by 1975 carrying three times the traffic of telegrams in the U.S. Adding them in with telegrams would reverse the picture; the U.S. and Japanese figures would be similar, with a somewhat larger U.S. volume.

There are a number of media where the data definitions are sufficiently different to suggest that one should not directly compare the absolute levels. The CATV data set is the least comparable. The data on education and on books are also hard to compare directly, partly because of the difference in handling of textbooks. Consumption figures for newspapers and magazines are also of dubious usefulness for direct comparison because of the weakness of the U.S. figures. Finally, data flows on computer networks were measured differently, so direct comparisons of absolute levels are surely misleading.

The striking finding in regard to the remaining media is that volumes of flow are much larger in the U.S.A. than in Japan. The volume supplied by the mass media tends to be two to ten times as much per capita in the U.S.A. as in Japan. The volume consumed there per capita is often reported at twice what it is in Japan.

Nonetheless, there is reason to believe that the difference in the volume of words consumed is not nearly the two-to-one suggested in Table 3.4. One factor which needs to be taken into account is the regular tendency of the American research to find a higher word rate per minute for reading or listening or viewing than did the Japanese. In many instances these differences are moderate. Japanese researchers found the reading rate for newspapers and magazines to be 192 words per minute (but 120 per minute for books); the Americans used a reading rate of 240 words per minute across the board. For radio also the results are fairly comparable: 64 words per minute consumed by listeners according to the Japanese estimate, 70 in 1973 according to the American. Telephone traffic is estimated at 100 words per minute in Japan and 120 in the United States. On the other hand, in some instances the differences are two to one or more. For education the Japanese estimate was 71 words consumed per minute; for the U.S., 120. For TV, a most important medium, the Japanese

**Table 3.2**
JAPANESE PER CAPITA ANNUAL FLOW AS PERCENTAGE OF COMPARABLE U.S. FIGURES

(a) Mass Media

|  | Volume Supplied | | Volume Consumed | |
| --- | --- | --- | --- | --- |
|  | 1960 | 1975 | 1960 | 1975 |
| Radio | 13% | 9% | 71% | 16% |
| TV | 17 | 38 | 21 | 47 |
| Movies | 105 | 33 | 83 | 18 |
| Education | 44 | 32 | NA | NA |
| Newspapers | 28 | 48 | 52 | 79 |
| Magazines | 24 | 43 | 54 | 66 |
| Books | 34 | 73 | 36 | 44 |
| Direct mail | 15 | 19 | 426 | 722 |

(b) Point-to-Point Media

|  | 1960 | 1975 |
| --- | --- | --- |
| First class mail | 36% | 46% |
| Telephone | 12 | 22 |
| Telex | 123,520 | 22,470 |
| Telegrams | 16 | 267 |
| Facsimile | — | 430 |

estimate was 63 words consumed per minute and in the U.S. 153.

The importance of such differences is highlighted by the TV figures. Daily viewing time in the two countries is almost the same: 210 minutes per person in Japan in 1975 against 223 in the United States. But given the remarkable difference in word rate, American TV word consumption is much higher. Is the difference real? In part it may well be. The style of broadcasting may be different. There is also the possibility discussed above that the concept of the word is not the same in the two languages. Yet, neither of these possibilities could account for the whole differences.

There are also differences in the way the figures were arrived at in the research. In the American study reading speed estimates were sought from experts on reading pedagogy. Radio and television word rates were the result of counting from taped samples of a day's broadcasting. For education and telephone a general speaking rate figure was again sought from experts. In Japan radio and television word rates were obtained from research at

48  SOME AGGREGATE TRENDS

NHK on the speaking speed of announcers. NHK research has also estimated reading rates and the word rate in educational broadcasts. That figure was applied to the Ministry of Education's figure on the lecture hours in schools. Some part of the difference may therefore be in the nature of the sources. Whatever the reason, the American figures are across the board somewhat higher, and if one questions this, then one would question the full two-to-one difference.

One might react to these large differences with incredulity and wonder whether they should be rejected as errors in the methodology. We have already warned of the risks of direct comparisons of the national figures and urged that more attention be given to comparison of the patterns within countries. We have also urged that small differences not be taken seriously. However, there is solid evidence that the differences between the two countries in the volume of flow are to a significant extent real and not artifacts of the research. While some of our data series are rather weak, some are very solid. Among those series which it would be hard to dismiss as artifactual are such items as number of phone calls, number of first class letters, and newspaper circulation. Translating these hard numbers into number of words supplied or consumed involves manipulations which are much less solid, such as estimating number of words sent or consumed per message.

For the moment let us neglect all those controversial manipulations and compare the U.S. and Japan on the hardest time series available. As Tables 3.3 and 3.4 show, the U.S. flow is very much larger than the Japanese flow by those measures too. The difference between these two information societies is apparently

**Table 3.3**
SOME "HARD" INDICATORS

| | Annual Number of Items Per Capita Per Annum | | | |
|---|---|---|---|---|
| | 1960 | | 1975 | |
| | U.S.A. | Japan | U.S.A. | Japan |
| First class letters | | | 291 | 71 |
| Direct mail units | | | 121 | 20 |
| Telephone calls | 748 | 131 | 1,298 | 516 |
| Newspapers circulated | | | 134 | 229 |

## Table 3.4
### COMPOSITION OF THE AGGREGATE FLOWS BY MEDIA

#### U.S.A.

| Medium | Words Supplied 1960 | Words Supplied 1980 | Words Consumed 1960 | Words Consumed 1980 |
|---|---|---|---|---|
| Radio | 74.5% | 71.8% | 17.5% | 18.8% |
| TV | 17.6 | 25.3 | 38.1 | 51.7 |
| CATV | 0.02 | 0.52 | 0.002 | 0.76 |
| Records & tapes | NA | 0.0003 | 0.12 | 0.08 |
| Movies | 0.12 | 0.02 | 0.97 | 0.44 |
| Education | 0.12 | 0.03 | 9.24 | 6.36 |
| Newspapers | 6.20 | 1.90 | 20.0 | 8.52 |
| Magazines | 0.98 | 0.28 | 4.40 | 3.15 |
| Books | 0.16 | 0.056 | 6.18 | 4.43 |
| Telephone directory | — | — | — | — |
| Direct mail | 0.30 | 0.09 | 0.12 | 0.10 |
| First class mail | 0.0089 | 0.0031 | 0.80 | 0.73 |
| Telephone | 0.033 | 0.019 | 2.70 | 4.27 |
| Telex | $6.6 \times 10^{-8}$ | $6.9 \times 10^{-7}$ | $4.2 \times 10^{-6}$ | $7.8 \times 10^{-5}$ |
| Telegraph | $3.8 \times 10^{-6}$ | $8.1 \times 10^{-8}$ | $3.1 \times 10^{-4}$ | $1.3 \times 10^{-5}$ |
| Mailgram | 0 | $5.1 \times 10^{-7}$ | 0 | $1.1 \times 10^{-4}$ |
| Facsimile | 0 | $1.3 \times 10^{-5}$ | 0 | 0.003 |
| Data | $9.1 \times 10^{-5}$ | 0.003 | 0.0075 | 0.57 |
| | 100% | 100% | 100% | 100% |

#### Japan

| Medium | Words Supplied 1960 | Words Supplied 1975 | Words Consumed 1960 | Words Consumed 1975 |
|---|---|---|---|---|
| Radio | 64.2% | 40.8% | 26.4% | 6.47% |
| TV | 19.8 | 50.2 | 17.2 | 46.1 |
| CATV | 0.34 | 0.76 | 0.23 | 0.85 |
| Records & tapes | — | — | — | — |
| Movies | 0.61 | 0.05 | 1.80 | 0.19 |
| Education | 0.73 | 0.18 | 19.3 | 11.5 |
| Newspapers | 11.9 | 6.43 | 22.5 | 20.4 |
| Magazines | 1.56 | 0.83 | 5.19 | 4.59 |
| Books | 0.37 | 0.29 | 4.87 | 4.28 |
| Telephone directory | 0.18 | 0.23 | 0.005 | 0.004 |
| Direct mail | 0.30 | 0.11 | 1.21 | 1.33 |
| First class mail | 0.02 | 0.01 | 0.62 | 0.70 |
| Telephone | 0.03 | 0.03 | 0.68 | 1.66 |
| Telex | $5.5 \times 10^{-6}$ | $5.5 \times 10^{-4}$ | 0.01 | 0.04 |
| Telegraph | $4.1 \times 10^{-6}$ | $1.2 \times 10^{-6}$ | 0.0001 | 0.0001 |
| Mailgram | — | — | — | — |
| Facsimile | $1.9 \times 10^{-5}$ | $1.2 \times 10^{-5}$ | 0.0005 | 0.013 |
| Data | — | 0.01 | — | 0.89 |
| | 100% | 100% | 100% | 100% |

a fact, not an artifact. If the faster Japanese growth continues, the difference in the level of flow between the two countries will gradually close, but as of the mid-1970s the U.S. flows were still much larger.

Hence, while we prefer not to treat the differences in absolute values found in the two studies as good estimates of the true ratios, there is little doubt that in volume supplied the difference in words is substantial. This is indicated even by "hard" data for newspapers, where the circulation per capita in 1975 was higher in Japan than in the U.S.A., because the average number of pages per paper in Japan then was 15, but in the United States, it was 57. In volume of words consumed, too, there is apparently a difference reflected in the total hours that the studies found for use of all media. Yet we do not wish to contend that it is as much as two to one.

### 3.2.2 Mass Media Compared to Point-to-Point Media

Given the way in which we counted words, the volume of point-to-point transmissions is tiny compared to the volume of the mass media. The point-to-point flows constituted less than 0.5 percent of the words supplied and were less than 6% of the words consumed.

Since the distinction between volume supplied and volume consumed does not apply to point-to-point media, quite different impressions may arise in comparing the rates of growth in point-to-point media with the rates of growth in mass media, depending on whether one makes the comparison with volume supplied or with volume consumed. For the entire period from 1960 to 1980, the annual growth rate for American words supplied by mass media was 8.4% and 3.2% for words consumed. These two values bracketed the 5.8% for words transmitted by point-to-point media. Thus from the perspective of the growth in traffic, the mass media (and particularly broadcasting) were growing faster, but in regard to communications that people actually consumed, point-to-point communication was growing faster. Furthermore, the growth in point-to-point communication has speeded up in the last few years, even as the growth in mass media has been slowing down.

In Japan, in contrast to the U.S.A., point-to-point traffic grew as fast as mass media words supplied, even though there was

MEDIA GROUPINGS  51

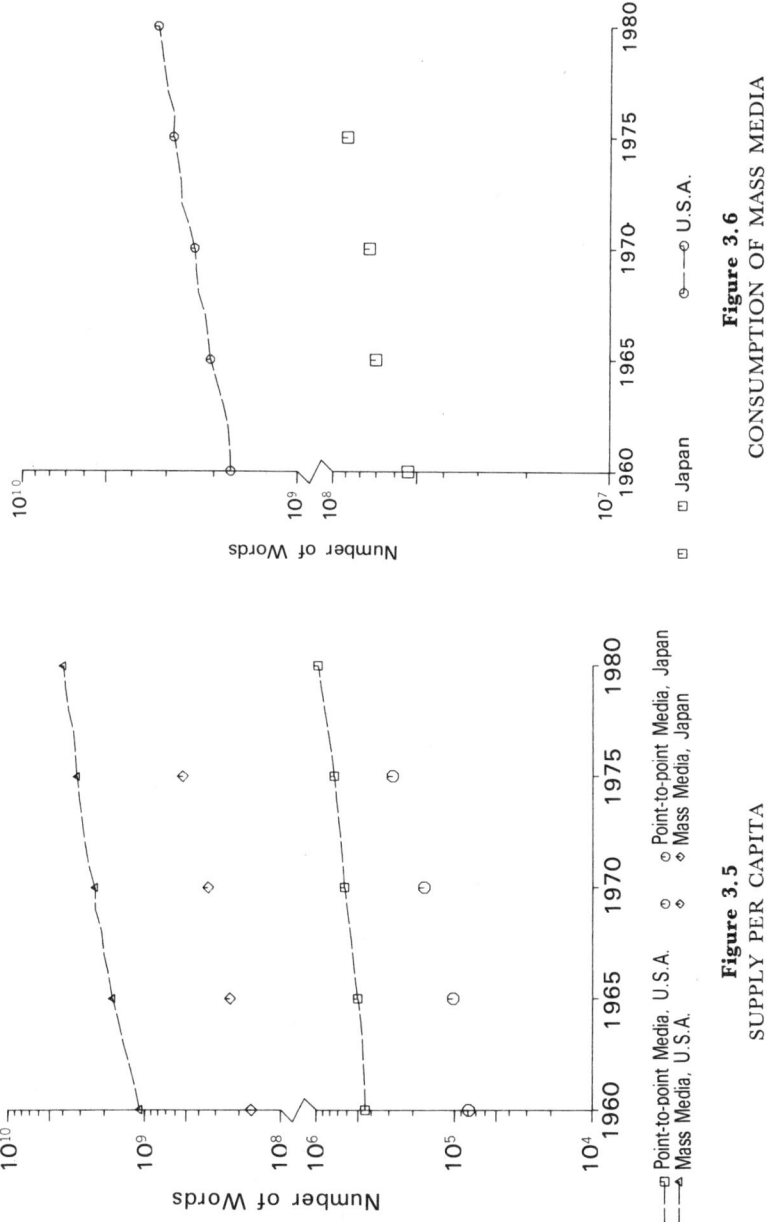

**Figure 3.6**
CONSUMPTION OF MASS MEDIA

**Figure 3.5**
SUPPLY PER CAPITA

## Table 3.5
### AMERICAN AND JAPANESE GROWTH RATES FOR MASS AND POINT-TO-POINT MEDIA

|  | Mass Media | | Point-to-Point Media |
|---|---|---|---|
|  | Words Supplied | Words Consumed |  |
| U.S.A. 1960–1980 | 8.4% | 3.2% | 5.8% |
| U.S.A. 1960–1975 | 9.3 | 3.4 | 5.4 |
| Japan 1960–1975 | 9.5 | 3.2 | 9.5 |

## Table 3.6
### POINT-TO-POINT TRANSMISSION AS PERCENT OF TOTAL FLOW

|  |  | 1960 | 1975 | 1980 |
|---|---|---|---|---|
| Volume Supplied: | U.S.A. | 0.04% | 0.02% | 0.03% |
|  | Japan | 0.05 | 0.05 | NA |
| Volume Consumed: | U.S.A. | 3.3 | 4.4 | 5.6 |
|  | Japan | 1.3 | 3.3 | NA |

## Table 3.7
### GROWTH RATES IN 1970s COMPARED TO FULL PERIOD

|  |  | Mass Media | | Point-to-Point Media |
|---|---|---|---|---|
|  |  | Words Supplied | Words Consumed |  |
| U.S.A.: | 1960–1980 | 8.4% | 3.2% | 5.8% |
|  | 1970–1975 | 8.2 | 3.8 | 5.3 |
|  | 1975–1980 | 5.9 | 2.6 | 6.9 |
| Japan: | 1960–1975 | 9.5 | 3.2 | 9.5 |
|  | 1970–1975 | 10.5 | 4.2 | 11.5 |

no deceleration apparent in broadcasting and mass media growth in Japan by 1975.

Tables 3.5–3.7 compare the trends in U.S. and Japanese mass media and point-to-point media. They document for each country the findings above.

### 3.2.3 Determinants of Point-to-Point Flows

The Japanese research team conducted a special study of the data on point-to-point communication to ascertain which economic factors most strongly affect the volume of such flows and also to develop measures of the communications flows between

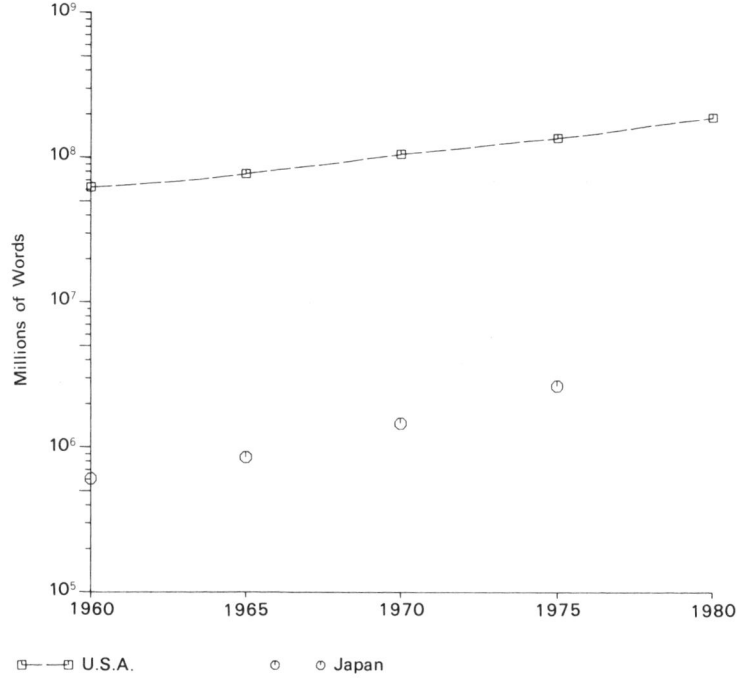

**Figure 3.7**
SUPPLY OF POINT-TO-POINT MEDIA

the United States and Japan.[3] In particular, the purpose of this study was to test how far the Gross National Product or levels of trade were major determinants of the volume of flows in domestic communications and in communications between the two countries.

For this particular study, the team used, in addition to the four Japanese data points, year-by-year data, which deviate in minor respects from the other data.

Figure 3.8 shows in linear scale the growth of total point-to-point information in Japan, the Gross Domestic Product (GDP) deflated by the price index, and the former divided by the latter. One could argue that the 1973 result suggests a constant relation, i.e., that the flow of point-to-point information grows fairly much

---

3) For a full report see Tadao Saito, Hiroshi Inose and Sei Kageyama, "A Comparative Study of the Mode of Domestic and Transborder Information Flows, Including Data," *Information Economics and Policy*, vol. 1, no. 1, 1983, pp. 75–92.

54 SOME AGGREGATE TRENDS

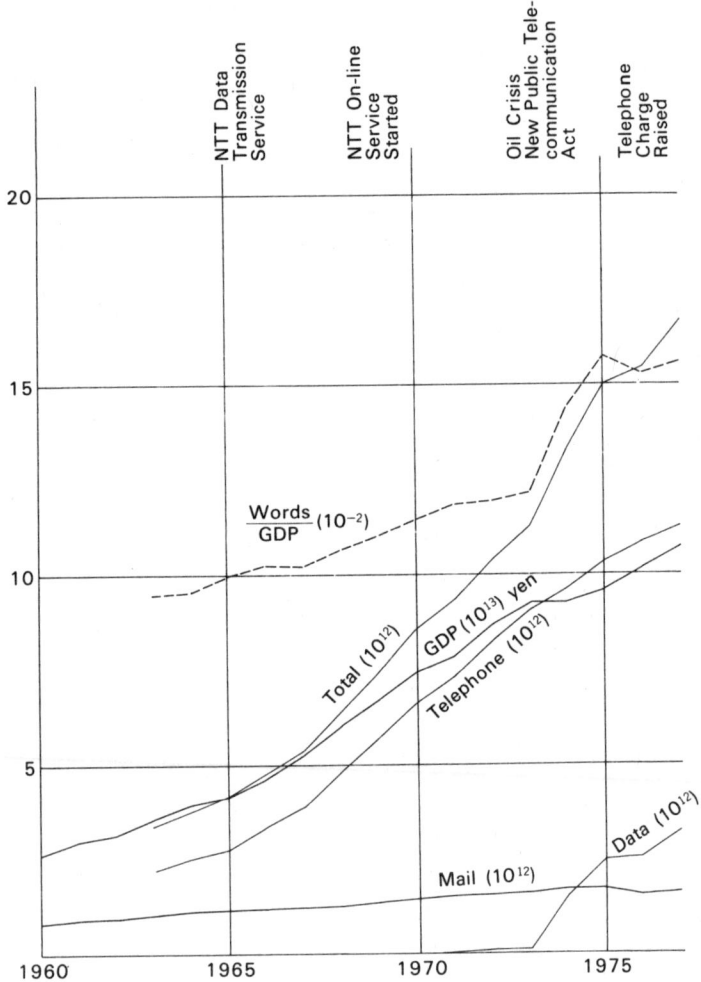

**Figure 3.8**
DOMESTIC INFORMATION FLOW AND GDP: JAPAN

in synchrony with the GNP. Then, however, there was a stepwise change, and it would seem more plausible to argue that communication activity is growing faster than the economy as a whole. The relationship of point-to-point communication to the GDP is less close in the United States. For the period studied the growth in total point-to-point communication (in Figure 3.9)

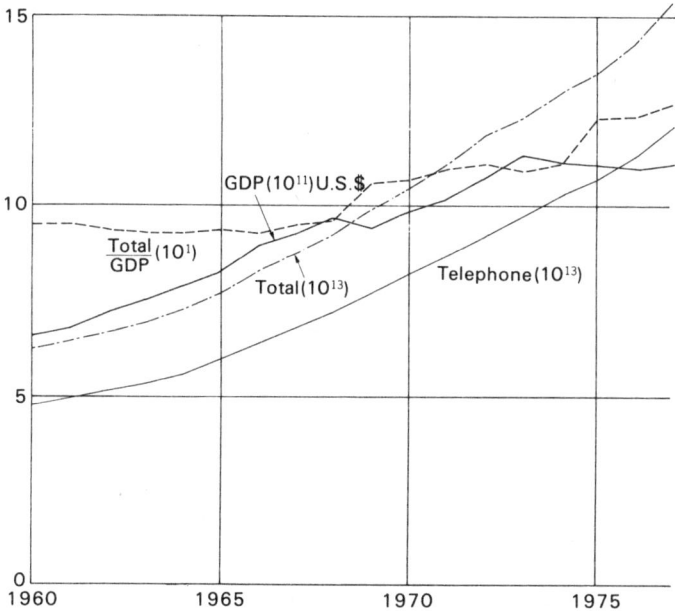

**Figure 3.9**
DOMESTIC INFORMATION FLOW AND GDP: U.S.A.

seems to expand regularly regardless of fluctuations in the economy.

The data for U.S.-Japan international communication were based on KDD statistics. For data communication the word count was based on the number of leased international telephone lines between the two countries. Statistics for international telephone calls were multiplied by a KDD estimate of 66 spoken words per minute. For international telex, transmitted words were calculated from holding time statistics, assuming a transmission speed of 66 words per minute. The mean number of words in an international letter was estimated at 500 in contrast to 300 for a Japanese domestic letter and 395 for an American domestic letter.

The total volume of this international traffic is several orders of magnitude smaller than the countries' domestic traffic, as can be seen from both Figures 3.7 and 3.8. The latter figure deals with the hypothesis that the volume of international point-to-

56 SOME AGGREGATE TRENDS

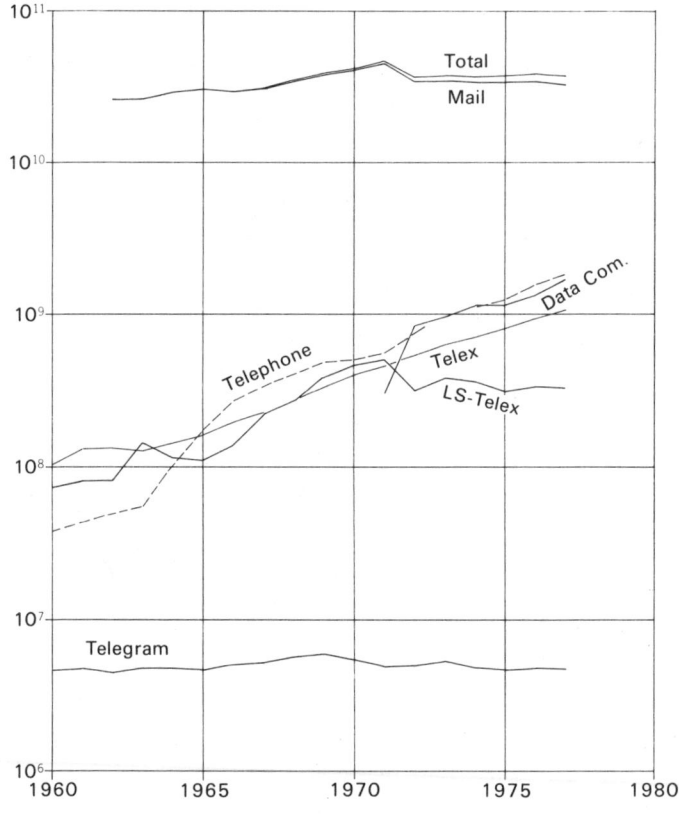

**Figure 3.10**
JAPAN-U.S. INFORMATION FLOW

point communication is a function of international trade. Indeed, both are growing, but the ratio between them reveals that electronic communication is growing faster and more smoothly than the volume of trade.

New facilities have been an important stimulus to international communications use. Sharp increases in growth of traffic occurred in the mid-1960s when the transpacific cable and then satellite communication was first introduced. Then another bend in the curve occurred in 1971 when KDD introduced voice-grade leased-line service. The advent of better and cheaper means of international communication has affected the means used. As we

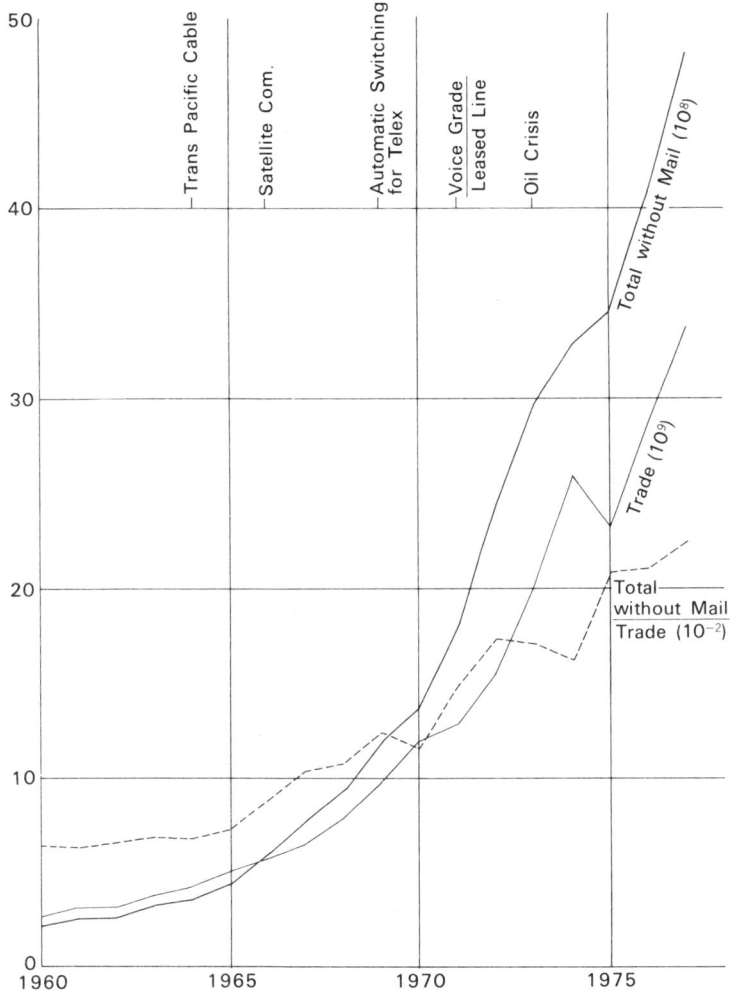

**Figure 3.11**
U.S.-JAPAN INFORMATION FLOWS AND FOREIGN TRADE

see from Figures 3.10 and 3.11, mail is still overwhelmingly the predominant channel for point-to-point communication between the United States and Japan, but it (as well as conventional telegrams) is giving way quite rapidly to telephone and now data communication.

### 3.2.4 Print vs. Electronic Media

The basic finding, already discussed in Chapter 2, is that electronic media have grown to be the dominant part of the information flow and are rapidly overwhelming the older flows. Growth in print media is far from over, but the substitution of new electronic technologies for that of Gutenberg is unmistakably apparent. (See Figures 3.12–3.13.)

The media for which we have been able to develop time series are based overwhelmingly on two technologies: that of the printing press and that of electronic signals. There are, however, media which rely on neither of these. Conversation, which we were not able to tabulate, is by far the most important. Among the media that we did tabulate, two also belong in this category of "other": motion pictures and teaching in the classroom, which are too heterogeneous to be discussed as any kind of group. One should note that in the discussion here of print media versus electronic media, we are excluding two media that fit in neither category.

There are several data problems in making the print/electronic comparison. One which we noted already is that in Japan, use of textbooks is included in education, while for the United States education includes only face-to-face interaction of teacher and students. Another is that we have no time series on office circulation of paper; over the period since 1960 this medium has undoubtedly been a growing part of the total information flow. Most important, however, is the fact that the consumption figures for American print media are among the least reliable ones that we have. Intercountry comparisons of trends in print words consumed are confounded by inherent uncertainty about what are the correct consumption figures for such words of print; there may or may not be a significant difference in trends in the two countries.

We noted earlier the reason for the unreliability of the print consumption data; the industry relies primarily on circulation data rather than on surveys of reader behavior. Circulation and audience data, which are reported annually, allow for calculation of reasonable estimates of words supplied. Consumption, however, is estimated from time budget studies, which tabulate how many hours people spend reading, and such studies on use of print are rare. In Japan NHK has produced time-budget studies every five

MEDIA GROUPINGS 59

**Figure 3.12**
SHARE OF COMMUNICATION MEDIA IN U.S.-JAPAN
COMMUNICATION

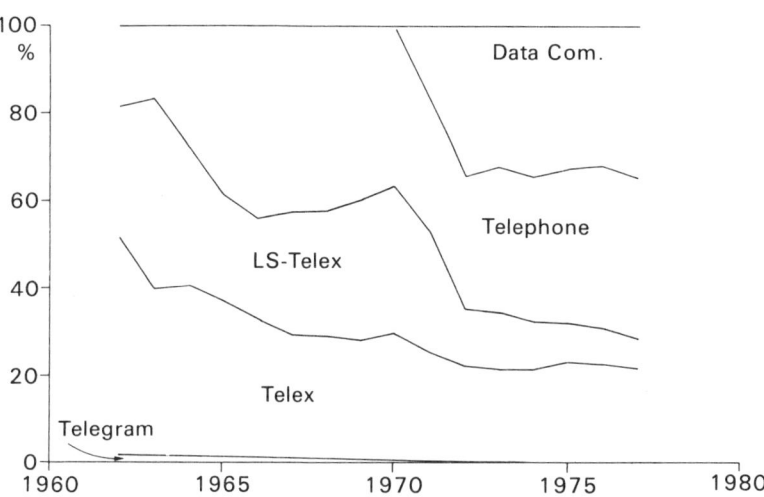

**Figure 3.13**
SHARE OF MEDIA, EXCLUDING MAIL, IN U.S.-JAPAN
COMMUNICATION

## Table 3.8
## CHANGES IN THE COMPOSITION OF THE AGGREGATE FLOWS FOR MASS AND POINT-TO-POINT MEDIA

### (a) Mass Media
#### U.S.A.

| Medium | Words Supplied | | | Words Consumed | | |
|---|---|---|---|---|---|---|
| | 1960 | 1975 | 1980 | 1960 | 1975 | 1980 |
| Radio | 74.6% | 75.1% | 71.8% | 18.1% | 21.3% | 19.9% |
| TV | 17.6 | 21.9 | 25.3 | 39.4 | 50.5 | 54.8 |
| CATV | 0.015 | 0.27 | 0.52 | 0.002 | 0.062 | 0.80 |
| Records & tapes | NA | 0.0003 | 0.0003 | 0.12 | 0.10 | 0.09 |
| Movies | 0.125 | 0.033 | 0.022 | 1.01 | 0.54 | 0.47 |
| Education | 0.12 | 0.043 | 0.028 | 9.57 | 7.88 | 6.74 |
| Newspapers | 6.20 | 2.19 | 1.91 | 20.7 | 10.9 | 9.03 |
| Magazines | 0.98 | 0.32 | 0.28 | 4.55 | 3.58 | 3.33 |
| Books | 0.16 | 0.065 | 0.056 | 6.40 | 5.04 | 4.70 |
| Telephone direc. | — | — | — | — | — | — |
| Direct mail | 0.30 | 0.091 | 0.091 | 0.13 | 0.10 | 0.11 |
| | 100% | 100% | 100% | 100% | 100% | 100% |

#### Japan

| Medium | Words Supplied | | Words Consumed | |
|---|---|---|---|---|
| | 1960 | 1975 | 1960 | 1975 |
| Radio | 64.4% | 40.8% | 26.7% | 6.70% |
| TV | 19.2 | 50.2 | 17.5 | 47.7 |
| CATV | 0.34 | 0.76 | 0.24 | 1.91 |
| Records & tapes | — | — | — | — |
| Movies | 0.61 | 0.06 | 1.83 | 0.19 |
| Education | 0.73 | 0.18 | 19.6 | 11.9 |
| Newspapers | 11.9 | 6.61 | 22.7 | 21.1 |
| Magazines | 1.57 | 0.83 | 5.27 | 4.74 |
| Books | 0.38 | 0.29 | 4.93 | 4.43 |
| Telephon direc. | 0.20 | 0.23 | 0.005 | 0.004 |
| Direct mail | 0.30 | 0.12 | 1.23 | 1.38 |
| | 100% | 100% | 100% | 100% |

### (b) Point-to-Point Media

| | U.S.A. | | | Japan | |
|---|---|---|---|---|---|
| | 1960 | 1975 | 1980 | 1960 | 1975 |
| First class mail | 22.9% | 16.0% | 13.1% | 47.0% | 21.1% |
| Telephone | 76.9 | 79.7 | 76.6 | 51.8 | 50.3 |
| Telex | 0.0001 | 0.0009 | 0.0014 | 1.11 | 1.08 |
| Telegraph | 0.009 | 0.0004 | 0.0002 | 0.008 | 0.002 |
| Mailgram | — | 0.0013 | 0.0020 | — | — |
| Facsimile | — | 0.02 | 0.054 | 0.038 | 0.24 |
| Data | 0.23 | 4.28 | 10.2 | — | 27.3 |
| | 100% | 100% | 100% | 100% | 100% |

years from 1960 through 1980 which provide the basis for the Japanese media consumption estimates.[4] In the U.S., in contrast, there were usually only one or two reliable estimates in the decades we covered. Thus our estimates of reading time are sometimes constants or modified constants rather than time series.

Since time spent reading newspapers is well over half of all reading time, this problem centers on the data about that. We found ourselves forced to consider two different estimates for American consumption of newspapers. The one we generally use in these aggregate statistics is based on a reported decline in the amount of time spent reading daily newspapers; the other assumes constancy in average reading time per person. The first newspaper estimate results in a growth rate of 0.2% since 1960 in print words consumed, while the second estimate results in an annual growth rate of 1.6%.

We resorted to these two boundary estimates because for the U.S. we have only two usable newspaper data points. In 1965, a survey of daily use of time was conducted as part of Alexander Szalai's comparative international time budget study. Reading time for newspapers was included, as well as for other media. In 1975, John Robinson replicated the earlier study and found that Americans were spending considerably less time reading newspapers than they did in 1965.[5] But a number of the media

---

4) NHK Public Opinion Research Institute, *How Do People Spend Their Time Survey*. Cf. Kenzo Yamada, "Leisure Activity of the Japanese," Radio and TV Cultural Research Institute, NHK, *Studies of Broadcasting*, 1983, pp. 93–118; Naomichi Nakanishi, "A Report on 'How Do People Spend Their Time' Survey in 1980," *Studies of Broadcasting*, 1982.

5) Cf. John P. Robinson, *How Americans Used Time in 1965*, Ann Arbor: U. of Michigan, Institute of Social Research, 1977. For the international study, cf. Alexander Szalai, *et al.*, *Use of Time* (The Hague: Mouton, 1972). John P. Robinson, *Changes in American Use of Time*: 1965–1975, Cleveland State University Communications Research Center, 1975. A 1961 national study sponsored by the Newsprint Information Committee reported 36 minutes of daily reading time per adult reader for newspapers of all sizes. See Chilton Bush, ed., *News Research for Better Newspapers*, vol. 1 (New York: American Newspaper Publishers Association Foundation, 1966), pp. 9–11. We did not use this data because of comparability problems. The result is a somewhat higher figure than that obtained from the time budget studies, even when it is assumed that this value is the average for only those who read newspapers and is adjusted accordingly. It was reached, however, through a different methodology, one which involved asking subjects a question rather than having them keep a diary. Nevertheless, along with numerous local studies that have touched on this matter, it does confirm the general order of magnitude of time spent on newspaper reading.

results from this latter study have come under criticism. The source of the problems is obscure. It could be nothing more than random variation causing the results of this one study to deviate from most, as is bound to happen from time to time.

The general conclusion that can be drawn from Robinson's findings does agree with the impressions of firms in the industry which sporadically in local studies ask people (the rather unreliable question) "about how much time do you usually spend reading the newspaper" or "how much time did you spend reading it yesterday?" Those who have been doing such local studies over the years have the impression that there is some decline, but not as much as Robinson's data suggest. Furthermore, there is every reason to expect a decline; the number of American cities with multiple newspapers has declined in this period. It is well documented in newspaper research that the number of persons reading more than one paper a day has declined for that reason; those who have dropped a second paper tend to read papers for fewer minutes a day. For these reasons we have chosen in our consolidated data to reflect the view that there has been a decline in the minutes of newspaper reading.

Nevertheless, even if Robinson's later results as well as his earlier ones are completely correct, two points do not give us a basis for estimating the shape of that trend. We have postulated exponential decay, and have projected such a trend back from 1965 to 1960 and forward from 1975 to 1980. That, however, is an arbitrary assumption. Perhaps we are in the presence of an S curve; what happened from 1965 to 1975 may not have been happening before or afterwards. There may be a levelling off. Or perhaps there were annual fluctuations and the two years of observation were off the main trend line.

If we were looking at supply figures there would be good reason for believing the last to be the case. In fact we find that in the mid-1970s there was a dip in newsprint use in the U.S.A., partly as a result of a rapid run-up in newsprint prices and partly because of economic recession. In contrast, the late 1970s leading up to 1980 were a period of relative prosperity, growth in advertising, and corresponding growth in the size of newspapers (if not their circulation). There was consequently growth in the supply of words in print. However, words consumed, which is our concern here, do not necessarily track the growth of words supplied.

**Table 3.9**
GROWTH RATES OF PRINT AND ELECTRONIC MEDIA SINCE 1960

|  | Words Supplied | | Words Consumed | |
| --- | --- | --- | --- | --- |
|  | U.S.A. | Japan | U.S.A. | Japan |
| Print media | 2.2% | 5.5% | 0.2%* | 2.7% |
| Electronic media | 8.7 | 10.3 | 4.7 | 5.1 |

* Using newspaper estimate 1.

**Table 3.10**
MOST RECENT DATA ON GROWTH RATES OF PRINT AND ELECTRONIC MEDIA

|  | Words Supplied | | | Words Consumed | | |
| --- | --- | --- | --- | --- | --- | --- |
|  | U.S.A. | | Japan | U.S.A. | | Japan |
|  | 1970-75 | 1975-80 | 1970-75 | 1970-75 | 1975-80 | 1970-75 |
| Print media | 2.8% | 3.2% | 0.8% | 0.3% | 0.1% | 5.2% |
| Electronic media | 8.3 | 6.0 | 11.9 | 5.4 | 4.0 | 4.6 |

* Using newspaper estimate 1.

Given these uncertainties, we have reported two series for newspaper consumption based on different assumptions. In the absence of more than one data point we also used an assumption of constancy in average time spent reading the much smaller media of magazines and books. For these reasons, the comparison of consumption with supply figures, like that of American with Japanese consumption figures, is particularly weak for the print media.

The data which we trust more, those on words supplied, present a clear picture: while print is far from dead, the contrast to the growth of the electronic media is striking (Tables 3.9 and 3.10 and Figure 3.14). In print media there was a break in the rate of growth in the late 1960s and early 1970s. As we discussed in the previous chapter, this was related in part to the oil crisis and the economy, in part to the competition of the new electronic alternatives. Although these conditions affected the use of expensive means of communication, that does not mean people stopped reading. On the contrary, in Japan from 1970 to 1975, growth in consumption of print media exceeded that for electronic media (something that was certainly not true in the United States). But in supply there was evidence in the early 1970s of at least a temporary arrest. The data for 1975 to 1980, which

64  SOME AGGREGATE TRENDS

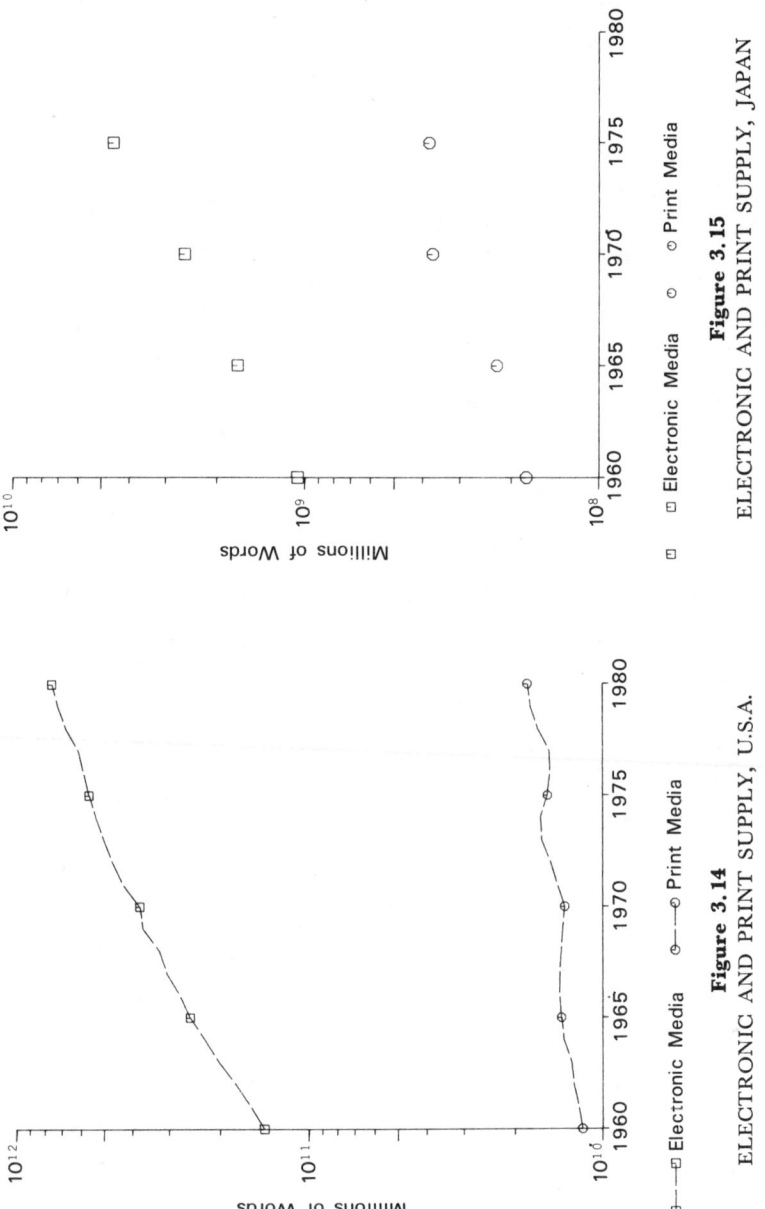

**Figure 3.14**
ELECTRONIC AND PRINT SUPPLY, U.S.A.

**Figure 3.15**
ELECTRONIC AND PRINT SUPPLY, JAPAN

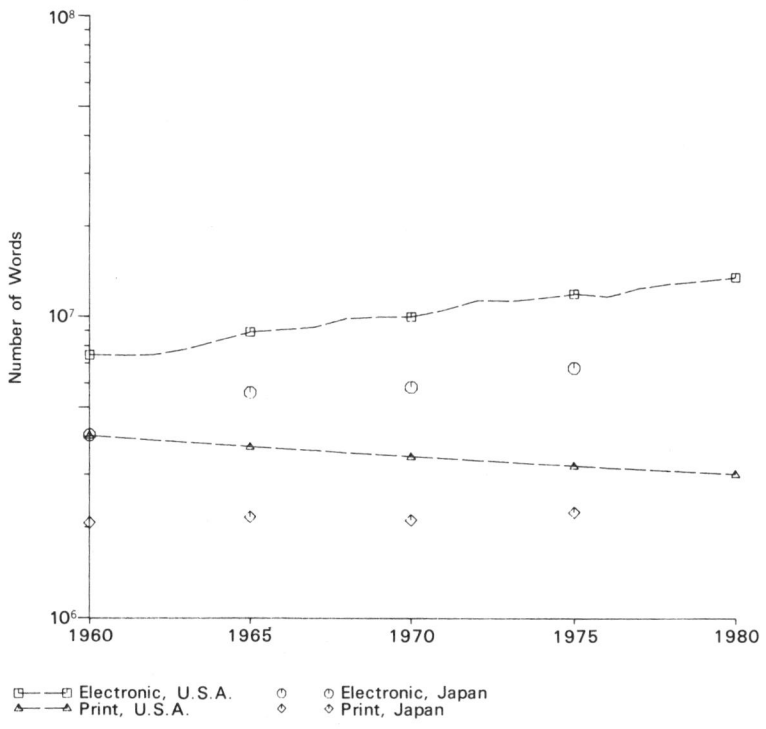

**Figure 3.16**
ELECTRONIC AND PRINT MEDIA CONSUMED PER CAPITA

we have only for the United States, make clear that the more rapid growth of the electronic media does not mean that printing in the Gutenberg mold will stop. The growth rates in the print media are, however, and are likely to remain, substantially lower than those for the new media.

### 3.2.5 Subgroups of Media

For additional analysis we have divided the media into four groups: print mass media, electronic mass media, print point-to-point media, and electronic point-to-point media. However, these subgroupings turn out not to be very useful since a subgroup may be dominated by one medium and also because the mass media are so dominant in the total flow. For the latter reason

66  SOME AGGREGATE TRENDS

**Table 3.11**
MAIL AMONG THE PRINT MEDIA

|  | % of Words Supplied | | % of Words Consumed | |
| --- | --- | --- | --- | --- |
|  | Japan | U.S.A. | Japan | U.S.A. |
|  | 1975 | 1980 | 1975 | 1977 |
| First class mail | 0.4% | 0.2% | 2.2% | 4.3% |
| Mass print media | 99.6 | 99.8 | 97.8 | 95.7 |
|  | 100% | 100% | 100% | 100% |

**Table 3.12**
POINT-TO-POINT MEDIA AMONG ELECTRONIC MEDIA

|  | % of Words Supplied | | % of Words Consumed | |
| --- | --- | --- | --- | --- |
|  | Japan | U.S.A. | Japan | U.S.A. |
|  | 1975 | 1980 | 1975 | 1977 |
| Point-to-point electronic media | 0.1% | 0.02% | 3.0% | 6.3% |
| Mass electronic media | 99.9 | 99.98 | 97.0 | 93.7 |
|  | 100% | 100% | 100% | 100% |

there can be very little difference between what we have already noted about trends in print and electronic media as a whole and what we now observe about print and electronic mass media. The above tabulations for words supplied by print or electronically will not be affected if we exclude the fraction of a percent for the point-to-point media. Similarly, for words consumed, excluding at most four percent of the words in print or six percent of the electronic words cannot alter the conclusions drawn above about electronic media in general.

A separate look at the point-to-point media could be more meaningful. However, among the point-to-point media only one is non-electronic, namely first class mail. In both countries the volume of mail words grew, but less rapidly than did electronic messages. For two decades of our American time series, first class mail volume grew at 2.8% per annum, while the electronic point-to-point volume expanded 6.3% per annum. In Japan from 1960 to 1975, first class mail volume grew at 4.1% per annum and the electronic point-to-point media at 12.8% per annum.

The more rapid electronic message growth in Japan than in the U.S. is explained mainly by the approach in the former country during that period to universal telephone penetration,

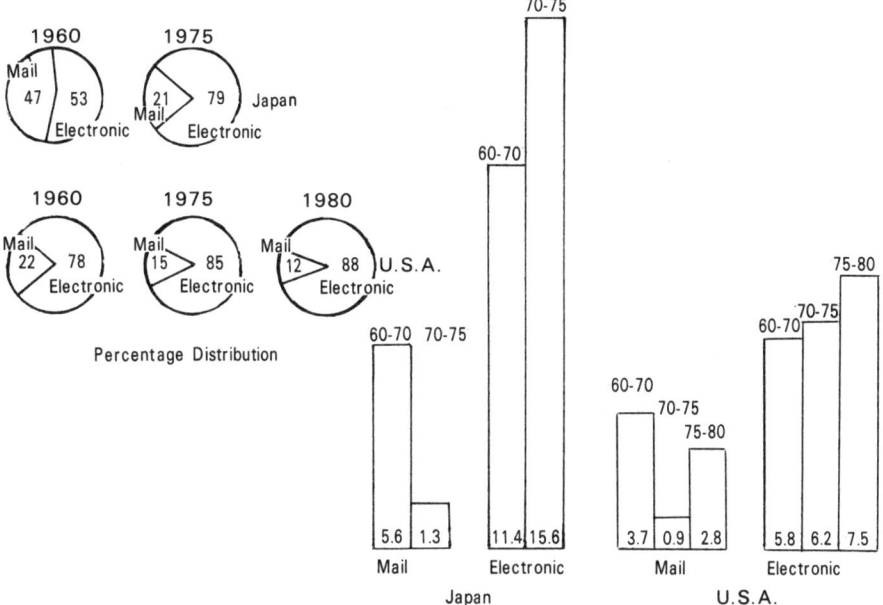

**Figure 3.17**
GROWTH RATES: MAIL VS. ELECTRONIC POINT-TO-POINT MEDIA

which had already been achieved in the United States by 1960. In the 1970s in both countries the rate of growth for first class mail declined, while that for electronic point-to-point media accelerated. This recent acceleration appears mostly due in both countries to the emergence of data communication, since voice telephony was a mature, universal medium in the U.S. and nearly so by then in Japan. Although the precise growth figures for data communication are non-comparable, the conclusion remains that first telephony and more recently data communication have kept electronic point-to-point media expanding vigorously.

### 3.2.6 Office Communications

Among the media of communication on which we have no adequate data, the most important, no doubt, are conversation and office communication. There are others too. The words that flow in the complex system of military reconnaissance, command, and control must be vast, but are unknowable to us. There are courier services which in the United States in the early 1980s handled an estimated 300,000 pieces per day or two-tenths of one percent of the first class mail. There are other small media such as the live theatre and churches. But the ones that we would like to have included in this census, had we been able, are above all conversation and office communications.

To the best of our knowledge, the only careful social research that has attempted to document the amount of conversation in which people engage was a Hungarian study, which had, as far as we know, no published results. A sample of individuals agreed to wear tape recorders strapped to their bodies for full days. The researchers were surprised at the small total amount of conversation in which their subjects engaged, but we have no figures. It is unlikely that this study will be replicated elsewhere without significant protection of the privacy of the subjects.

Office communication has become the subject of a follow-on study by the American research team, and some preliminary results can be reported here. Time series of the sort that we required for this flow census do not exist. But with the assistance of the Xerox Corporation we have been able to use a series of studies on the flow of information in offices. These, along with basic data on the amount of office employment and types of activity, allow us to make some estimates of the size of the office word flow.

Had it been possible to generate time series data for the past two decades on office communications, we would undoubtedly have found rather robust growth curves. During that period, both the number and proportion of workers who were engaged in information processing activities at their place of work was growing substantially.[6] So, even if there were no change in document handling per employee, the yearly addition of employees in managerial, clerical, and administrative activities would imply expanding volumes of words supplied and consumed. On top of that, however, the development of reprographics has drastically increased the numbers of document copies distributed to each such employee.

---

6) Fritz Machlup, *The Production and Distribution of Knowledge in the United States*, Princeton, N.J.: Princeton University Press, 1962; Organisation for Economic Co-operation and Development, *Information Activities, Electronics and Telecommunications Technologies: Impact on Employment, Growth and Trade*, Paris: OECD, 1981; M. U. Porat et al., *The Information Economy*, Washington, D.C., U.S. Department of Commerce Special Publication, 1977.

One cannot assume that this unmeasured growth curve of the past two decades will continue unchanged into the future. While technical advance in the ease and cheapness of making copies probably will continue, the structure of the workforce may show quite different trends.

Charles Jonscher, in a major work on that last point, observes that with 80% of the information sector workers being engaged in management and co-ordination, and with that sector now constituting about half of the total workforce, the economic incentive for improving productivity in information and management activities has become very strong indeed.[7] At the same time, the computer and information handling technology in general has made possible significant increases in the productivity of such workers. As a result, starting in the last decade, the growth in the information workforce has begun to slow relative to the previously expected values which Jonscher calculated from a structural analysis of information activities in the economy. That is to say, a rise in productivity per employee in information activities has begun, and it can be expected to continue.

So any forecast of wordflow in business information has to take account of two opposite and interacting factors: a probable decline in the proportion of the workforce engaged in information activities—Jonscher forecasts a drop of about four points by the year 2000—and an increase in the ease and economy with which those employees will be able to produce information traffic. One can anticipate, perhaps, that the growth in office words supplied and available to office workers will continue to grow at a fairly rapid rate, despite a reversal of the trend of growth in the number of such workers.

Some of the information supplied and consumed in American offices is already included in our tabulations on various media, particularly point-to-point media such as telex and the public telephone network. But the vast majority of the office information flow is unmeasured because it is composed of words on paper sent through the firm's internal mail, telephone words transmitted through private branch exchanges (PBX's), and words spoken at office meetings.

This conclusion is based on a substantial number of surveys

---

7) Charles Jonscher, "Information Resources and Economic Productivity," *Information Economics and Policy*, vol. 1, no. 1, 1983, pp. 13–35.

(most of them proprietary) of the flow of work within offices. One 1978 study of office procedures at the headquarters of a large American corporation found that published material like books and magazines constituted only 6% of filed material, while documents, reports, computer print-outs and punched cards took up 75%. That result appears in line with the findings in other studies that, on average, 85% to 95% of incoming and outgoing mail was received from or directed to locations within the firm.[8] Moreover, the series of studies also showed that the Postal Service transmitted at most 10% to 15% of such mail and other hardcopy work inputs or additional information used by managers, professionals and clerical workers. The rest was transmitted by internal mail, hand carried or picked up.

A similar picture emerges for telephone use. A rule of thumb in the PBX industry suggest that 60% of calls originating within such a system are within the system. The office studies support a still higher estimate of the proportion of calls to persons within the firm. One may infer from data in the series of studies that 70% of all calls are internal to the firm; while a different proprietary study reports that only 13% of incoming and outgoing calls handled by managers and professionals and 12% of those handled by clerical personnel were external. Of course, many of the intracompany calls may be made over the public network, especially since only a third of total business telephones in the U.S. are in some PBX. Nevertheless, it seems inevitable that as the number of such systems and the number of stations in them grow, the public network will supply a diminishing share of the telephone words in the office flows. A possible exception to this pattern of communications is the office of the most highly placed executive. Henry Mintzberg found that more than half the mail received by his small sample of chief executive officers was from outside the organization, and about half of their contact time, including telephone calls, was spent with outsiders. Slightly less than half of outgoing mail went to outsiders. But there are very few chief executive officers.[9]

Paper constitutes the primary means for the flow of informa-

---

8) Data from Xerox Office Profile (an unpublished compilation of 62 office studies) and from two other proprietary studies.

9) Henry Mintzberg, *The Nature of Managerial Work*, New York: Harper & Row, 1973, pp. 244 ff.

tion among office workers. Managers, professionals, and clerical workers spent, on average, close to 70% of their time with work inputs and additional information in hard copy, 10% in telephone conversation, and somewhat more than 10% in meetings. In the decade of the 1970s, when the studies were done, less than 5% of their aggregate time involved other electronic media including computer-generated or related material like visual displays, printouts, and punched cards. Very likely, the use of computer-mediated material has already increased with the diffusion of visual display terminals and, more recently, personal computers in American offices. Indeed, a comparison of studies in the series with more recent but methodologically similar ones suggests that the time managers and professionals spent with such materials rose from 2% to 3% during the 1975-80 period.

The distribution of work time among use of paper, telephone, and meetings is fairly uniform across occupational levels except for those at the highest managerial level, who seemed to spend half or more of their time in meetings. There is also some evidence from the office studies that at various levels, the percent of time spent on the telephone and in meetings increased during the 1970s. However, since these cannot be considered representative of the office population period by period, one may hesitate to accept the results in the earlier and later studies as fully comparable.

Whatever the growth of other means of communications, there is strong evidence of substantial growth of paper-based information flows in the office. From 1960 to 1980, the yearly average growth of bond and writing paper supplied in the U.S. was 8.1%, and it was 9.1% for form bond.[10] Consumption in the form of reading from the paper-based flow takes up about 10% of the aggregate work hours of managers, professionals, and clericals. Average reading time remained fairly constant during the 1970s, but it should be noted that the minutes workers spend reading tends to rise with their occupational level. Ten per cent of work time amounts to about twice the 1980 figure for newspaper reading time, but because the office population is only about a fifth of the general population, office reading averaged across the whole population amounts to much less than newspaper reading; it

---

10) American Paper Institute, *Statistics of Paper, Paperboard and Wood Pulp*, 1981, New York, 1981, pp. 6-9.

represents approximately the level of word consumption from magazines. In terms of amount of time spent, reading, telephoning, and participating in meetings are nearly equivalent activities; but since reading rates are about twice speaking rates in words consumed, reading results in about twice as large a consumption of words.

The data we have reported on office communications reflects many of the same trends that we have noted elsewhere in this study: e.g., growth, fast growth in electronic communication, faster growth in words supplied than in consumption. Time spent reading, being roughly constant per capita, the growth in reading is more or less linear with the growth in the office population. At the same time the figures on paper supply suggest a fast exponential growth of words supplied. Strangely then, there seems to have been at most only a linear growth in the number of original documents produced, since the most striking time trend in the series of office studies is a decline in the time spent writing.[11] Word processing, which only just got under way in the 1970s would permit at least a partial maintenance of the number of different documents produced in a lesser amount of time. Reprographics would help account for an increase in the number of copies and of the supply of writen information at an exponential rate, despite the slow growth in the number of originals. One proprietary study found that even ordinary letters and memos averaged four addressees.

This analysis is written at a point of time which represents the very beginning of office automation. We find the office communications system to be much more paper-based than the communications system of the general public. We also find the same trends as in the rest of the society toward an explosion of words supplied, and a resulting information overload. This may well force information consumers to use the very technologies of information handling which were a major factor in the growth of supply, to manage such supply more efficiently than was possible in the past.

### 3.2.7 Functions of Communication

In one of its studies using the basic flow census data, the Japa-

---

11) The raw figures suggest a reduction by half, but that result must be viewed with caution because of the non-comparability of the early and late samples.

nese team sorted out the different uses made of communications, and their relative growth rates. These uses were classified into three functions: information for work, information for living, and entertainment; and each medium was examined to arrive at some estimate of how its flow was allocated among those three.

The trichotomy actually results from a two-way classification leading to a four-fold table. The various media were grouped into those providing information for work and those providing information for living and also into entertainment and nonentertainment media. These two cross-cutting dichotomies allow four possible cells, one of which has no member.

|  | Non-Entertainment | Entertainment |
| --- | --- | --- |
| Information for Work |  | Nonexistent |
| Information for Living |  |  |

"Information for work" refers to communications related to production, commerce, etc. "Information for living" consists of communications that socialize individuals and direct their personal consumption and development. Finally "entertainment" refers to communications that are intended to divert. For example, a feature film is entertainment, professional literature is information for working, and a public affairs TV program is non-entertainment information for living.

Some media tend to fall entirely into one or another of the three cells. Thus telex carries information for work and movies are entertainment. Other media have a mixed character. Mail, for example, carries business and personal messages, as do telephone calls. Newspapers provide both "hard news," which nurtures world views, and human interest and comic strips, which entertain. Some magazines and books are intended to entertain while others are professional literature or work instructions. Primary and secondary schools are principally socializers, but higher educational institutions devote many of their class hours to professional training. That is, they dispense information for work. Finally, TV, radio, and even cable television mix public affairs and cultural programming, which is information for living, with entertainment programs.

To permit comparison of the U.S. and Japanese data, the American media were classified in the same way as the Japanese, insofar as possible. The Japanese study made rough estimates of how each of the mixed media divided among cells, and similar estimates were made for the U.S.[12] For example, the estimate that American newspapers are half information for living and half entertainment is based upon a content survey of several 1981 issues of two local newspapers. The disaggregation rules for the mixed media and the quantitative results are presented in Appendix 2.

With these limitations, tentative and somewhat surprising comparisons and contrasts can be made. First, in both Japan and the U.S.A. the volume of information for working is a minuscule part of the total volume supplied and a very small part of the volume consumed. The tabulated media, however, did not include office communication. In neither country did it exceed 0.3% of the volume supplied for any observed year. In both, however, it constituted an increasing part of the volume consumed, rising from 3.8% in 1960 to 5.2% in 1977 for the U.S.A. and from 1.4% in 1960 to 3.0% in 1975 in Japan.

The U.S.A. and Japan apparently differ greatly in the breakdown of the remaining material. In the U.S.A., 73% to 75% of total volume supplied and 58% to 60% of the total consumed is entertainment. Lest those who deplore the kitsch entertainment carried by the mass media be too depressed by the dominance of that material in the U.S.A., they should note that information for living was nonetheless a large and also more rapidly growing component of the total flow. In Japan, on the other hand, the bulk of the total supplied is considered information for living (63.4% in 1960; 71.7% in 1975), while information for living and entertainment compose equal shares of the volume consumed. Moreover, in Japan the share of information for living in total volume supplied has increased, while the share of such information in total consumption has decreased. Put another way, the Japanese appear to be increasing their consumption of entertainment relative to their entire media consumption, despite the

---

12) There are nevertheless differences between the decision rules used in the American and Japanese studies, and in this part of the analysis it was not possible to make the transformations of the data that we made above to bring them in line. So the Japanese data on the volume supplied of information for working, information for living, and entertainment are based on counting formulas which measure volume produced, not volume supplied.

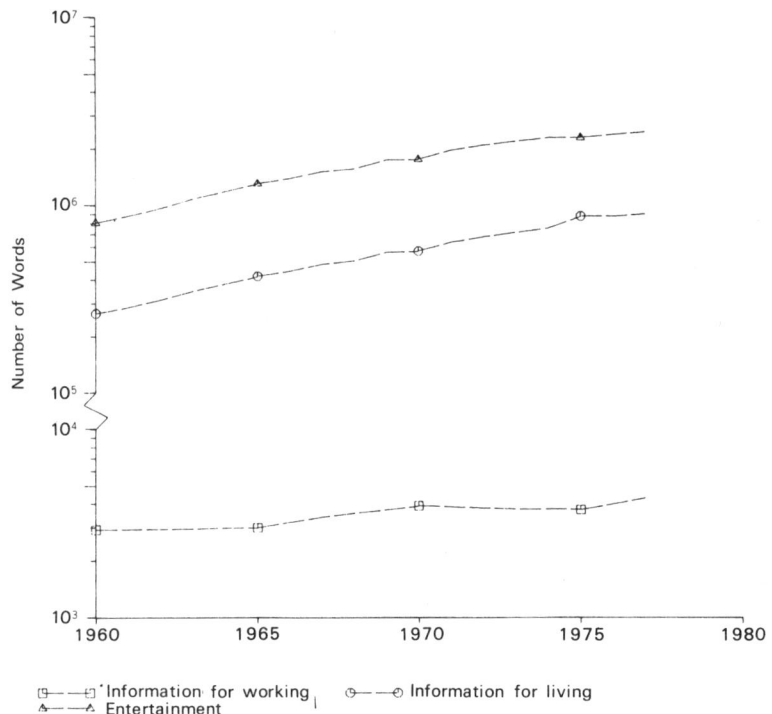

**Figure 3.18**
PER CAPITA SUPPLY OF INFORMATION BY FUNCTION, U.S.A.

fact that their media are carrying more non-entertainment than in the past. The notable fact remains that non-entertainment material constitutes a substantially larger proportion of Japanese than of American media content.

# Chapter 4
# THE INDIVIDUAL MEDIA

78 THE INDIVIDUAL MEDIA

After first presenting the basic Japanese data, this chapter discusses the data for each medium included in the study. We summarize and comment upon the trends in each case and any major problems encountered with the data. Graphs are used to show the trends from 1960 on the volume of words supplied and consumed, production costs, transmission cost, and consumption cost in 1972 dollars. There are also graphs comparing Japanese and American trends on a per capita basis.

In the Appendices will be found a description of the datasets from which the graphs are derived: the equations used and the definitions of the variables in them; notes on the variables, including bibliographic identification of the data sources, and the data year by year for each American variable.

The basic Japanese data are in Tables 4.1 and 4.2 and Figures 4.1, 4.2, and 4.3.

## 4.1 Radio Broadcasting

From about 1950 to 1954 in the United States and a few years later in Japan, radio, which had been the dominant medium in communications flow, was hard hit by the coming of TV. The amount of listening declined in both countries; advertising revenues dropped in the United States, and in Japan, the volume of words produced by radio grew only slowly. In 1960, when TV saturation had already been reached in the U.S. but not yet in Japan, radio listening in the two countries was farily similar, 108 minutes per person per day in the former, 95 minutes in the latter. Listening continued to decline moderately in the U.S. for the next several years, but in Japan it fell by 1965 to only a quarter of the amount five years earlier.

The decline in radio proved in part temporary. In both countries, despite the decline in consumption, the volume of material broadcast grew, and in Japan the growth after 1965 was more rapid than for 1960–1965 (4.3% vs. 2.4% per annum). More important, after the sharp drops listening began picking up again. That was in part due to the penetration of cheap, small transistor sets among young people. In Japan, an apparent shift from more serious to entertainment programming may have stimulated additional listening. However, the recovery in radio usage has been much greater in the U.S. than in Japan. The difference in

## Table 4.1
## VOLUME OF PRODUCTION OF WORDS BY MEDIUM IN JAPAN

| Media \ Year | 1960 | 1965 | 1970 | 1975 | Growth rate per annum (%) |
|---|---|---|---|---|---|
| Telephone | 31,250 | 42,193 | 89,853 | 124,389 | 9.6 |
| Telegram | 5 | 5 | 5 | 6 | 1.2 |
| Telex | 672 | 1,095 | 2,721 | 2,672 | 9.6 |
| Facsimile | 23 | 72 | 174 | 603 | 24.3 |
| Data Transmission | | 35 | 1,707 | 67,360 | 65.6 |
| Mail | 28,380 | 41,070 | 48,760 | 52,090 | 4.1 |
| Direct Mail | 98,300 | 142,800 | 168,900 | 177,000 | 4.0 |
| Newspaper Preprinted Inserts | — | — | — | 227,000 | — |
| Radio | 21,150,000 | 24,430,000 | 44,920,000 | 68,710,000 | 8.2 |
| Television | 6,536,000 | 23,478,000 | 35,375,000 | 84,585,000 | 18.6 |
| CATV | 110,500 | 383,400 | 728,000 | 1,282,100 | 17.8 |
| Newspapers | 3,919,000 | 5,364,000 | 9,910,000 | 10,835,000 | 7.0 |
| Books | 121,400 | 220,300 | 374,700 | 483,300 | 9.6 |
| Magazines | 514,100 | 660,500 | 1,133,400 | 1,400,900 | 6.9 |
| Telephone Directory | 59,500 | 99,000 | 282,000 | 392,000 | 13.4 |
| Movie | 1,196 | 746 | 521 | 392 | −7.2 |
| Education | 70,500 | 77,200 | 68,600 | 72,600 | 0.2 |
| Total | 32,640,826 | 54,940,416 | 93,104,341 | 168,412,412 | 11.6 |

## Table 4.2
## VOLUME CONSUMPTION OF WORDS BY MEDIUM IN JAPAN

| Media \ Year | 1960 | 1965 | 1970 | 1975 | Growth rate per annum (%) |
|---|---|---|---|---|---|
| Telephone | 31,250 | 42,193 | 89,853 | 124,389 | 9.6 |
| Telegram | 5 | 5 | 5 | 6 | 1.2 |
| Telex | 672 | 1,095 | 2,721 | 2,672 | 9.6 |
| Facsimile | 23 | 72 | 174 | 603 | 24.3 |
| Data Transmission | | 35 | 1,707 | 67,360 | 65.6 |
| Mail | 28,380 | 41,070 | 48,760 | 52,090 | 4.1 |
| Direct Mail | 55,500 | 80,700 | 95,400 | 100,000 | 4.0 |
| Newspaper Preprinted Inserts | — | — | — | 269,600 | — |
| Radio | 1,859,000 | 508,000 | 543,000 | 749,000 | −5.9 |
| Television | 1,215,000 | 3,993,000 | 4,474,000 | 5,337,000 | 10.4 |
| CATV | 16,410 | 75,720 | 106,830 | 214,160 | 18.7 |
| Newspapers | 1,027,600 | 1,138,000 | 1,119,900 | 1,263,200 | 1.4 |
| Books | 223,000 | 248,000 | 272,000 | 322,000 | 2.5 |
| Magazines | 238,000 | 263,000 | 289,000 | 345,000 | 2.5 |
| Telephone Directory | 244 | 272 | 290 | 304 | 1.5 |
| Movie | 82,700 | 30,400 | 20,800 | 14,200 | −11.1 |
| Education | 885,000 | 923,000 | 801,200 | 863,300 | −0.2 |
| Total | 5,662,179 | 7,344,562 | 7,865,640 | 9,724,884 | 3.7 |

Unit: $10^8$ words.

80 THE INDIVIDUAL MEDIA

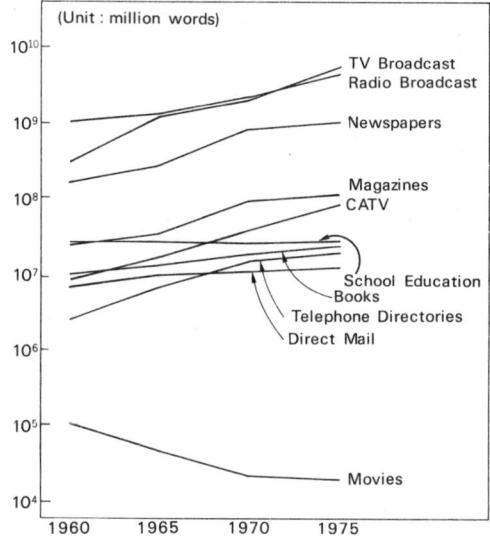

**Figure 4.1**
WORDS SUPPLIED BY EACH MASS MEDIUM: JAPAN

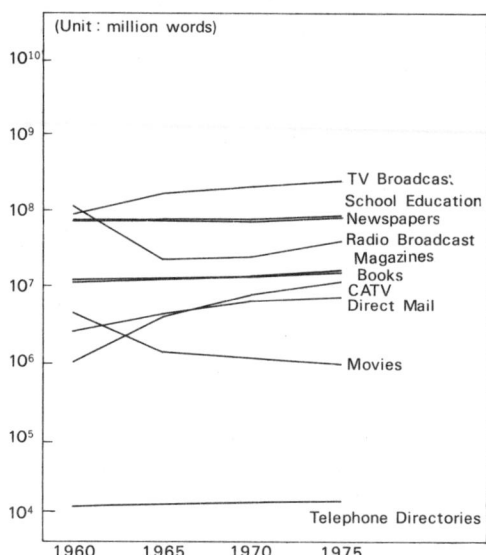

**Figure 4.2**
WORDS CONSUMED FROM EACH MASS MEDIUM: JAPAN

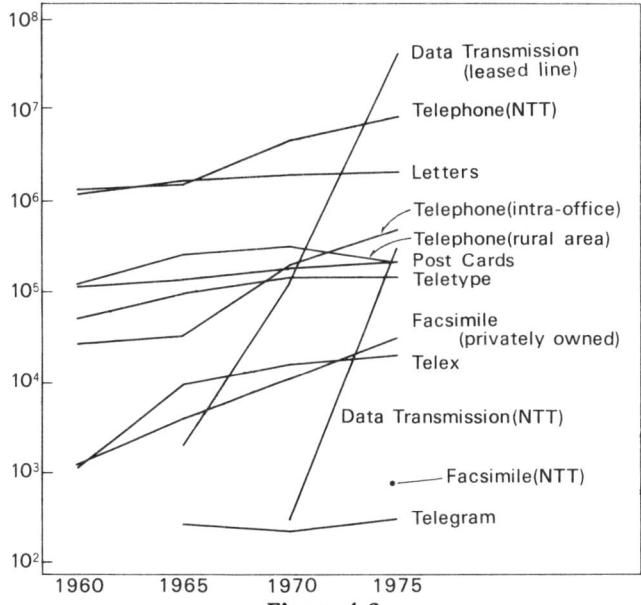

**Figure 4.3**
WORDS SUPPLIED BY POINT-TO-POINT MEDIA: JAPAN

volume of radio words supplied is partly a function of national policy. In the U.S., the FCC has sought to make as many licenses available as possible, with the result that there are many more stations on the air.

In the U.S., radio listening bottomed out in 1962: by 1965 it was significantly higher than in 1960 and continued rising through 1980. Although the individual daily average in Japan was also rising by 1970, the rate of rise was much slower. As a result of these differences, radio consumption in Japan fell by more than half from 1960 to 1975 while in the U.S. it grew by an average of 4.5% per annum, and 3.7% per annum for the full period 1960–1980. Still, the rate of growth in American radio consumption fell off in the 1970s: from 1972 to 1980 it was only 1.5% per annum.

One factor behind the difference between the two countries was the earlier universal penetration in the U.S. of the automobile radio. A Japanese commuter may spend two hours every day in a crowded train, while many of his U.S. counterparts travel in a car with the radio on for a similar length of time.

A more fundamental reason for the growth in radio is its cheapness. As shown in Figures 2.1 and 2.3, radio is the least expensive of all the media we studied, with a cost per word supplied, an order of magnitude less than for TV and several orders less than that for print media. As the figures show, the average yearly decline in such cost was 4.0% and it was paralleled by the average annual decline in production costs of 4.4%. Consumption cost per word likewise fell, at an annual rate of 5.4%.

Production costs of radio broadcasts are defined as programming, while transmission costs include all the rest of the broadcaster's expenditures. Consumption costs are what the public spends for radio sets, and do not include any estimate for radio repairs, which have fallen almost to zero in the U.S.

These declines in radio costs arise from the replacement of expensive programming formats with such cheap ones as playing of records and also from advances in electronic technology. The transistor revolution made radio sets so cheap and small that households can own several.

A consequence of the extreme cheapness of radio broadcasting is that the ratio of words supplied to words consumed is higher than for any other medium. In 1960 radio words consumed in America were three-tenths of one percent of words supplied, and in 1980 just one-tenth of one percent. The costs were such that broadcasters could afford to put out all that material despite its low consumption.

For broadcasting, our definition of words supplied is the number of receiving sets multiplied by the average number of stations available per community, multiplied by the average hours of broadcasting by a station and by the words contained per unit of broadcasting time, times the number of persons over 10 years old per household. All these figures, except for the number of words spoken per minute of broadcasting, come from published sources. The words spoken per minute on U.S. radio were estimated by taping random minutes from the Boston radio stations and counting the words said or sung. The basic Japanese figures for words produced do not multiply the words broadcast by the number of receivers in a household, though in comparative tables and charts we have applied that factor to the original figures. The logic of the equation for words supplied is that it counts the broadcast material which is there to be heard by any grown member of the household if he or she chooses to turn a set on. In principle, if a word could be heard by a person simply by tuning to it, it has been supplied.

Words consumed is the hours per day an average person spends listening to radio, times the number of persons over 10 years old, times the number of words broadcast per minute, all reduced by a factor for inattention. Since we are unaware of any radio research that measures inattention, we used an estimate made on attention and inattention to TV broadcasts. Because the basic Japanese figures do not include such a factor, for comparative purposes we applied the same value to those data.

One weakness in the radio consumption data in the United States is the fact that estimates of hours of daily listening for different years were made by different research organizations using somewhat different methodologies. TV has been rich enough to afford a highly regular and detailed set of Nielsen ratings. Ever since radio lost its preeminence as an adveratising medium, radio ratings have had to be done inexpensively, and organizations doing radio ratings have come and gone. Also, for a number of years the only American data reported were household sets-in-use figures rather than the individual listening figures we needed. Estimates of individual listening were made for those years by applying the ratio of household figures to individual figures found it those years when both existed. The result is a radio consumption time series in which we can have a fair but limited confidence.

## 4.2 Television

By the end of the time period that we have studied, television was the source of far more words consumed than any other medium. Universal penetration of television came later in Japan than in America. In 1960 in Japan 21%, and in the U.S. 38%, of all words consumed from the tabulated media already came from TV, and by 1975 that had risen to 55% in Japan and 48% in the U.S. By 1980, it had risen to 52.1% in the U.S. The growths follow the typical pattern for a new medium, with initial rapid growth followed by slower growth as some level of saturation is approached (see Table 4.3).

**Table 4.3**
TV GROWTH RATES

|  | Words Consumed | | Words Supplied | |
| --- | --- | --- | --- | --- |
|  | Japan | U.S.A. | Japan* | U.S.A. |
| 1960–1970 | 13.9% | 5.1% | 16.4% | 11.8% |
| 1970–1975 | 3.6 | 5.1 | 17.3 | 8.9 |
| 1975–1980 | NA | 4.5 | NA | 9.1 |
| 1960–1975 | 10.4 | 5.1 | 16.7 | 10.9 |
| 1960–1980 | NA | 4.8 | NA | 10.4 |

* Adjusted by household factor.

**Table 4.4**
TV VIEWING TIME

|  | Japan | U.S.A. |
| --- | --- | --- |
| 1960 | 61 min. | 156 min. |
| 1965 | 180 min. | 170 min. |
| 1970 | 191 min. | 196 min. |
| 1975 | 210 min. | 222 min. |
| 1980 | NA | 258 min. |

TV, while not as inexpensive as radio broadcasting, is still a low-cost medium. The ratio of words supplied to words consumed is, therefore, high, though an order of magnitude less than that for radio. By 1975, using parallel measures, television words consumed were but 1.4% of words supplied in Japan and 1.1% (0.9% in 1980) in the U.S.

Words supplied grew much faster than words consumed. The recent slowing of growth in U.S. television supply could be misleading, for there is a new explosion of video material coming through CATV. Multi-channel CATV systems (as well as some additional conventional TV stations and new low-power TV stations) could keep the supply of video growing at a substantial rate for some time into the future, even if the mechanism of delivery changes.

If that happens, while words consumed via video media will probably grow only modestly, the consequence will be the widely discussed "fragmentation of the mass audience" as more varieties of video are available.

Changes in consumption of TV words are a function of change

in the time people spend viewing. Although universal TV diffusion occurred later in Japan than in the United States, by 1965 the daily averages in the two countries were very close.

In our definition of words consumed or supplied by TV, which is similar to that described above in the section on radio, all the figures except for the number of spoken and written words per minute in American broadcasting come from published sources. To estimate the last, we taped random minutes from the Boston TV stations and counted the words spoken or displayed on the screen. We found 131 spoken words and an astonishing 22 written words per minute. A large proportion of the latter appeared during commercials or credits.

The calculations of production costs (i.e., programming costs), transmission costs, and consumption costs follow the same logic as in the case of radio broadcasting, except that a set repair figure also enters consumption costs. The TV data base is probably the most robust one for any mass medium. Advertisers' need to know who and how many people are out there viewing has resulted in remarkably complete information about the TV audience.

## 4.3 CATV

Cable television viewing data can be differentiated from those for television in either of two ways. One way is to count viewing of TV broadcasts received over cable as CATV and subtract those from the figures for TV viewing. The other way is to count such broadcasts as TV, whether they are received over the air or via cable, and to count as the separate CATV medium only that programming which was never broadcast over the air and which is only available on the cable. By the latter definition, CATV consists of syndicated cable services, access programming, locally originated, and rotating bulletins of news, weather and advertising, and pay-TV. The Japanese team used the first alternative; the American team used the second, partly for practical reasons of data availability and partly because in Japan CATV systems have generally been community antennas for TV, without any original programming. As a result the two time series are not comparable. Most CATV viewing is of broadcast programs, so the method used in Japan results in high figures being

## 86 THE INDIVIDUAL MEDIA

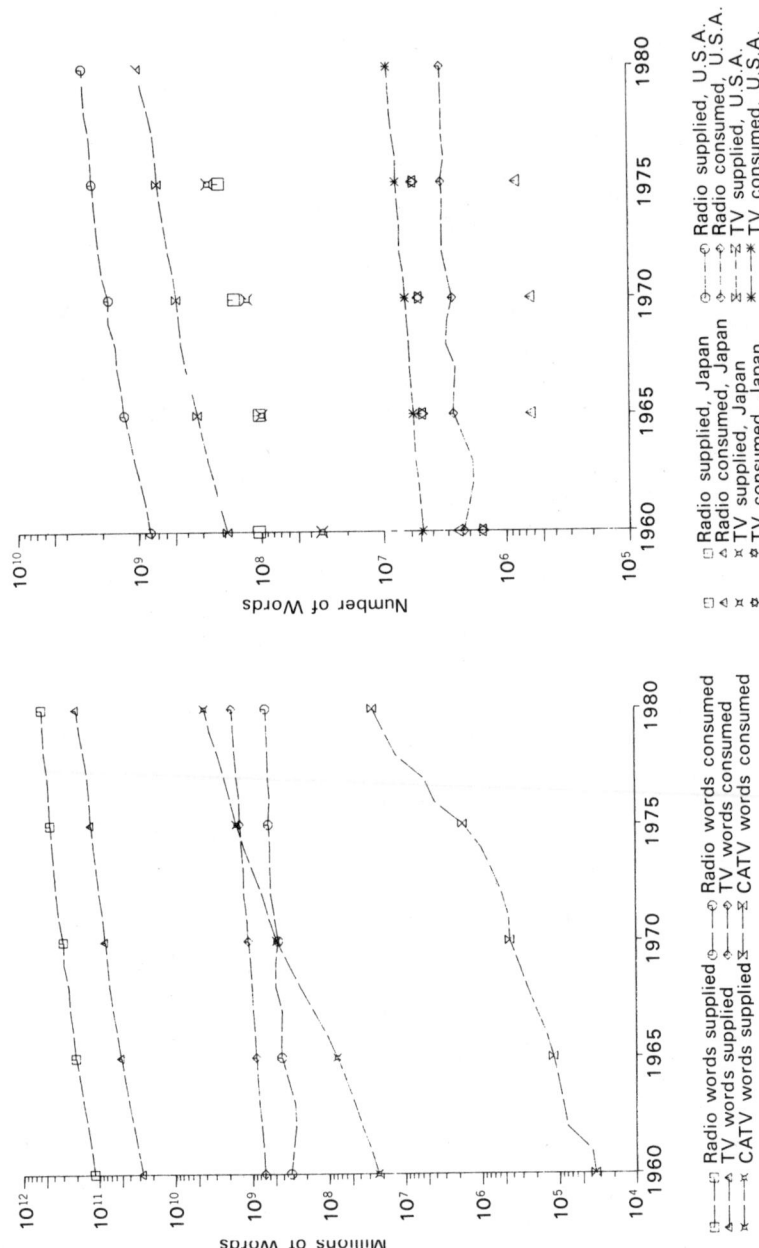

**Figure 4.4**
BROADCASTING TRENDS, U.S.A.

**Figure 4.5**
BROADCASTING PER CAPITA, JAPAN AND U.S.A.

CATV 87

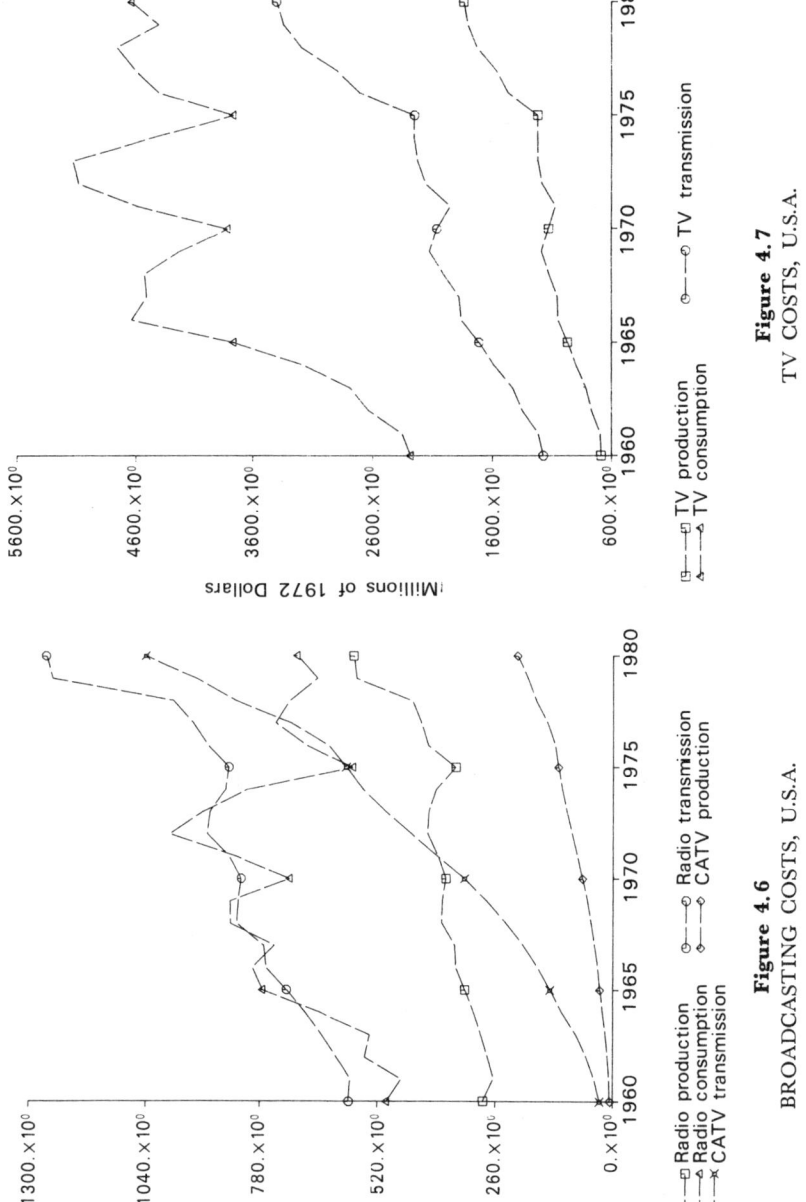

**Figure 4.7**
TV COSTS, U.S.A.

**Figure 4.6**
BROADCASTING COSTS, U.S.A.

88 THE INDIVIDUAL MEDIA

reported. Counting only original cable programming, on the other hand, makes CATV in the U.S.A. a small medium until about 1980, when pay-cable began to attract large numbers of subscribers.

In the U.S., two key regulatory developments contributed to the emergence of CATV as a significant medium. In 1972, the Federal Communications Commission adopted new cable rules which encouraged CATV in general and local origination in particular, and in 1977, the decision of the Court of Appeals for the District of Columbia in the Home Box Office case[1] opened the doors to pay-TV. With some small lag these regulatory decisions are reflected in the U.S. trend data.

Nevertheless, CATV, as defined for the U.S., was still a small medium, though its recent growth is extraordinary. In 1980 only one-half of one percent of the tabulated words supplied, and three-quarters of one percent of the words consumed, were delivered over CATV. But since 1971 the words supplied by CATV have grown at 23.3% per annum and the words consumed from CATV at 56.9% per annum. Such growth rates can only continue for limited periods and when rising from a very low base. Yet even if those extraordinary numbers must inevitably shrink somewhat, they indicate important further expansion for this new medium.

Our conceptualization of words supplied and words consumed via CATV essentially parallels that for broadcasting. Words are supplied if a CATV channel conveys material and there is a subscribing TV set, whether or not the set was turned on. Words are consumed if the set is turned on, though an inattention factor is applied so as not to posit that every word that comes out of the set is attended to.

Production cost, as in the case of TV, is equated to programming cost. Since that is calculated as a fixed percentage of total CATV expenses, the estimated growth rates of production costs and transmission costs are artificially identical. No consumption costs were assigned since it was assumed that the CATV viewers have already paid for their TV set and that extra monthly cost of watching the special cable programming is included in transmission costs.

Data on access, local origination, and rotating bulletin pro-

---

[1] Home Box Office vs. FCC, F. 2d (D.C. Cir. 1977).

gramming are rather weak for this new medium. Only recently have the Nielson procedures been changed to take account of viewing of material that was not picked up from broadcasts, and except for viewers of Home Box Office, the audiences are usually too tiny for reliable measurement.

## 4.4 Records and Tapes

The relatively small mass medium of records and tapes is presented only for the U.S. study. The data are poor. Hard data exist only on yearly sales, but since the owner may replay these materials over many years, sales figures are not a good basis for flow calculations. Nevertheless we have used those figures as one factor in the estimate of the U.S. supply. Even so, usable unit sales figures do not exist for before 1966, nor do extrapolations produce sensible results. Our supply series consequently begins with 1966. For the U.S., time spent listening to records and tapes was estimated in the Szalai time budget study.[2] Since that was at only a single time point, the only variable term in the consumption equation is the size of the population, and the growth estimate simply tracks it. Although the Japanese team did not find usable supply figures for records and tapes, NHK time budget studies in Japan do show a trend of growing consumption of these media.

For aggregate calculations, the weakness of the data on records and tapes does not matter since they are such a small part of the total flow. They account for less than one-tenth of one percent of the words consumed and only three-ten-thousandths of words supplied, as we calculate them.

There is a peculiarity in the relation of words supplied and consumed for this medium: consumption figures for this medium are higher than supply figures. This is because words supplied are calculated as record and tape sales, which means words in one playing of each record and tape, while words consumed are calculated on a time-budget basis, which allows for multiple playings.

One obvious reason for the small flow of words in records and tapes is that many are of instrumental music. A tabulation based

---

[2] A constant of 1.0 minutes per person per day was estimated, A. Szalai *et al.*, *The Use of Time*, The Hague: Mouton, 1972, p. 453.

90 THE INDIVIDUAL MEDIA

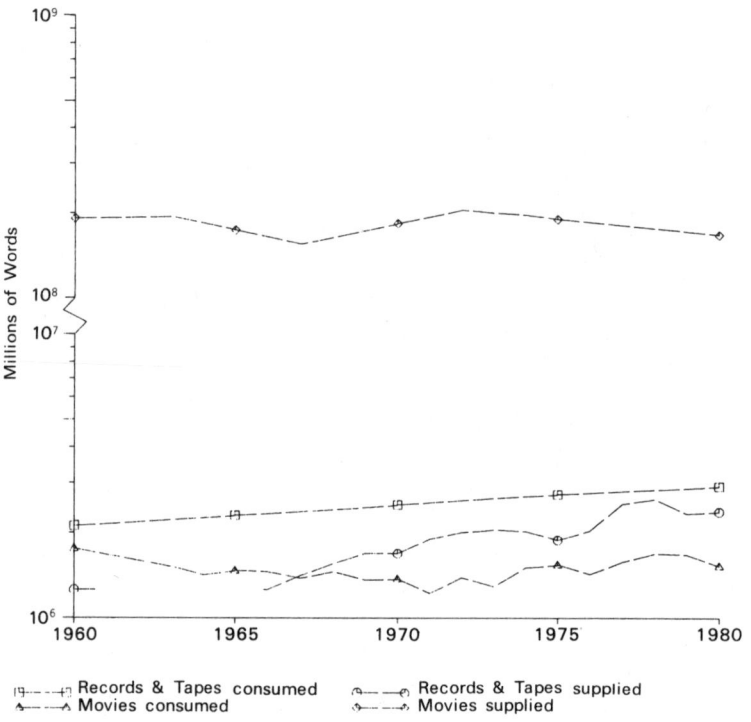

**Figure 4.8**
TRENDS IN MOVIES AND RECORDS & TAPES, U.S.A.

on records played on Boston radio stations led to a count of 41 words per minute of play. We used that figure for home use of records and tapes although this assumes, perhaps questionably, that the mix of songs and instrumental music played on radio is the same as what is played at home.

We defined consumption costs as consumer purchases of the phonographs and tape players. The revenues of the industry from sales of records and tapes encompass the production and transmission costs. Royalties to artists approximate what we consider to be production costs, i.e., costs of creating the message content, independent of its dissemination. The total revenues from sales, minus the production costs, are treated as transmission costs.

## 4.5 Movies

In both Japan and the United States movies, like radio, were hard hit by the coming of TV in the 1950s and early 1960s, but in the U.S. they have enjoyed a partial recovery since 1967 in words supplied, and since 1971 in words consumed. In Japan the decline in moviegoing and in the number of theaters has been more severe and prolonged. In 1960, before Japanese TV viewing approached that in the U.S., per capita motion picture consumption in the two countries was nearly equal. By 1975, however, the American per capita consumption was five times that in Japan and per capita supply was three times as great. The cinema business today is in many ways different from what it was in its heyday. Giant movie palaces have given way to multiple small theatres in a single building. The double feature has vanished and so have the shorts.

A number of these changes are not quantitatively documented. We found no time series of the average length of a movie show or the average number of shows per week. The National Association of Theatre Owners was helpful in providing informed estimates. The most important time series, and one for which data do exist, is attendance. Unfortunately, however, there is no one consistent data series, and there are substantial discrepencies among sources.

As with radio, TV, and records, we made an estimate for movies of words per minute by sampling and counting. The U.S. data are from a subsample of the TV word count consisting solely of movies shown on TV.

The conception of movie supply assumes that every seat in every theatre could be filled at every showing; in other words, supply is what the public could receive if it chose to attend.

Words consumed, on the other hand, are calculated on the basis of the number of persons who actually attended. No inattention factor is used; that is reserved exclusively for broadcasting (radio, TV, and CATV). We have made this distinction because broadcating is used in a quite passive way: after the set is turned on, people sometimes pay attention to what comes over it, and sometimes not. But when people makes a more active choice to use a medium, they tend to pay attention to it. Thus for movie attendance and for reading, we assume consumption of all the

## 92 THE INDIVIDUAL MEDIA

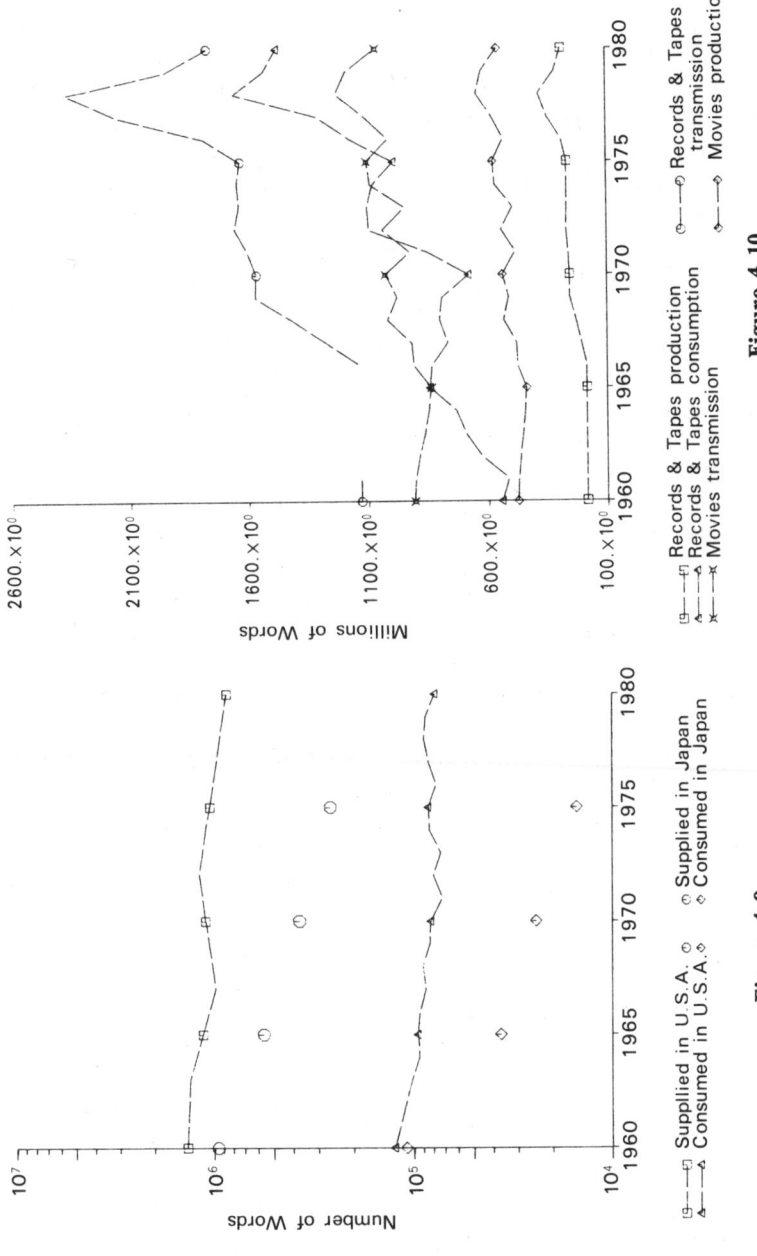

**Figure 4.9**
MOVIES PER CAPITA, U.S.A. AND JAPAN

**Figure 4.10**
MOVIE, RECORD & TAPE COSTS, U.S.A.

words heard or seen during that activity. In short, we disregard as trivial such behaviors as falling asleep in the theater.

The decline in movie supply and consumption does not imply the end of the single subject, relatively long visual narrative. Movies in that sense are supplied to and consumed by Americans and Japanese via televevision, CATV, and even prerecorded video tapes as well as in theatres. It is the future of the mode of delivery that is in question.

There are no consumption costs in going to the movies, i.e., there is no investment in equipment that the public has to make. Production costs are construed as what the theatre owners have to pay to the movie producers. Transmission costs are the rest of the theatre owners' revenues.

## 4.6 Education

Education is rarely treated as a mass medium, though indeed it is one. Classroom presentation is perhaps the largest remaining face-to-face oral institution of communication in our society.[3] Education also makes very extensive use of the book. In Japan the research team included use of textbooks under education. The American team, however, put books together as one medium, whether read for pleasure, education, or other purposes. Thus in the U.S. the education time series is essentially what goes on in the classroom.

The definition of words supplied in classroom education is arrived at by looking at what teachers do: how many of them there are, how many hours they teach, how much do they say per unit of time, and, in the U.S., how many students they have in a class at the same time.[4] The definition of words consumed is arrived at by looking at what students do: how many there are, how much time they spend in class, and how many words they

---

[3] Since our census deals with communication by persons 10 years old and older, we have excluded the first few years of education. We have revised published statistics to eliminate portions applying to children under 10.

[4] As in other mass media, there is a difference between the two national supply series, in that the Japanese figures refer to words produced by teachers, with no multiplier for the number of students. (This is analogous to the non-application of a household size factor for media delivered to homes.) One result of this approach, as seen from the Japanese basic figures (Tables 4.1 and 4.2), is that volume supplied figures are less than those for volume consumed.

receive in a unit of class time. As already noted, the teachers' estimated speaking rate was lower in Japan than in the U.S. Also, a main reason for the difference in education consumed is the proportions of the age cohorts continuing to higher education.

In contrast to media like broadcasting, education is very expensive. Because of its costliness, teaching is not dispensed casually, without regard to whether students are consuming what is taught. The institution is designed to force attention: attendance is taken; silence is required while the teacher speaks. In general the words emitted are treated as having substantial value.

As a result of their cost, the ratio of words emitted in education to words consumed is close to unity. Our data for the U.S. assert that in 1960 91.1% of the words supplied were consumed and in 1980, 93.1%. Yet those figures are misleading. Lacking any basis for an estimate, we used no measure of inattention in the classroom, such as was used for broadcasting. Clearly there is inattention. The American figures for consumption of education do take absenteeism into account—but only absenteeism. Yet, even if inattention in the classroom approximated or exceeded that to TV, the level at which education is consumed would still be distinctive. While most mass media supply tens or hundreds of times as many words as are actually taken in, for education the question is whether the ratio is closer to unity or to two or three to one.

In the U.S., the supply and consumption of education grew quickly in the early 1960s, slowed in the late 1960s, and then flattened out and declined in the 1970s with the passing of the wave of the post-war baby boom.

In Japan, the trends were less definite. Both student consumption of words and the production of them by teachers, which had grown moderately in the early 1960s, declined sharply in the late 1960s, but were growing again by 1973. The dominant factors affecting the trends, are first, the size of successive school-age cohorts and, second, the proportion of students who continue their education.

In the U.S. the cost of education did not show a decline equivalent to its volume. Cost in constant dollars grew faster in the late 1960s than in the early 1960s, and continued to grow, even if slowly, in the 1970s. While demographics were the main reason for the trends observed in the supply and consumption of educa-

EDUCATION  95

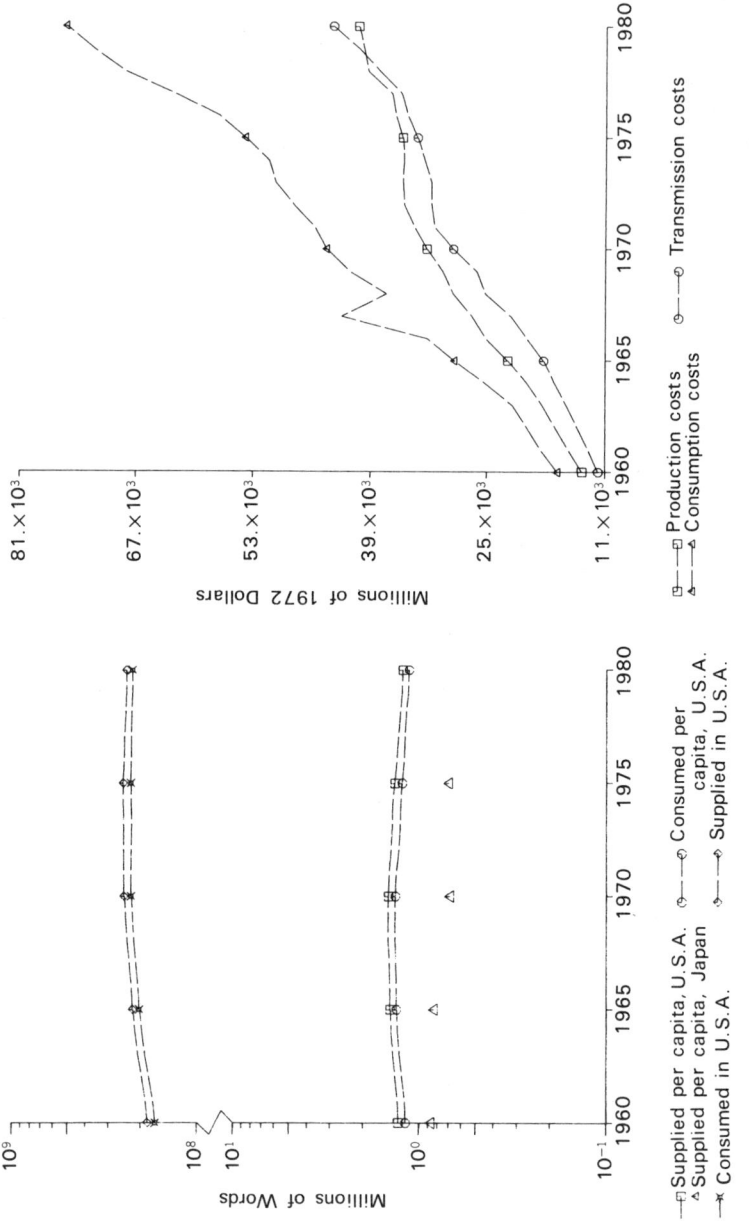

**Figure 4.11**
TRENDS IN EDUCATION

**Figure 4.12**
EDUCATION COSTS, U.S.A.

tion, cost may also have contributed to slowing educational growth. Educational budgets are inelastic; they do not expand and, indeed, decline proportionately to the numbers of students.

Our conception of transmission costs in education is instructional expenditures as reported in Ministerial statistics. In the U.S. instructional expenses reported in the Department of Health, Education and Welfare (DHEW) Digest of Educational Statistics are subtracted from the total budgets of schools and colleges, leaving a remainder which we call production costs, including, for example, the cost of physical plant. In other words, transmission costs are conceived as the variable costs of putting out instruction, while production costs are fixed expenses needed in order for that transmission to occur.[5]

What we call the consumption cost of education includes two elements of cost borne by students of higher education. One of these is room and board; the other is an opportunity cost, the earnings which students forgo by going to school instead of working. These are certainly relevant to the choices people make for more or less education, and per student they have been rising at an average American annual rate of 1.1% in constant dollars. However, if we restrict our attention to the direct transmission and production costs of education which fall on school and university budgets, costs have been growing rapidly. From 1960 till 1980 American education supplied grew at 1.3% per annum, education consumed at 1.4% per annum, production costs at 5.6% per annum, and transmission costs at 5.5% per annum.

## 4.7 Newspapers

Supply figures for newspapers, as for print media in general, are rather robust. Circulation figures are generally precise and word counts are easy. The total supply of words via newspapers shows growth in both Japan and the U.S., but the rate of growth is far greater in Japan. Indeed in the United States per capita supply has actually declined. There is a striking trend toward convergence in the time levels of newspaper reading in the two countries.

---

[5] These definitions are somewhat at variance with those used for the other mass media, where production costs generally represent only the cost of creating the program.

The dominant factors affecting supply of newspaper words are circulation and the size of newspapers. Circulation of daily papers in the United States rose from 58.9 million in 1960 to 63.1 million in 1973, and then fell to 60.7 million by 1975, rising again to 62.2 million in 1980. The number of words in an average newspaper has had a more complex history, affected primarily by the cost of newsprint and the rises and declines in advertising associated with the business cycle. From 1970 on, but particularly from the oil crisis of 1973 until 1977, there was a nearly catastrophic run-up in newsprint prices (see Figure 4.13) which reached in 1977 an index of 329 from a base of 100 in 1970.

With national economies hit by the oil shock, advertising dropped off. Newspapers were reduced in size, publishers turned to lighter paper, and in the U.S. changes were made in columnar arrangements to allow for more words on the same page.[6] With these changes and with an upturn in ad revenue due to the economic recovery in the late 1970s, U.S. newspapers toward 1980 resumed growing in size.

Thus, a parallel trend in the United States and Japan is the peaking of the rate of growth in words supplied around 1970, followed by a slippage in the 1970s. In the former country there was growth at the rate of 2.7% per annum from 1960 until 1973 and then a lower expansion at 1.3% per annum from 1973 to 1980. In Japan there was a much more rapid rate of growth. From 1960 to 1965 the rate was 6.5% per annum (4.8% using a household correction factor); from 1965 to 1970, 13.1% (10.9% using a household factor); and from 1970 to 1975, a period of rising newspaper prices, the rate fell to 1.8% (0.3% using a household factor). For the period as a whole the data indicate a hefty per capita growth in Japan, but an anemic one in the United States, with the former more than six times the latter.

Newspapers are the dominant print medium. In 1960 they provided 83% of all the words supplied in print in both the U.S. and Japan. In 1975, the figure was 80% for Japan and 82% for the U.S. and in 1980 it was again 82% for the U.S.

While figures on words supplied by publishing are fairly reliable, consumption figures for print media are scarce and unreliable.

---

6) That particular change was unfortunately not caught in our statistics, which treated words per page as a constant. The yearly volumes of newspaper words supplied in the U.S.A. in recent years are therefore slightly underestimated.

98 THE INDIVIDUAL MEDIA

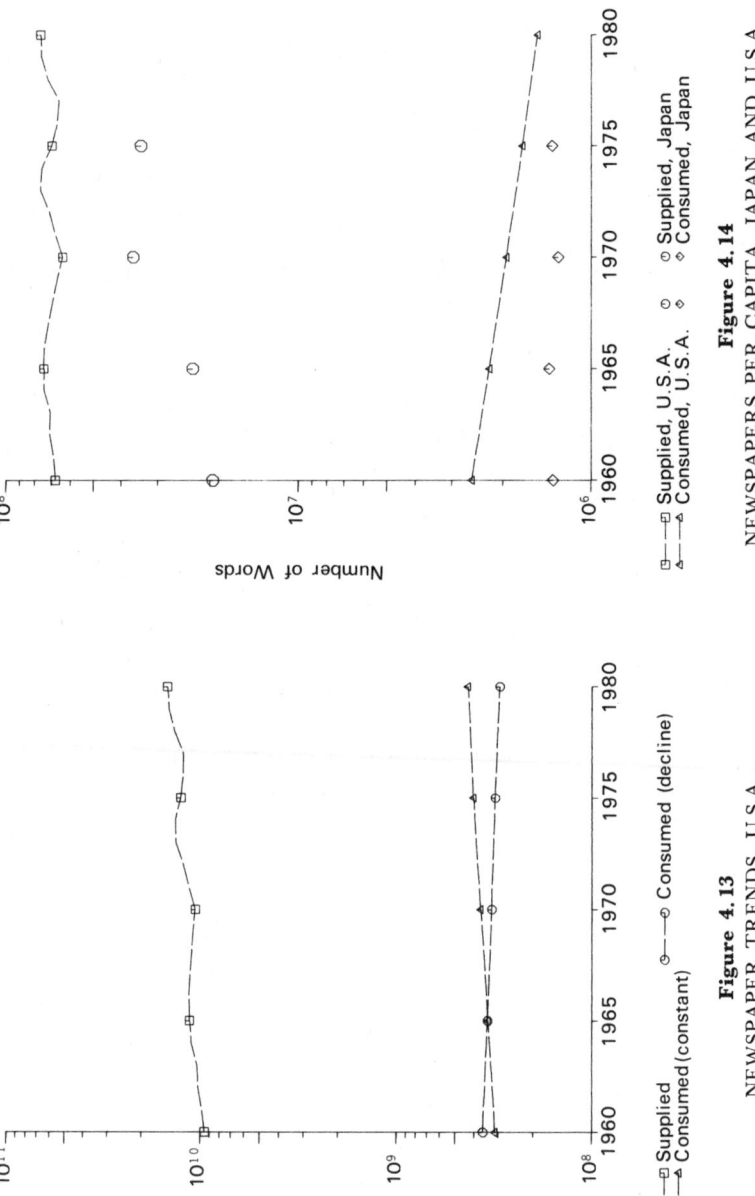

**Figure 4.13**
NEWSPAPER TRENDS, U.S.A.

**Figure 4.14**
NEWSPAPERS PER CAPITA, JAPAN AND U.S.A.

NEWSPAPERS  99

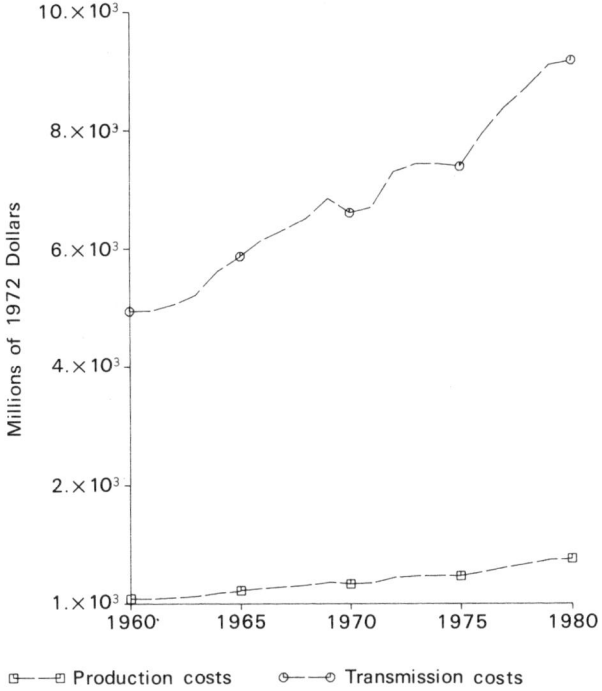

**Figure 4.15**
NEWSPAPER COSTS, U.S.A.

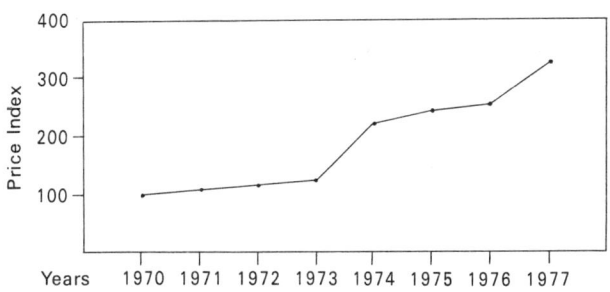

**Figure 4.16**
NEWSPRINT PRICE INDEX 1970-1977
From Pauline Wingate, "Newsprint From Rags to Riches and Back Again," in Anthony Smith, ed., *Newspapers and Democracy*, M.I.T. Press, 1980, p. 71.

100 THE INDIVIDUAL MEDIA

The advertising industry uses circulation figures and so has no great need to create the kind of audience data that broadcasters use. Few careful studies exist of time spent reading newspapers. Frequently an American audience researcher will ask "about how much time did you spend reading the paper?" or "how much time did you spend yesterday?" The subjective replies are unreliable, and in any case, coming in different towns without regularity, they provide no national time series. In Japan, however, the quinquennial NHK time budget studies show substantial stability, ranging from 18 to 20 minutes a day of newspaper reading, with no trend. As described in Chapter 3, we have in the U.S. but two time points on newspaper consumption derived from time-budget studies.[7] They show a decline of one-third in reading time from 1965 to 1975, a result which most newspaper researchers challenge as being too steep. In any case, we lack any independent data to permit us to make a choice among the various claims. For that reason, we have presented two estimates of newspaper consumption trends, one based on an exponential extrapolation of Robinson's data, and the other assuming constancy in average individual reading time.[8]

Our first estimate, which follows Robinson in the decline in reading time for daily papers but postulates constancy for Sunday papers, results in a 1.0% per annum decline in consumption of newspaper words, and a total decline of 17.9% since 1960. The second estimate, which postulates constancy in reading time per capita, would result in an actual growth in words consumed corresponding to the growth in the population, at a rate of 1.6%. Since we believe there probably has been some per capita decline in newspaper reading time, we have used estimate 1 in aggregate statistics in the previous chapters. In any case, we hope that raising these questions will lead newspaper audience researchers to investigate the unresolved questions about individual reading time.

---

7) Robinson, *op. cit.*

8) The Newspaper Advertising Bureau has done a further survey which will be appearing shortly. It denies that there has been a decline in reading time. It finds constancy in reading time for any one paper and finds that the decline in multiple papers read has had a trivial effect. The NAB study claims that average reading for newspapers came to 44 minutes a day in 1982, down only four minutes from 1971, because there were fewer multi-paper cities in 1982.

Newspaper costs in constant dollars continue to rise, and indeed rose especially in the years of the runup in newsprint prices. No consumption costs are applied to newspapers. Production costs are construed to be editorial costs; the remaining costs of a newspaper are construed as transmission costs.

## 4.8 Magazines

Much of what we have to say about magazines parallels what we have said about newspapers, though some of the time series are even less robust.

The magazine supply figures, which are based on circulation, are fairly solid. Some effort went into ascertaining the words per copy in the U.S.A., though not year by year. Because of the great variety of formats of American magazines, we did a sample tabulation of pages and words per page for general magazines, trade magazines, college magazines, religious magazines, agricultural magazines, foreign language magazines, and other magazines.

In Japan the four NHK time budget studies found time spent reading magazines growing from 4 minutes 40 seconds a day, on the average, to 5 minutes 18 seconds. American consumption figures are badly lacking. We have no time series, so we used the Szalai-Robinson time budget datum of 6.4 minutes of magazine reading each person per day as a constant. Hence the only variable in the U.S. consumption equation is the growth of population.

Words supplied by magazines increased at a healthy rate until 1970, but there was a slowdown in both countries in the early 1970s. There was even some decline in the U.S. in the mid-1970s. Though more recently, the American supply has begun to grow again. The growth for magazines has been much faster in Japan, as can be seen from the comparison of the Japanese and American trends in Table 4.5. In Japan, monthlies have continued to grow, while weeklies stopped growing.

Costs, as in the case of newspapers, have risen sharply, even in constant dollars, and more rapidly in recent years. No consumption costs are tabulated; production costs are considered to be editorial costs, and all other costs are transmission costs. Since our data on editorial costs consist only of a constant factor applied

**Table 4.5**
PER ANNUM GROWTH RATES IN WORDS
SUPPLIED BY MAGAZINES

|           | Japan* | U.S.A. |
|-----------|--------|--------|
| 1960–1970 | 6.4%   | 2.7%   |
| 1970–1975 | 2.8    | −1.2   |
| 1975–1980 | NA     | 3.1    |

* Adjusted for household factor.

to total costs, rates of growth of production and transmission costs come out as identical, as is true also for books and direct mail.

## 4.9 Books

In both Japan and the United States, among the major print media, book publishing seems to have suffered least from the impact of new electronic competition. Words supplied by books grew by 9.6% per annum from 1960 to 1975 in Japan, and by 2.9% per annum from 1960 to 1980 in the United States.

There are, however, some problems with the data. The Japanese data include textbook use under education as we have noted, while the U.S. study includes it here. That constitutes a large part of book reading. We estimate that in the U.S. 39% of the book words consumed and a clear majority of the time spent reading are in study. (The reading rate for such purposes is lower than the normal one.[9]) Second, as with magazines, the only useful time budget figure we have in the U.S. is from 1965. So the only variable in the consumption equation is population. Data from Japanese time budget studies hint that this assumption of constancy in book reading has some rough accuracy. They show that in Japan average individual reading increased only one minute from 1960 to 1975, from 6 minutes 45 seconds to 7 minutes 56 seconds, or 1% per year. There also are some problems peculiar to books, records, and tapes, for these are media that are apt to

---

9) Our figure of 9 minutes a day reading books is considerably higher than Robinson's figure of 5.5 minutes; he did not include study. He did estimate study as averaging 17.5 minutes a day across the population, of which about 7 minutes was essentially reading. However, the usual reading rate for such material is slower than for casual reading because of such intermittent activities as note-taking. These factors entered our word consumption estimate.

**Table 4.6**
ANNUAL GROWTH RATES IN BOOK USE

|  | Japan | | U.S.A.** |
|---|---|---|---|
|  | Volume Supplied* | Volume Consumed | Volume Supplied |
| 1960–1970 | 10.0% | 2.0% | 3.3% |
| 1970–1975 | 3.8 | 3.4 | 2.1 |
| 1975–1980 | NA | NA | 2.7 |

\* Adjusted for household factor.
\*\* Volume consumed time series data not available for the U.S.A.

be used more than once. No allowance has been made for passing on the publication from household to household. That is a particularly restrictive assumption for books which are in fact sold at second hand, given to friends, and circulated by libraries. However, we have no good data on such pass-on circulation.

The ratio of words consumed to words supplied is higher for books than for other print media. Our Japanese data report 67% of words produced in 1975 being consumed. Our U.S. data say that in 1960 46% of the words supplied in books were read, and in 1980 35%. This contrasts to 5% in both years for magazines and 3% in 1960 and 2% in 1980 for newspapers. Even if pass-on of books justified doubling or trebling the supply figure, the supply of words in the relatively high-cost medium of books is, as we would expect, relatively sparing in relation to consumption.

The average number of words per page and the average number of pages in American books was estimated by drawing a sample of books on the shelves of the Boston Public Library. We found no consistent trends in the values for either of these variables. The volume supplied figure in the U.S. thus primarily reflects the number of books sold.

Use of books continued to grow steadily into the 1970s. In Japan the consumption of book words grew more rapidly in the last five years of our data than before. In the United States, growth in supply, after slowing in the early 1970s, was more rapid in the most recent period (see Table 4.6).

As in the case of newspapers and magazines, costs have been rising even in constant dollars, especially recently. Production costs are measured by royalties to authors; transmission costs are the rest of book publishing costs. Since royalties are estimated as

104 THE INDIVIDUAL MEDIA

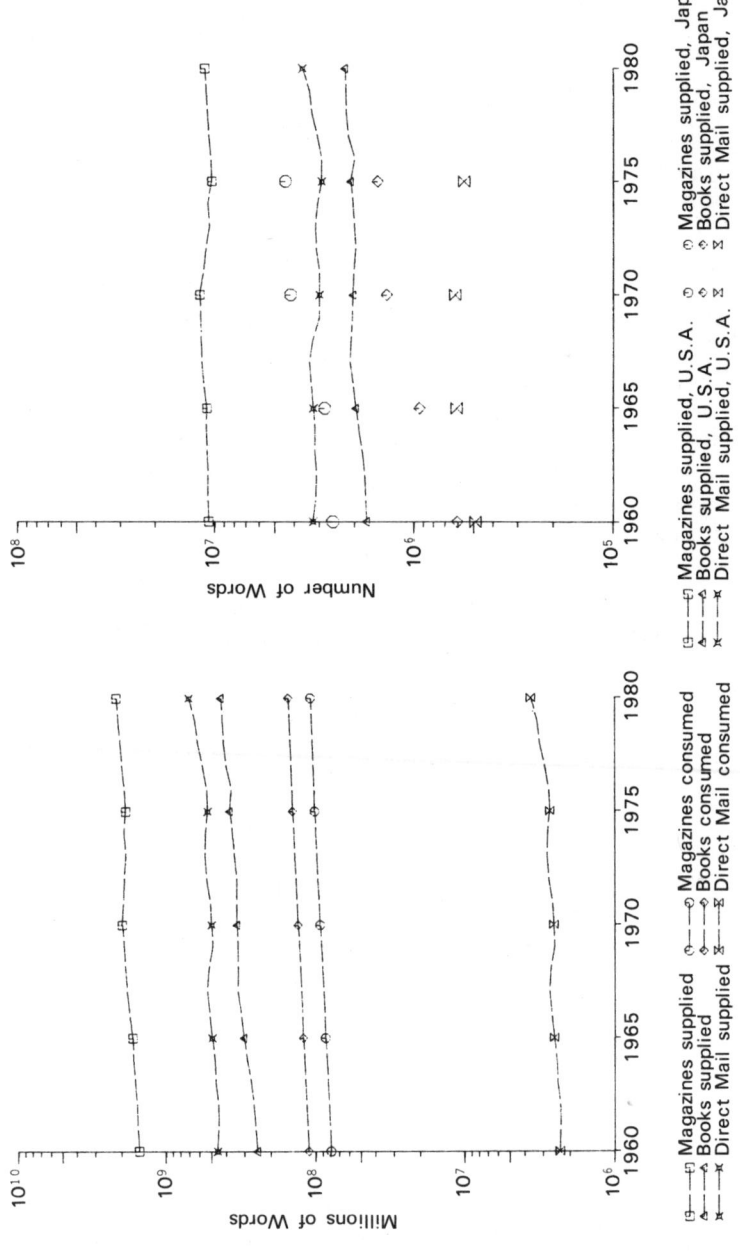

**Figure 4.17**
OTHER PRINT MASS MEDIA, U.S.A.

**Figure 4.18**
OTHER PRINT MASS MEDIA PER CAPITA

a constant percentage of publishers' revenues, growth rates come out the same for production and transmission costs.

One important medium which was tabulated in Japan, but for which we lacked data in the U.S., was telephone directories. In Japan, these were tabulated separately from books, and indeed, their physical character aside, such directories are quite different in their use from books of running text. Unlike books in which words supplied are only modestly greater than words consumed, for directories the ratio is large. In 1960 words consumed were estimated at four-tenths of a percent of words produced, and in 1975 one-tenth of a percent of words produced. There are a lot of words in this widely circulated print medium, but no one of us ever reads more than a few of them.

From 1960 to 1975 the words produced for the public in Japanese telephone books grew at an annual rate of 13.4%. The surge was largely in the period 1965–1970, as phone penetration and service grew.

## 4.10 Direct Mail Advertising

What proportion of direct mail (often called junk mail) is read by those who receive it? At first glance, the Japanese and U.S. results seem quite irreconcilable. According to the Japanese data, 28 percent of the words in junk mail are read (with half the words read in the 56% of pieces that are read at all). The U.S. data puts the figure at half of one percent of the words being read. But this difference can be resolved; the exercise serves to warn how careful researchers must be in interpreting data.

In the first place, recall that the basic Japanese data are words produced, without multiplying for all potential readers in the household that receives them. In fact, two possible readers were assumed for each piece of Japanese direct mail. Allowing for this factor brings the Japanese figure to 20% of the words being read on the basis of the calculation used in the U.S.A.

The nature of direct mail in the two countries has been different. In the U.S., direct mail is dominated, in number of words if not items, by thick advertising catalogues. A large proportion are thrown away unread, but consider the reading behavior of those receivers who actually buy from one. They thumb through it

106 THE INDIVIDUAL MEDIA

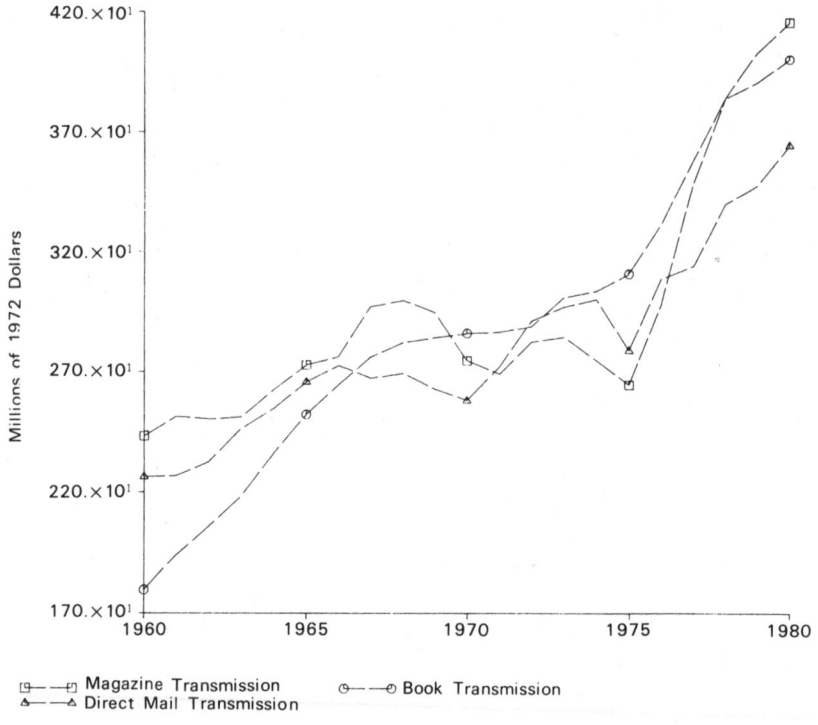

**Figure 4.19**
MAGAZINE, BOOK, DIRECT MAIL COSTS, U.S.A.

quickly, come to a picture of something that interests them, read that description closely, fill out and sometimes mail the order form. Most of the words in the catalogue remain unread.

In Japan, direct mail of the catalogue type has recently been increasing, but leaflets and postcards were more generally prevalent during most of the period studied.

Also, and most important, the average American receives about six times as many pieces of direct mail as the average Japanese. Since we have no analysis of various subcategories of direct mail in Japan and the United States, we cannot provide a figure on how much of the discrepancy between the two national figures is now accounted for, but probably most of it. Whatever residual remains may indeed be a genuine difference in reader behavior and/or errors of research.

Let us note how the American estimate of 0.5% of words supplied being consumed was arrived at. There is a Nielsen study which gives figures for the proportion of direct mail pieces that were "read fairly thoroughly," just "glanced at," or "not read." To translate these qualitative findings into actual numbers of words, we asked a few experimental subjects to look at a sample of direct mail that we collected. We grouped their behavior into these three types and determined for each such act how many words read it implied. That gave us a rough measure of what those categories might mean in counted words.

The use of direct mail in both Japan and the United States rose continuously during the two decades studied, but with somewhat different trajectories. In Japan the rate of growth was faster in the earlier years as Japan's economy moved into its present high state. From 1960 to 1965 the growth rate was 7.8% per annum. From 1970 to 1975 it was 0.7% per annum. In the U.S., irregularities in the rate of growth are largely accounted for by fluctuations in the economy and therefore in advertising, and by fluctuations in postage rates.

Direct mail costs, like those of most print media, have been rising at a faster rate than the volume supplied or consumed, even in constant dollars, and particularly so in the most recent years. We have no reported data on the split between editorial and other costs for direct mail, so we used the newspaper constant. Since it is a constant, growth rates for production and transmission costs come out the same.

## 4.11 First Class Mail

We note quite different patterns of growth in words transmitted by first class mail in Japan and in the United States. In Japan the growth rate was 7.7% per annum from 1960 to 1965, 3.5% from 1965 to 1970, and 1.3% from 1970 to 1975. Clearly the big surge was in the period when Japan was still moving from its post-war economy into its present affluent economy. Since then telephoning has partly substituted for letter writing, and postage rates have risen sharply. One Japanese response to this rise in postal rates was to send postcards instead of letters, so the less costly part of the traffic grew more. In 1976 the average cost per phone call was 38 yen, per letter 35 yen, per postcard 13 yen.

In the United States, first class mail has grown at a fairly steady three and a half percent[10] except for a period of stagnation from 1971 till 1976 when the growth rate was 0.6%.

The cost of postage also rose rapidly in the U.S., which may be part of the explanation for the temporary 1970s halt in mail growth; but that did not stop a later recovery. In 1960 a one-ounce letter took a 4-cent stamp; in 1980 it took 15 cents. The increase came mainly between 1968, when the postage was 6 cents, and 1975, when it reached 13 cents. One might hypothesize that when total postal costs from first class mail started rising at 13.6% per annum (compared to 6.1% from 1960 to 1971), the first transient reaction to this mail shock was to hold back on using postal service, and this response was reinforced a couple of years later by reaction to the oil shock. But after the shocks were absorbed and the economy recovered, the growth of American usage apparently resumed.

All Post Office expenses are classed as transmission costs. Production costs are the costs that business senders incur in producing letters before they mail them.

The most reliable data on first class mail is from Post Office records on sales of stamps and on the envelopes it delivers. Next most reliable is information collected in surveys of origin and destination, and which distinguish mail going from business to business, business to private individual, private individual to private individual, etc. Less reliable is information about what is inside the envelope, and most particularly the number of words. Also at the unreliable end of the scale is information about the cost of production of a letter. Yet these topics too have been studied in research on cooperating subjects. We have used both the Post Office information and these other studies for our data.

Since first class mail is a point-to-point medium, we do not distinguish words supplied from words consumed. More accurately, these are treated as equal, so in any aggregate data which contains mass media as well as point-to-point media, the latter is added both to the words supplied and to the words consumed. Whatever may happen in a future world of electronic mail, con-

---

10) 3.7% from 1960 to 1971; 3.4% from 1976 to 1980.

sumption of first class mail is still growing moderately, but it is not experiencing the explosion of traffic reflected by the supply of electronic words.

## 4.12 Telephone

The growth in telephone traffic has been substantial in both Japan and the United States, but has followed quite different patterns. In the mature U.S. phone system, which had achieved virtually universal penetration during the decade after World War II, the growth in telephone usage has been remarkably regular. For the period since 1960 the total growth has been 5.7% per annum. In Japan, where universal penetration was achieved only in the late 1970s, we find a logistic growth curve with the period of explosive growth occurring between 1965 and 1970, as the telephone became a normal part of all of Japanese life. The per annum rates of growth were: 1960–65, 6.2%; 1965–70, 16.3%; 1970–75, 6.7%.

The telephone figures are solid ones. Telephone traffic is accurately tabulated by the phone companies for billing and engineering purposes, but even in the telephone figures there are problems of detail. The American figures are calls placed through public carriers required to report to the FCC. Small rural and private systems did not report, and by 1980 many calls were taking place inside PBX's and over private lines. So both the volume of calls and the rate of growth are being underestimated.

The original Japanese data did distinguish inter-office phone traffic, which has grown fast, from rural area co-operative and muncipal phone systems, which have declined, and the public NTT network, which is by far the largest. On that, as the number of lines have grown the telephone traffic per line has declined, while total traffic has, of course, grown.

Production costs reported in the U.S. data have to do with what it costs businesses to pay their employees who are using the phone. The bills to the phone company are entirely transmission costs. Total U.S. transmission costs in constant dollars have been growing since 1960 at 4.9% per annum, a lower rate than the growth of traffic. In contrast to the print media, whose unit costs have been rising per word, and to some other electronic media, for telephone, unit costs have been falling, at least in

110 THE INDIVIDUAL MEDIA

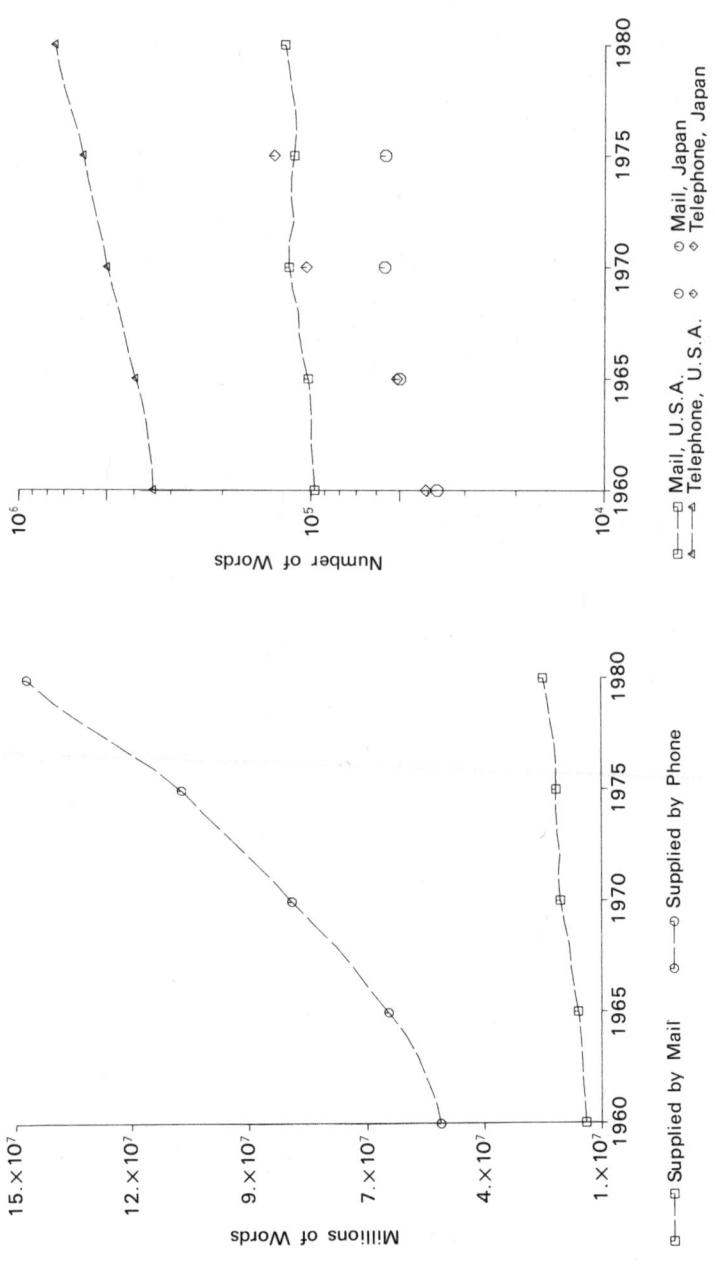

**Figure 4.20**
FIRST CLASS MAIL AND TELEPHONE, U.S.A.

**Figure 4.21**
MAIL AND PHONE PER CAPITA, U.S.A. AND JAPAN

TELEPHONE  *111*

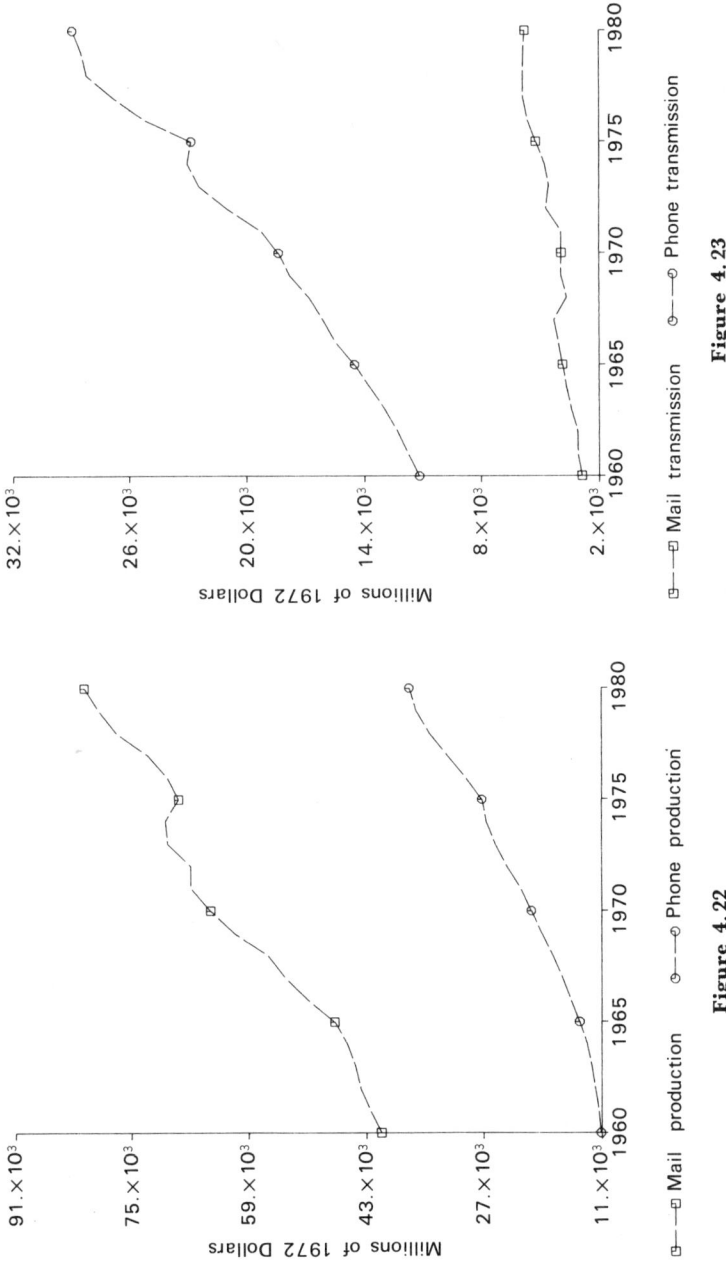

**Figure 4.23**
MAIL AND PHONE TRANSMISSION COSTS, U.S.A.

**Figure 4.22**
MAIL AND PHONE PRODUCTION COSTS, U.S.A.

## 112  THE INDIVIDUAL MEDIA

constant dollars. There is substantial controversy in the United States at the present time as to whether phone costs will rise under the 1982 divestiture decree, but in the past, falling real costs have been the experience.

### 4. 13  Telex, Telegrams, and Mailgrams

These three media are to such an extent substitutes for one another that we comment on them together. Telegraphy came first and at one time was very important. Western Union at the end of the nineteenth century was the largest company in the United States. But by 1960, the date our census begins, telegraphy was already in precipitous decline. Burdened by the high labor costs involved in entering and delivering telegrams, telegraphy could not compete with the superior technologies and lower cost of instant communication by telex and telephone.[11] So telegrams have declined to near disappearance in the United States.

In Japan, as well, telegram volume is the smallest of all the media here reported. In the 1950s, as telephone service spread, telegraphy had declined markedly, but since then it has not declined further because Japanese law requires NTT to maintain a delivered telegram service, even at a very large loss. No such requirement is imposed on Western Union, and that company no longer delivers ordinary telegrams; it instead phones them and then sends a hard copy through the mail. Given the availability of service in Japan, telegrams continue to be used by the public at a low, fairly steady rate. The length of the average Japanese congratulatory telegram has, for some reason, tended to increase substantially.

The yearly volume of international cables remained level longer than that for domestic telegraphy, but following 1967 the volume of such telegrams in international business collapsed too, as international telex and telephony became more readily available.

Telex as a whole has shown a strong growth in both countries, for the whole time series 9.6% in Japan and 19.8% in the U.S. Such a summary is misleading because it masks several separate and different trends. In Japan, volume of telex traffic displayed

---

11)  For cost figures see Table 2. 2.

the same logistic pattern as for telephone, but in this case the curve ended in decline instead of continuing growth, but the average annual growth rates were: 1960–65, 10.3%; 1965–70, 20.0%; 1970–75, −0.4%. That small decline might be dismissed as an insignificant fluctuation, but while we have no Japanese word counts after 1975, we know that NTT telex susbcribers have declined from 72,900 in 1977 to 52,000 in 1981.

In the United States, domestic telex traffic grew at 17.7% per annum from 1960 to 1970 but then declined almost as fast: at 12.8% per annum from 1970 to 1980. More economical computer networks (and also facsimile) replaced such telex traffic in both countries.

However, even as the domestic telex business was disappearing, international telex started to boom. Outside the United States telex is much more highly developed than in the U.S.; both in advanced industrial countries and in developing countries practically all significant businesses use it. On the other hand, telephone service and computer networks are not as well developed even in most advanced industrial countries as in the U.S. and are more expensive. Telex therefore remains a standard method for instantaneous international communication, though it is now being affected by computer data networks. The rate of growth for international telex from 1960 to 1980 was 27.5% per annum. From 1974 to 1980 it was lower, but still a vigorous 18.4% per annum.

In the Japanese word count there is no separate measurement of international telex, though the special study of Japanese-U.S. communication in Chapter 3 found a fairly steady growth rate in telex of 14.5%. KDD, the Japanese international communications company, reports number of international telex messages handled growing from 1960 to 1973 at a rate of 29% per annum and from 1973 to 1979 at 19%.[12] These rates and changes are similar to the American trends. Thus international telex still retains its vitality despite the beginnings of international computer networks.

Transmission costs for international telex grew for the whole period in the U.S. at 15.8% per annum in constant dollars and since 1974 at only 7.5%. Thus unit costs were falling especially

---

12) KDD, *Japan's Progress in International Communications*, Tokyo, 1980, p. 117.

114 THE INDIVIDUAL MEDIA

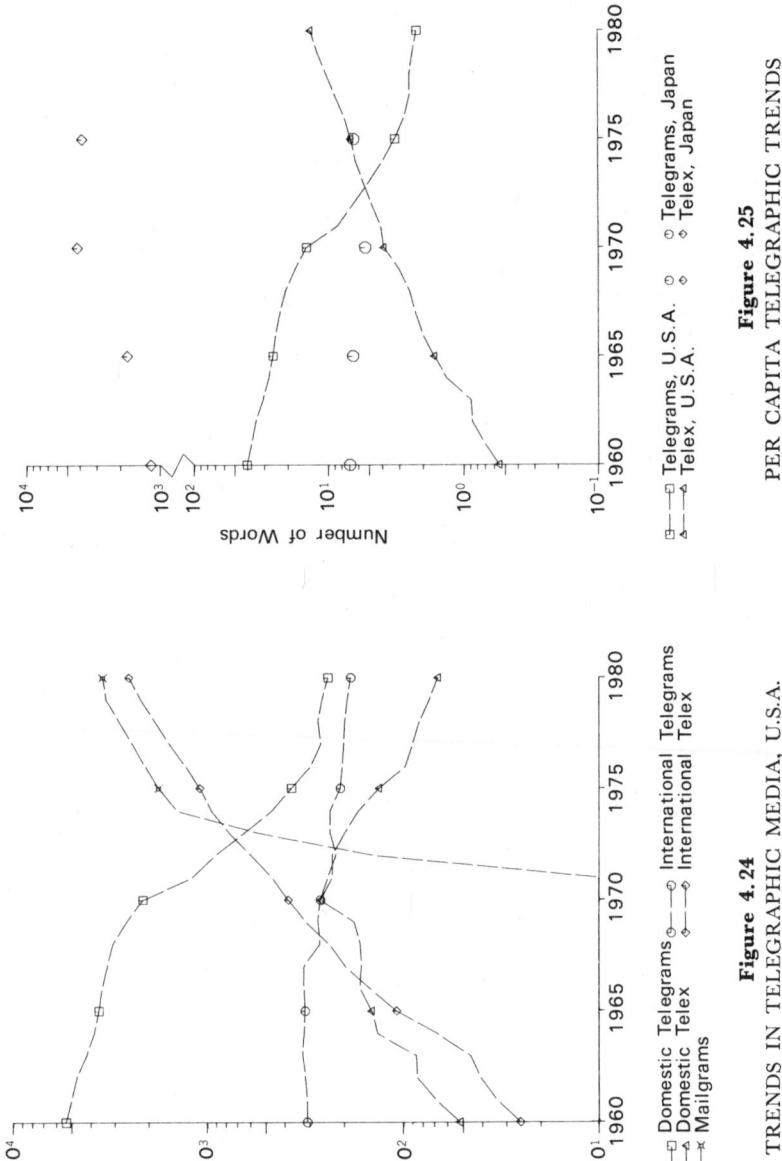

Figure 4.24
TRENDS IN TELEGRAPHIC MEDIA, U.S.A.

Figure 4.25
PER CAPITA TELEGRAPHIC TRENDS

TELEX, TELEGRAMS, MAILGRAMS *115*

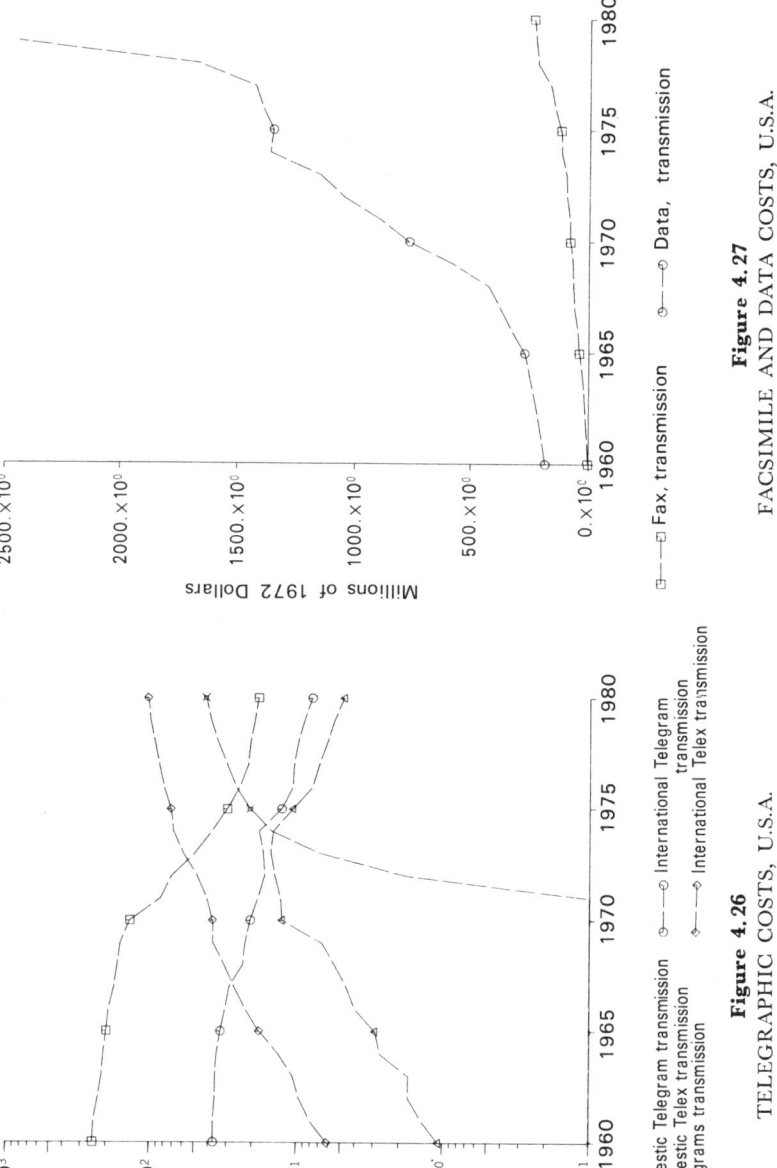

**Figure 4.26**
TELEGRAPHIC COSTS, U.S.A.

**Figure 4.27**
FACSIMILE AND DATA COSTS, U.S.A.

in the last few years. As we saw in Table 2.2, telex costs per word had fallen to less than half of telegram costs. But since the 1970s telex has faced competition from still cheaper means of communication.

Production costs for telegrams, telex, mailgrams, and facsimile are calculated, just as for mail, to be the estimated labor cost of writing the messages.

Starting in 1972 a new domestic telegraphic service, mailgrams, started in the United States. While not providing instantaneous delivery, it solved the problem of local delivery by combining local postal delivery with telegraphy for the long haul. By 1977 it had reached the volume that domestic telegraphy was carrying in 1969 at about one-fifth the cost in constant dollars. There is no parallel service in Japan, since telegrams are still delivered immediately.

## 4.14 Facsimile

In both Japan and the United States, facsimile is one of the most rapidly growing media. In Japan from 1960 to 1975 its annual growth rate was 24.3% per annum. In the U.S., starting at near zero in 1960, the rate of growth since 1961 has been 34.8% per annum, and even since 1974 it has still been growing at 28.5% per annum. The transmission cost per word is very low because a facsimile machine reproduces a whole page at the same cost regardless of the number of words on it. So the marginal cost of extra words on the page is zero. A telex, on the other hand, costs for each word, so there is an economy in brevity; this affects sender behavior. A person with a typed memo and a facsimile machine will put the memo in as it is. If he has a telex machine he may well write a short summary message instead of the original. The American cost of a word transmitted by facsimile in 1977 was only 2.7% of the cost per word of telex. That, however, disregards the fact that a 10-word message by facsimile costs the same as a 500-word message. So if a 10-word message will do, telex will be more economical.

Facsimile is particularly convenient and widely used in Japan since it can transmit handwritten non-alphabetic characters.

FACSIMILE  117

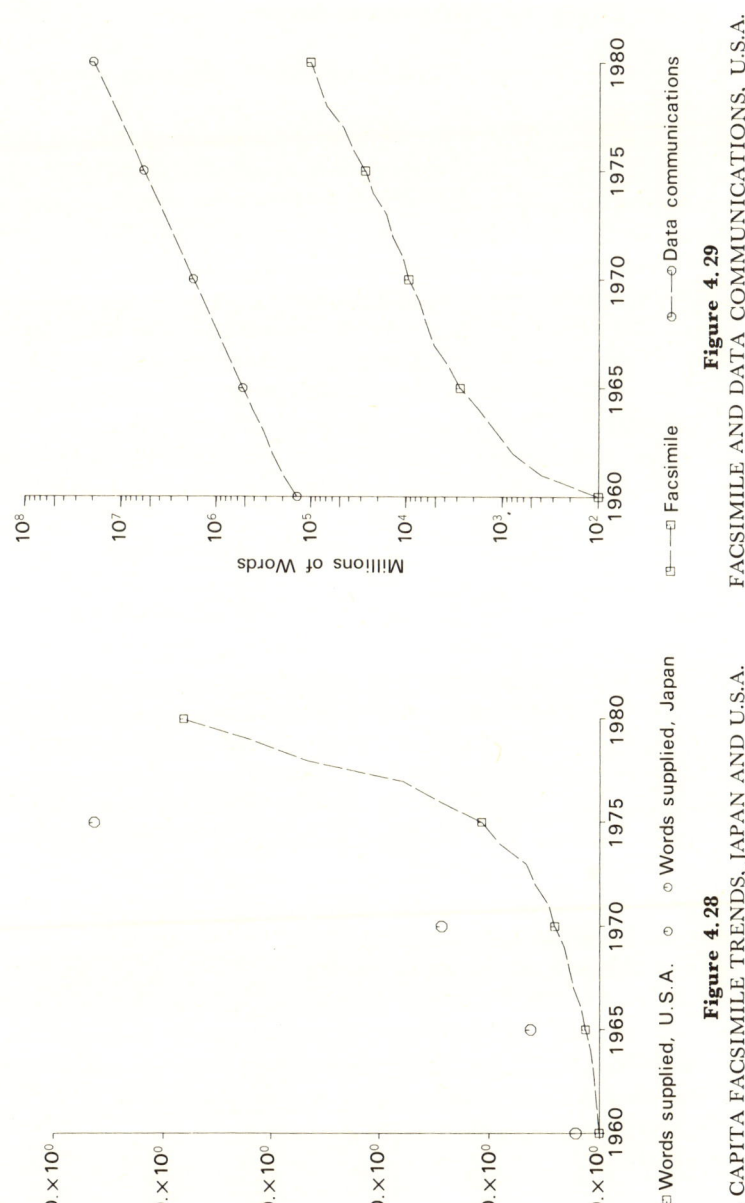

**Figure 4.28**
PER CAPITA FACSIMILE TRENDS, JAPAN AND U.S.A.

**Figure 4.29**
FACSIMILE AND DATA COMMUNICATIONS, U.S.A.

## 4.15 Data Communication

Of the new media of communications the most significant is that called "data networks" or "computer networks." Its significance was discussed in the last section of Chapter 2, where we outlined our main conclusions. We noted the cheapness of data communication, and how that allowed it to be used almost as a mass medium, though it is in fact a point-to-point medium. We considered the possibility that data communication might lead to another order of magnitude or more of growth in the volume of communication. We noted the revolutionary potential of a medium that can create and transform messages by artificial intelligence as well as just delivering them. Among other things, the definition of the volume of communication may be conceptually different when the system can generate messages that are transmitted but not to a human receiver nor sent by a human sender.

In the literature on office automation an estimate can be found that electronic communication involves a network overhead for formatting, synchronization, headers, and acknowledgement that may be as much as 40% of the original message size.[13] That upper bound, which could be reduced in the future by advances in compression and protocols, is not, however, the growth that we are talking about. The point here is not just that the identical messages sent electronically may take some additional communications overhead, but that intelligent machines will increasingly be used to create and generate messages that would never have been authored in a purely human-to-human system.

We shall not develop these points again, but will here discuss some of the data problems we had with this very new medium. Time series reports for data transmission do not exist, so other expedients had to be tried. The Japanese and U.S. time series were developed by different methods which make them not really comparable. The Japanese estimate was 9% of the capacity of leased lines. That procedure rests upon a solid figure for available capacity, though on a weaker one for percentage of

---

[13] John F. Shoch and Jon A. Hupp, "Measured Performance of an Ethernet Local Network," CACM 23, no. 12, pp. 711–721, Dec. 1980; Stephen A. Smith and Robert I. Benjamin, "Projecting Demand for Electronic Communications in Automated Offices," ACM Transactions in Office Information Systems, 1983.

use. However, to the American team that did not seem to be appropriate to a country in which much data traffic is on dial-up phones and leased lines need not be distinguished between voice and data. The American team, therefore, chose to rely on traffic projections that had been made by other analysts.

Five estimates of traffic were collected and projected either forward or backward for years not covered, using the same growth rate as the analyst established in the reported years. Representatives of corporations involved in the data transmission industry were asked to assess these estimates and also asked to supply other estimates, if they knew of any.

The team received a verbal report of a proprietary study from representatives of the American Telephone & Telegraph Co. (AT&T). This study, conducted in 1976, projected U.S. domestic data communication traffic, providing estimates for the total volume of traffic in bits per year for years 1975, 1980, and 1985. The data points for 1975 and 1980 corresponded closely to the team's earlier estimates. The AT&T study estimated the 1975 to 1980 growth rate to be 27 percent. In light of the plausibility of these results, its modal fit among the other studies, and considering that the bulk of data communication transmissions are handled by AT&T, we chose the AT&T study as the basis for an estimate of traffic trends in this medium. Data points were interpolated for the intervening years between 1975 and 1980, and extrapolations based upon this growth rate were performed back in time from 1975 to 1960. Bits were converted into words according to the commonly used ratio of 50 to 1.

The AT&T representatives indicated that they believed the extrapolations were legitimate, but the growth rate during the early years may have been considerably higher as the primitive computer technologies were first being introduced on a large scale. However, a comparison of the exponential curve produced by these derived data points with curves published in *EDP Industry Report* representing data communication revenues, data sets in use, terminals in use, and domestic software expenses indicated that a single exponential rate of growth was a reasonable assumption. We know that neither a uniform growth curve nor a uniform percentage of capacity represents an accurate portrayal of the historical growth of data communication, but it is the best we can now do.

Production costs for data transmission would include those for equipment, such as terminals, modems, data concentrators, needed to produce a message for transmission and also the requisite software. We have failed to find data that would allow us to estimate what percent of each year's expenditures for computer hardware and software was devoted to equipment for data communication purposes.

Transmission costs are defined as the revenues of common carriers for transmitting the bits. In Japan the revenues from leased lines were taken as the basis for this cost estimate. U.S. telephone revenues do not segregate data transmissions. However, from several disparate estimates we compiled a rough time series of the growth of data transmission expenditures. Despite the weakness of these estimates, they leave no doubt that data communication has now become the seminal medium in the changing world of communications.

# Appendix I
# AMERICAN DATA SETS

For each medium, this Appendix lists:
1: The equations used in estimating:
   Volume supplied
   Volume consumed
   Production costs
   Transmission costs
   Consumption costs
2: The definitions of the symbols used in the above equations
3: The sources of the data used
4: Time series of the major variables from 1960 to 1980

Appendix I  AMERICAN DATA SETS

## Frequently Used Variables

P: total resident population over ten years old in thousands.
TH: total number of households in the U.S.
GDPDEF: Deflator used to convert from current to constant dollar value. All dollar time series with "72" attached to the label are in 1972 dollars.

## Sources

1. U.S. Bureau of the Census, Current Population Reports series P-25, nos. 519, 614, 643, 721.
2. Predicasts, Basebook 1978 (Cleveland: Predicasts, Inc., 1978), p. 6.
3. Basebook 1977, (Cleveland: Predicasts, Inc.), p. 37; Basebook 1982 (Cleveland: Predicasts, Inc.), p. 72.

## Radio Broadcasting

### Equations

1. VS (volume supplied) = {[IPAM X ST X (AMST/TST) X AMTH X RIU] + [IPFM X ST X (FMST/TST) X FMTH X RIUFM]} X 60 X 365 X (P/TH)
2. VC (Volume consumed) = IC X LY X 365 X P X RA
3. PC (Production Costs) = (PGCPR X RVPR) + (PGCCR X RVCR)
4. TC (Transmission Costs) = RVPR + RVCR - PC
5. CC (Consumption Costs) = CEXPR

### Definitions of Symbols

### Equation 1

IPAM: average number of words spoken per minute on AM radio broadcasts.(1)
ST: average number of radio broadcasting stations available per household.(2)
AMST: total number of AM radio stations.(3)
TST: total number of radio stations.(3)
AMTH: average number of broadcast hours per day for AM radio stations.(4)
RIU: total number of radio sets.(5)
IPFM: average number of words spoken per minute on FM radio.(6)
FMST: total number of FM radio stations.(3)
FMTH: average number of broadcast hours per day for FM radio stations.(7)
RIUFM: total number of radios in use which receive FM.(8)

### Equation 2

IC: average number of words consumed per minute of radio listening.(9)

Appendix I  AMERICAN DATA SETS

LY: amount of radio listening per individual per day in minutes.(10)
RA: rate of attention given to radio broadcasts.(11)

Equation 3

PGCPR: programming cost as a percentage of total expenses for U.S. public radio stations.(12)
RVPR: total revenues for all public radio stations.(13)
PGCCR: programming costs as a percentage of total expenses for commercial radio stations.(14) RVCR: total revenues for commercial radio stations.(15)

Equation 4

RVPR: total revenues for all public radio stations.(13)
RVCR: total revenues for all commercial radio stations.(15)
PC: production costs for radio; the result of equation 3.

Equation 5

CEXPR: total consumer expenditures on purchasing radio sets.(16)

Sources

(1) A constant of 87 words per minute, estimated by measuring a sample from 19 AM stations broadcasting in the Boston area during mid-January, 1979.
(2) Standard Rate and Data Service, Radio Spot Sales (New York: Standard Rate and Data Service, 1970, 1975, 1978) provided data for 1970, 1975 and 1978. Other years' data are interpolations or extrapolations.
(3) Christopher H. Sterling and Timothy R. Haight, The Mass Media: Aspen Institute Guide to Communication Industry Trends (New York: Praeger

and the Aspen Institute for Humanistic Studies) 1978, pp. 43-44; Television Factbook, 1981-82 ed., no. 50,(Washington, D.C.: Television Digest, Inc.) p. 75-a.
(4) Data for 1970 and 1975 are results of sample studies in Standard Rate and Data Service, Radio Spot Sales for the corresponding years. For other years a constant of 16.8 hours per day was estimated.
(5) Television Digest, Television Factbook loc. cit.
(6) A constant of 48 words per minute was estimated by measuring a sample from 22 FM stations in the Boston area during mid-January, 1979.
(7) Data for 1970 and 1975 are results of sample studies in Standard Rate and Data Service, Radio Spot Sales for the corresponding years. For other years a constant of 19.8 was estimated, this being the average of the two real data points.
(8) RIUFM = RIU − (RIU X PAM) where PAM is the percentage of radios in use that are AM only. Time series data for PAM is in Consumer Electronics (1978).
(9) Data are averages of the words supplied per minute by AM and FM stations weighted in each year by the percentages of AM and FM receivers of total receivers for that year.
(10) A.C. Nielsen Co., Radio Audience (Northbrook,IL; A.C. Nielsen, 1962, 1963) (for 1962, 1963). The yearly estimates are derived from measures of average national radio audience per 15 minute intervals of broadcast (from 6 AM to 12 midnight) for 1967, 1969, 1971, 1973, 1975, 1977, 1982 in Radio Advertising Bureau, Radio Facts (New York; RAB, 1980, 1982) p. 3.
(11) A constant of .650 was adopted from the computed rate of attention for television watching. See television dataset, footnote 10. No comparable data exists for radio.
(12) The estimates for 1960 and 1970, 33% and 31% are based on data from surveys, reported in

Sterling and Haight, The Mass Media, p. 202.
The estimate for 1975, 31% is the value reported
there for FM stations. For all other years an
estimate of 31.3% was made.
(13) Sterling and Haight, The Mass Media, p.
196, for 1976, 1979 and 1980; Corporation for
Public Broadcasting, Summary Statistical Report of
Public Radio Stations 1980/1981 (Washington 1981).
(14) The data for 1960, 1970 and 1975, i.e., 33%
31% and 29%, respectively, are in Sterling and
Haight, Mass Media, p. 202 with the last being
that for AM stations only. For all other years an
estimate of 31.3% was made.
(15) Sterling and Haight, p. 203, and
Broadcasting-Cablecasting Yearbook (Washington,
D.C.: Broadcasting Publications 1982), p. A-2.
(16) Sterling and Haight, pp. 361-362, for
1960-1976; Electronic Market Data Book 1983 ed., p.
23 for 1977-1980.

## Television

### Equations

1. VS (Volume supplied) = IP X ST X
   [(365 X 60 X COMM  X  (COMS/TS))
   + EDM X (EDS/TS))] X TTV X (P/TH)
2. VC (Volume consumed) = IP X WY X 52 X P X
   (TVH/TH) X RA
3. PC (Production costs) = (PGCED X RVED)
   + (PGCCM X RVCM)
4. TC (Transmission costs) = RVED + RVCM - PC
5. CC (Consumption costs) = CEXPT + CE 2

## Definitions of Symbols

### Equation 1

IP: average number of words per minute, both spoken and written, transmitted by television.(1)
TTV: total number of television sets.(2)
ST: average number of television stations available in each community.(3)
COMM: average number of broadcast hours per day for commercial television stations.(4)
COMS: total number of commercial TV stations.(5)
TS: total number of television stations.(5)
EDM: average number of broadcast minutes per year for educational television stations.(6)
EDS: total number of educational television stations.(7)
TS: total number of television stations (TS = COMS + EDS).

### Equation 2

IP: number of spoken and written words per minute transmitted by television.
WY: average number of television viewing minutes per week per person.(9)
TVH: total number of households equipped with television.(8)

### Equation 3

PGCED: total programming cost as a percentage of total operating costs for educational television stations.(11)
RVED: total income of public television stations.(12)
PGCCM: total programming cost as a percentage of total operating expenses for commercial television stations.(13)
RVCM: total income of commercial TV stations.(14)

## Appendix I  AMERICAN DATA SETS

### Equation 4

RVED: total revenues of public TV stations.(12)
RVCM: total income of commercial TV stations.(14)
PC: the production cost of the television industry, the result of equation 3.

### Equation 5

CEXPT: total of consumer expenditures on TV sets.(15)
CEXRT: total of consumer expenditures on the repair of television and radio sets.(16)

### Sources

(1) This constant, 153 words (131 spoken, 22 written) per minute, was estimated by means of sampling the programming on 8 Boston television stations (4 VHF, 4 UHF) during the last week of January, 1979. The results 158 words/minute/VHF (134 spoken, 24 written), 140 words/minute/UHF (121 spoken, 19 written) were weighted by total number of VHF and UHF stations.
(2) Television Factbook. 50, p. 75-a.
(3) Sterling and Haight, The Mass Media p. 49. Datum for 1980 was estimated on basis of A.C. Nelson Co., Nielsen Report on Television, 1981 (Northbrook, Il., 1980).
(4) Standard Rate and Data Service, Spot Television Rates and Data (New York: Standard Rate and Data Service, 1970, 1975, 1978). Data were derived using a sample of 50 stations. Data are for years 1970, 1975, and 1978. Others years are extrapolations and interpolations.
(5) Television Factbook, op. cit., p. 67-c.
(6) U.S. Department of Commerce, Bureau of the Census, Statistical Abstract of the United States (Washington: U.S. Government Printing Office, 1976), p. 536; 1982 ed., p. 559.

(7) *Television Factbook*, op. cit., Stations Volume, p. 67-d.
(8) Broadcast Publications Company, *Broadcasting-Cablecasting Yearbook*, 1983 (Washington: Broadcast Publications Co., 1976), p. G-16.
(9) A.C. Nielsen, Co. *Television Audience 1978* (Northbrook, Ill.: A.C. Nielsen Co., 1978), p. 12, for years 1972-1977; *Broadcasting Yearbook*, 1976 for years 1960 and 1965. Data for 1978-1980 were computed on basis of *Nielsen Report on Television, 1981*.
(10) A constant of .650 is based on Robert B. Bechtell, et al., "Correlates Between Observed Behavior and Questionnaire Responses on TV Viewing," *Television and Social Behavior* Volume 4: *Television in Day-to-Day Life: Patterns of Use*, E. Rubinstein, G. Comstock & J. Murray, eds. (Washington, D.C., 1972), p. 294. Their data is for rates of attention by program type. Our constant is a weighted average of these rates where the respective weightings were the percents of total viewing time spent on each program type.
(11) Sterling and Haight, *The Mass Media*, p. 196. Data were available only for years 1970 through 1975. For other years, the average of these, 14% was used as an estimate.
(12) Ibid. Corporation for Public Broadcasting, *Summary Statistics of Public Television Licenses, 1980-1981*, for 1976, 1979, and 1980. The data are for years 1966, 1968, 1970 to 1975. Other years were interpolated or extrapolated.
(13) Sterling and Haight, p. 207. Data are from 1960 and 1970. Other years were the average of those two.
(14) *Television Factbook*, op. cit., pp. 59-a to 60-a.
(15) Ibid., p. 79-a.
(16) U.S. Department of Commerce, Bureau of Economic Analysis, *The National Income and*

Appendix I  AMERICAN DATA SETS

Product Accounts of the United States (Washington: U.S. Government Printing Office, n.d.), p. 91 for 1960 through 1974; Basebook 1981 (Cleveland: Predicast's, Inc., 1982) p. 736.

## Cable Television

### Equations

1. VS (Volume supplied) = IP X 60 X 52 X [((AW + SW) X SR) + PAYBW X PAYSR] X P/TH
2. VC (Volume consumed) = IP X 52 X ((AV X SR) + (PAYV X PAYSR) + (SV X SR)) X (P/TH) X RA
3. PC (Production costs) = REV X PROG
4. TC (Transmission costs) = REV-PC

### Definitions of Symbols

#### Equation 1

IP: average number of words supplied per minute of cable TV broadcasting.(1)
AW: average weekly broadcasting hours of automated origination per cable TV system.(2)
SW: average weekly broadcasting hours of studio-originated programs per cable TV system.(3)
SR: total number of cable TV subscribers.(4)
PAYBW: average weekly broadcasting hours per pay-TV system.(5)
PAYSR: total number of pay-TV subscribers.(6)

#### Equation 2

IP: average number of words per minute of cable TV broadcasting.(1)

AV: average number of minutes spent viewing automated origination cable TV programming per cable TV household per week.(7)
SR: total number of cable TV subscribers.(4)
PAYV: average number of minutes spent viewing pay-TV per pay-TV household per week.(8)
PAYSR: total number of pay-TV subscribers.(6)
SV: average number of minutes spent viewing studio-originated programming per household per week.(9)
RA: rate of attention given to cable TV broadcasts.(10)

Equation 3

REV: total revenues of cable TV industry.(11)
PROG: TV programming costs expressed as a percentage of total cable TV revenues.(12)

Equation 4

REV: total revenues of the U.S. cable TV industry.(11)
PC: production costs, is the result of Equation 3.

Sources

(1) This constant, 153 words per minute, is the value estimated for average number of words per minute supplied by commercial television. See television dataset, footnote 1.
(2) Data was estimated for 1967, 1970, 1975 and 1978 and 1980 by measuring programming statistics for a sample of approximately 100 CATV systems randomly from "Broadcasting Cable Sourcebook" (Washington: Broadcasting Publications, 1972, 1976, 1979) and Broadcasting Yearbook (Washington: Broadcasting Publications, 1967); Television Factbook, 1980-1981, no. 49. Data for years 1960 and 1961 are treated as 0). Other years are interpolations or extrapolations.

*132* Appendix I  AMERICAN DATA SETS

(3) See footnote 2 above. For this variable, data for 1960-1965 are considered zero, data for years other than 1967, 1970, 1975 and 1978 are interpolations or extrapolations.
(4) <u>Television Factbook</u>, no. 48 (1979) Services Volume (Washington: Television Digest, Inc., 1979), p. 83-a; Sterling and Haight, <u>The Mass Media</u>, p. 58; <u>Broadcasting-Cablecasting Yearbook 1982</u>, p. D-2, for 1979, 1980.
(5) Data for 1960-1971 are treated as zero; for 1972-1978 a constant of 64 hours was estimated on the basis of <u>Broadcasting Cable Sourcebook</u> 1972 and 1979.
(6) For 1960-1970 the variable's value is 0; Sterling and Haight, <u>The Mass Media</u>, p. 58 for 1972-1976; <u>Broadcasting-Cablecasting Yearbook</u>, <u>loc. cit.</u>
(7) An estimated constant of 3 minutes per week on the basis of J. Ruckinsas ("The Consumer in the Electronic Market" Media '90 Research Report 79-2, mimeo: 1979, p. 26) survey result that the average viewer watches such programming 3 times per week. We assumed 1 minute per viewing.
(8) A constant of 297 minutes was estimated for the years 1972-1978 on the basis of J. Ruckinsas' report, finding that the average viewer watches 8.8 movies per month, the average length of a movie having been estimated by us as 120 minutes, based on the movie dataset, footnote 2, but excluding trailers and shorts.
(9) An estimated constant of 5 minutes per week.
(10) A constant of .650 was adopted from the computed rate of attention for television viewing. See television dataset, footnote 10.
(11) Don R. LeDuc, <u>Cable TV and the FCC, a Crisis in Media Control</u> (Philadelphia: Temple U. Press, 1973), p. 114 for 1961-1965; M. Seiden, Cable Television, U.S.A.: An Analysis of Government Policy (New York: Praeger, 1972), p. 20 for 1971; <u>Cablevision</u> Dec. 17, 1979, p. 180 for 1974-1978;

*Broadcasting-Cablecasting Yearbook*, 1982 p. D-3,
for 1979, 1980.
(12) A constant of 17% was estimated following data
in *Cablevision*, Dec. 17, 1980, p. 180 and
also Seiden, op. cit., pp. 32-33.

## Records and Tapes

### Equations

1. VS (Volume supplied) = IP X [(TDS X NDS) + (TDL X NDL) + TT X NT)] X P/TH
2. VC (Volume consumed) = IC X TRT X 365 X P
3. PC (Production costs) = R X ASRI
4. TC (Transmission costs) = ASRI - PC
5. CC (Consumption costs) = CPH + CTR

### Definition of Symbols

#### Equation 1

IP: average number of words per minute on records and tapes.(1)
TDS: average minutes per single 45 rpm record.(2)
NDS: total number of single 45 rpm records sold.(3)
TDL: average number of minutes per LP (33 rpm) record.(4)
NDL: total number of LP records sold.(5)
TT: average number of minutes per tape.(6)
NT: number of pre-recorded tapes sold.(7)

#### Equation 2

IP: average number of words per minute of record and tapes.(1)
TRT: average time in minutes per day per person of listening to records and tapes.(8)

## Appendix I  AMERICAN DATA SETS

### Equation 3

R: percentage for artists' royalties of total annual sales of the recording industry.(4)
ASRI: total annual sales of the recording industry.(10)

### Equation 4

ASRI: total annual sales of the recording industry.(10)
PC: production costs, the result of equation 3.

### Equation 5

CPH: total annual sales of phonographs.(10)

CTR: total annual sales of tape recorders.(11)

### Sources

(1) A constant of 41 words per minute was estimated through a January, 1980 sample study of records played on Boston area AM and FM stations.
(2) A constant of 7 minutes (3.5 minutes on average per side) was estimated from the study cited in footnote 1.
(3) Sterling and Haight, *The Mass Media*, p. 40, Standard and Poor's, Inc., Industry Survey: *Leisure Time Basic Analysis* (N.Y.: 1982) p. 1-31, for 1977-1980. Values for 1966-1970 are derived from data in Sterling and Haight, p. 191, for total sales revenue of single 45 rpm records in each of those years, by dividing by the average price of a single 45 rpm record. This price was estimated on the basis of the data for 1971-1976, with adjustment for price changes on the basis of the consumer price index. Because no sales revenue data was found for years before 1966, that extrapolation procedure could not be used to yield unit sales values for those years.

(4) An estimate was based on a January, 1980 sample study of LP records in Ms. Sophia Wang's personal record library.

(5) Sterling and Haight, The Mass Media, p. 40, for 1971-1976; Standard and Poor's, loc. cit. for 1977-1980. Values for 1966-1970 were derived through an extrapolation procedure similar to that described in footnote 3 above, on the basis of LP sales revenue data in Sterling and Haight, p. 191.

(6) A constant of 45.5 minutes was estimated by the sample study cited in footnote 4.

(7) Sterling and Haight, op. cit., p. 40, for 1971-1976, Standard and Poor's, loc. cit. for 1977-1980. Values for 1966-1970 were derived through an extrapolation procedure similar to that described in footnote 3, on the basis of pre-recorded tapes sales revenue data in Sterling and Haight, p. 191.

(8) A constant of 1.0 minute per person per day was estimated, see A. Szalai et al, The Use of Time (The Hague: Mouton, 1972), p. 543 (the reported data is from the Jackson, Michigan study). (9) A constant of 14% was estimated on the basis of recording industry expenditure breakdowns in Sterling and Haight, op. cit., pp. 192-193.

(10) Billboard International Buyer's Guide 1978/79; Standard and Poor's, loc. cit. for 1979-1980. Data are for 1970 to 1978. Data for earlier years are extrapolated.

(11) Electronic Market Data Book (Washington, D.C.; Electronic Industries Association, 1973), p. 35, for 1960-1972. Data for 1973-1980 are based on Electronic Market Data Book (Washington, D.C.; Electronic Industries Association, 1983), p. 31, figures for imports, which constituted approximately 95% of the retail market during those years. The data here excludes sales of automotive tape recorders and players, which may lead to an automotive underestimate. But conversely it does not distinguish tape recorders used for office

*136* Appendix I  AMERICAN DATA SETS

purposes and thus may lead to an overestimate of consumption costs for records and tapes.

## Movies

### Equations

1. VS (Volume supplied) = IP X MS X (NS X 52) X (MIN + 4XMDR)
2. VC (Volume consumed) = IP X N X MS
3. PC (Production costs) = MRV X PRH
4. TC (Transmission costs) = MRV - PC

### Definition of Symbols

#### Equation 1
IP: average number of words per minute, both spoken and written in motion pictures.(1)
MS: average length of one movie in minutes.(2)
NS: average number of movie shows per week per theater.(3)
MIN: total number of seats in four-wall movie theaters.(4)
MDR: total number of car spaces in drive-in movie theaters.(4)

#### Equation 2
IP: average number of words per minute in movies.(1)
N: total number of admissions to movies per year.(5)
MS: average length of one movie in minutes.(2)

Equation 3

MRV: total revenues of motion picture theaters.(5)
PRH: cost of film rental and handling as a
percentage of total revenue of movie theaters.(6)

Equation 4

MRV: total revenues of motion picture theaters.(6)
PC: production costs, the result of equation 3.

Sources

(1) A constant of 110 words per minute in
U.S. movies, distributed between the years 1960
and 1978, was found by measuring a sample of such
movies broadcast on Boston area television stations
during the spring, 1980.
(2) A constant of 135 minutes, which includes time
of trailers and shorts as well as a feature movie,
was estimated by Mr. Joseph G. Alterman of the
National Association of Theater Owners.
(3) An estimate of 19.35 shows per week, treated as
a constant, was provided by Mr. Joseph G. Alterman.
(4) Sterling and Haight, The Mass Media, 1963,
1967 and 1972; Bureau of the Census, 1977 Census of
Service Industries, vol. 1, p. 4-21, for 1977.
Other values are extrapolations or interpolation
with the values for 1960, 1961 and 1962 being
interpolations on the additional base of data
reported in Sterling and Haight for 1958 (6,994,800
for four-wall theaters and 1,428,600 for drive-in
theaters).
(5) The values for 1966-1978 are found in Paine,
Webber, Mitchell, Hutchins, Inc., Research Dept.,
"Leisure" (mimeo) (New York, n.d.), p. 24; Standrad
and Poor's, op. cit., p. L-23 for 1979-1980. They
are based on Motion Picture Association of America
(MPAA) data for total movie theater revenue and
average ticket price by year. Values for 1960-1965

are based on "National Income and Products in the United States" data for total motion picture theater revenues and average ticket price by year. These time series are found in Predicasts, <u>Basebook 1973</u> (Cleveland: Predicasts, Inc., 1973), p. 385. This second source was not utilized for years after 1965 because the reported revenues were extremely high in comparison to the MPAA provided figures for the same years.

(6) A constant of 34.4% was estimated on the basis of Sterling and Haight, <u>The Mass Media</u>, p. 189. This value is given for 1970. It was substantiated since it closely approximated values reported in the same source for 1931, 1947 and 1956.

## Education

<u>Equations</u>

1. VS (Volume supplied) = IP X [(PTD X CL X ((STT - STT10)/STT) X SCRS X ST) + (HTW X TF X HCRS X NWY)]
    where SCRS = (PSD/PTD) X (STT/CL)
    and   HCRS = (HSW/HTW) X (HST/TF)
2. VC (Volume consumed) = IP X 60[(PSD X (STT - SST10) X STA) + (HSW X HST X NWY)]
3. PC (Production costs) = [(PEX - PTC + NPEX - NPTC) X [(STT - STT10)/STT)] + HEX - HTC
4. TC (Transmission costs) = (PTC + NPTC) X ((CSTT - STT10)/STT) + HTC
5. CC (Consumption costs) = (RBTP X PS) + (RBTNP X NPS) + (I X HST)

## Definitions of Symbols

### Equation 1

IP: average number of words produced per minute of teaching.(1)
PTD: average number of hours spent in primary and secondary school classes per teacher per day.(2)
CL: total number of classroom teachers in elementary and secondary schools.(3)
STT: total number of students enrolled in elementary and secondary schools.(3)
STT10: estimated number of school children under 10 years of age (4).
SCRS: estimated average number of students in a fully attended elementary or secondary school classroom (where PSD is the average number of hours spent per student per day for elementary and secondary schools.(9)
ST: average length of elementary and secondary public school terms per year in days.(5)
HTW: average time in minutes spent on teaching per teacher per week in colleges and universities.(7)
TF: total teaching faculty at colleges and universities.(7)
HCRS: estimated average number of students in a college or university class, where
    HST is the total number of students enrolled in colleges and universities in millions (13), and HSW is the average time in hours per week spent during term time on classwork per college and university student.(11)
NWY: average number of weeks per college and university academic year.(8)

### Equation 2

IP: average number of words consumed per minute of schooling.(1)
PSD: average time in hours spent in school per student per day for elementary and secondary schools.(9)

STT: total number of students enrolled in elementary and secondary schools.(3)
SST10: estimated number of schoolchildren under 10 years of age.(4)
STA: average number of days attended in public elementary and secondary schools per student per year in the U.S.(10)
HSW: the average time in hours spent during term time on classwork per college and university student per week.(11)
HST: total number of students enrolled in colleges and universities.(12)
NWY: average number of weeks per college and university academic year.(8)

### Equation 3

PEX: total expenditures for public elementary and secondary schools.(13)
PTC: transmission costs of public elementary and secondary education.(14)
NPEX: total expenditures for private elementary and secondary schools.(15)
NPTC: transmission costs of private elementary and secondary education.(16)
STT: total number of students enrolled in elementary and secondary schools.(3)
STT10: estimated number of school children under 10 years of age.(3)
HEX: total current-fund expenditures of colleges and universities.(17)
HTC: transmission cost of colleges and universities.(17)

### Equation 4

PTC: transmission costs of public elementary and secondary education.(14)
NPTC: transmission costs of private elementary and secondary education.(16)

STT: total number of students enrolled in elementary and secondary schools.(3)
SST10: estimated number of school children under 10 years of age.(4)
HTC: transmission costs of colleges and universities.(17)

Equation 5

RBTP: average cost of room and board for students attending public colleges.(17)
PS: total number of students in public colleges.(17)
RBTNP: average cost of room and board for students attending private colleges.(17)
NPS: total number of students in private colleges.(17)
I: average annual income of 18 to 24 year old men with a high school education.(17)
HST: total number of students enrolled in U.S. colleges and universities.(12)

Sources

(1) This constant, which approximates the normal speaking rate at 120 words per minute, was drawn from the sources cited in note 1 of the telephone dataset.
(2) On the basis of informed experience.
(3) Predicast, Basebook 1973 (Cleveland: Predicast, 1973), p. 337; Predicast, Basebook 1982 (Cleveland: Predicast, 1978), p. 755.
(4) U.S. Bureau of the Census, 1960, 1970, and 1980 Census. Data for other years were estimated on the basis of population trends adjusted by school enrollment trends.
(5) Department of Health, Education, and Welfare, Digest of Education Statistics (Washington: U.S. Government Printing Office, annual). Since no trend was visible, this variable was averaged and treated as a constant for those years for which actual data points were not available. Data points were

obtained for years 1961, 1963, 1967, 1971, and 1973. The average of these values, 179 days per term, was used for all years.
(6) Ibid (years 1970 and 1977). This constant, 556.5 minutes, is the average of data points found for 1969 and 1972, the only data points found.
(7) Ibid.
(8) This constant was estimated to be 30 weeks per year on the basis of our own academic experience.
(9) A constant of 4.6 hours per day was estimated on the basis of a survey of Boston area elementary, junior high school and high school administrators, conducted April, 1981. Respondents were asked to estimate time spent daily for lunch break, recesses, homeroom, study hall, physical education and similar activities. In each case the cumulated average daily time was subtracted from the corresponding official length of the school day. The results ranged from slightly under 4 hours to 5 hours with some convergence between 4.5 and 4.75 hours.
(10) HEW, Digest of Educational Statistics (years 1964, 1967, 1970, 1974, and 1975). Data were available for years 1961, 1963, 1967, 1971, and 1973. Other years represent interpolations or extrapolations. The equation thus adjusts consumption by attendance rate averaged over the school year.
(11) This constant, 15 hours per week, was estimated on the basis of academic experience.
(12) Predicast, Basebook 1973, p. 338, and Basebook 1982, p. 756.
(13) Predicast, Basebook 1978, p. 625 to 1977. Other years represent interpolations or extrapolations.
(14) HEW, Digest of Education Statistics (annual). Raw data on total expenditures by elementary and secondary schools and their expenditures on instructional staff were used to compute expenditures for instruction as a percent of total expenditures for the years 1960, 1961, 1963,

1965, 1967, 1969, 1971, 1973, 1975, 1977 and 1979. Extrapolations and interpolations completed the time series for PPTC, the instructional cost as a percentage of total expenditures for public elementary and secondary education. This data was then multiplied by the time series for total educational expenditures found in Basesbook 1973 and 1982. I.e., PTC = PPTC X PEX.
(15) Basebook 1978, p. 625; Basebook 1982, p. 755. Data were available for years 1965 and 1967 to 1977. Other years represent extrapolations or interpolations.
(16) This variable was calculated in the same way as was PTC, see note 14 above, except that PPTC was multiplied by NPEX instead of PEX.
(17) Digest of Education Statistics (annual).

## Newspapers

Equations

1. VS (Volume supplied) = [(CD X 313 X PD X WD)
    + (CS X 52 X PS X WD) + (CW X 52 X PW X WW)
    + (NW X NP X NI)] X (P/TH)
2. VC (Volume consumed) = IC X [(DNT X 313)
    + (SNT X 52)] X P
3. PC (Production costs) = (NEC X NEX X NRV)
    + (ECP X ADEX)
4. TC (Transmission costs) = NRV - PC - (1-ADEXP)
    X ADEX

## Appendix I  AMERICAN DATA SETS

### Definitions of Symbols

#### Equation 1

CD: total circulation U.S. daily newspapers.(1)
PD: average number of pages in a U.S. daily newspaper.(2)
WD: average number of words per page in daily newspapers.(3)
CS: total circulation of all Sunday newspapers.(1)
PS: average number of pages in Sunday papers.(4)
CW: total weekly circulation of all weekly newspapers.(5)
PW: average number of pages in weekly papers.(6)
WW: average number of words per page in weekly newspapers.(7)
NW: average number of words per page in pre-printed newspaper inserts.(8)
NP: average number of pages per pre-printed newspaper insert.(9)
NI: total number of pre-printed newspaper inserts (i.e. total circulation for the year).(10)

#### Equation 2

IC: average number of words consumed per minute of newspaper reading.(11)
DNT: time spent in minutes per day on reading daily newspapers.(12)
SNT: time spent in minutes on reading Sunday newspapers.(13)

#### Equation 3

NEC: editorial costs of the newspaper industry as a percentage of total expenditures.(14).
NEX: total expenditures of the newspaper industry as a percentage of total revenues.(13)
NRV: total receipts for all newspaper products.(13)
ECP: editorial costs of pre-printed newspaper inserts as a percentage of the total for

advertisers' pre-printed newspaper inserts(ECP=NEC).
ADEX: total advertisers' expenditures on
pre-printed newspaper inserts.(17).

Equation 4

NRV: total receipts for all newspaper products.(16)
PC: production costs of U.S. newspapers, the result
of equation 3.
ADEXP: percentage of advertisers' expenditures for
preprinted newspaper inserts that are paid to
newspapers.(18)
AEDX: total advertisers' expenditures on pre-printed
newspaper inserts.(17)

Sources

(1) Sterling and Haight, The Mass Media, pp.
332-333; Statistical Abstract of the United
States, 1982, p. 562.
(2) Statistical Abstract of the United States
1982, p.562.
(3) Estimated by us by measuring in a random sample
of pages in newspapers listed in Editor and
Publisher. This is a constant. Its value is 3048
words per page.
(4) Statistical Abstract of the United States,
loc. cit.
(5) Data points for 1960, 1965, 1970 measured by
sample survey of weekly, semi-weekly and tri-weekly
newspapers circulations listed in Ayer's Directory
of Publications for corresponding years.
(6) Estimated by measuring a sample of weekly
newspapers listed in Ayer's Directory of
Publications. The value of this constant is 36
pages.
(7) Estimated by measuring in a random sample of
pages in weekly newspapers listed in Ayer's
Directory of Publications. The value of this
constant is 1295 words per page.

(8) Estimated by measuring in a random sample of pages of pre-printed newspaper inserts appearing in Boston newspapers during February, 1980. The value of this constant is 385 words per page.
(9) Following advice of Theodore Knecht of the Newspaper Advertising Bureau, the value of this constant is estimated to be 12 pages.
(10) Personal communications from Theodore Knecht and Joseph Wallis, Newspaper Advertising Bureau. The data provided were for years 1960 and 1970 to 1980.
(11) This constant (240 words per minute) is the estimate of Sanborn Associates, a speed-reading firm in Brookline, Massachusetts. A representative of Evelyn Woods Reading Dynamics estimates the figure to be 250 words per minute.
(12) Two different estimates of this variable are used in our calculations. The first is based on John P. Robinson, "Toward A Post-Industrious Society," Public Opinion 2 (August-September, 1979): 43, which reports a much lower value for 1975 (14 min.) than for an earlier 1965 finding (22 min.). This suggested to us an exponentially declining trend reflected in the time series DNT1. Robinson's two data points yields an annual decline which appears too high. We estimated the highest plausible value as -3.6% per annum. The second estimate DNT2 holds as constant Robinson's value for 1965 daily reading. This choice thus produced 2 estimates of volume consumed with the lower VC1 corresponding to the use of DNT1.
(13) A constant of 45 minutes was estimated.
(14) Sterling and Haight, The Mass Media, p. 164. Data are available only for the years 1972 to 1976. These were averaged and treated as a constant throughout the time period of the estimate (14.8%).
(15) Ibid., pp. 163-164. This was treated as a constant (78.65%).
(16) Ibid., p. 158. Basebook 1982, p. 295 for 1975 to 1980.
(17) Estimates by Theodore Knecht of Newspaper

Advertising Bureau for 1960 and 1970 through 1980. (18) A constant of 50% was estimated on the basis of Newspaper Advertising Bureau information.

## Magazines

### Equations

1. VS (Volume supplied) = (WG + WT + WC + WR + WA + WF + WM) X P/TH
   where $W_i$ = $NW_i$ X $PW_i$ X $CW_i$,
   and i = G,T,C,R,A,F,M
2. VC (Volume consumed) = IC X RD X 365 X P
3. PC (Production costs) = PE X PX X RVMG
4. TC (Transmission costs) = RVMG − PC

### Definitions of Symbols

#### Equation 1

WG: total volume of words supplied per year by general magazines. (WG = NWG x PWG x CWG).
NWG: average number of words per page in general magazines.(1)
PWG: average number of pages per issue in general magazines.(2)
CWG: total annual circulation of general magazines.(3)
WT: total volume of words supplied per year by trade magazines. (WT = NWT x PWT x CWT).
NWT: average number of words per page in trade magazines.(4)
PWT: the average number of pages per issue in trade magazines.(5)
CWT: total annual circulation of trade magazines.(6)
WC: total volume of words supplied per year by

college magazines. (WC = NWC x PWC x CWC).
NWC: average number of words per page in college magazines.(7)
PWC: average number of pages per issue in college magazines.(8)
CWC: total annual circulation of college magazines.(9)
WR: total volume of words supplied per year by religious magazines (WR = NWR x PWR x CWR).
NWR: average number of words per page in religious magazines.(10)
PWR: average number of pages per issue in religious magazines.(11)
CWR: total annual circulation of religious magazines.(9)
WA: total volume of words supplied per year by agriculture magazines. (WA = NWA x PWA x CWA)
NWA: average number of words per page in agriculture magazines.(12)
PWA: average number of pages per issue in agriculture magazines.(13)
CWA: total annual circulation of agriculture magazines.(9)
WF: total volume of words supplied per year by foreign language magazines (WF = NWF x PWF x CWF).
NWF: average number of words per page in foreign language magazines.(14)
PWF: average number of pages per issue in foreign language magazines.(15)
CWF: total annual circulation of foreign language magazines.(9)
WM: total volume of words in millions supplied per year by other magazines. (WM = NWM x PWM x CWM).
NWM: average number of words per page in other magazines.(16)
PWM: average number of pages per issue in other magazines.(17)
CWM: total annual circulation of other magazines.(9)

Equation 2

IC: average number of words consumed per minute of reading.(18)
RD: average magazine reading time per day in minutes.(19)

Equation 3

PE: magazine editorial costs as a percent of expenditures.(20)
PX: expenditures of the magazine industry as a percent of revenue.(21)
RVM: the total annual revenue of magazines.(22)

Equation 4

RVMG: total annual revenue of magazines.(22)
PC: production costs, the result of equation 3.

Sources

(1) A constant of 436 for the average number of words per page of general circulation magazines, was derived by us from a September, 1979 sample study of 15 general circulation magazines randomly selected from Ayer's Directory of Publications, 1979 ed., (Bala Cynwyd, Pennsylvania: Ayer Press). Figures for each magazine were weighted by its relative level of circulation, so the number of words on a page of large circulation magazine determined the constant more than did a magazine with small circulation.
(2) A constant of 185 pages was estimated from the study described in footnote 1.
(3) On the basis of information from the Magazine Publisher's Association for 1960 through 1975. 1980 datum interpolated from Ayer's data for 1982.
(4) A constant of 836 words was derived from a

*150* Appendix I AMERICAN DATA SETS

September, 1979 sample of 25 technical and trade magazines randomly selected from Ayer's Directory of Publications 1979 ed. The weighting method described in footnote 1 was used.
(5) A constant of 70 pages was estimated from the above sample.
(6) Ayer's Directory of Publications for 1960, 1965, 1970, 1975 and 1978 provided data for the corresponding years. Other years are interpolations and extrapolations.
(7) A constant of 1423 words was estimated from a September, 1979 sample study of 20 college publications selected randomly from Ayer's Directory of Publications 1979 ed. The weighting method described in footnote 1 was used.
(8) A constant of 29 pages was estimated from the above sample.
(9) Ayer's Directory of Publications, 1960, 1970, 1978, 1982; for the corresponding years. Other years are interpolations.
(10) A constant of 1013 words was estimated from a September, 1979 sample of 19 religious magazines selected randomly from Ayer's Directory of Publications 1979 ed. The weighting method described in footnote 1 was used.
(11) A constant of 27 pages was estimated from the above sample.
(12) A constant of 830 words was estimated from a sample study of 30 agricultural publications selected from Ayer's Directory of Publications. Figures for each magazine were weighted by its relative level of circulation, see footnote 1.
(13) In the study cited above, a constant of 45 pages was the average number of pages per agricultural publication.
(14) A constant of 1169 words was estimated from a sample study of 11 foreign language magazines randomly selected from Ayer's Directory of Publications. Figures for each magazine were weighted by the relative level of circulation.

(15) A constant of 22 pages was estimated from the sample cited in footnote 16.

(16) A constant of 1332 words per page was estimated from a September, 1979 sample of 28 Black, Jewish and fraternal publications selected randomly from Ayer's Directory of Publications 1979 ed. Figures for each magazine were weighted by its relative level of circulation.

(17) A constant of 36 pages was estimated from the sample cited in footnote 19.

(18) An average of 240 words per minute was estimated by Sanborn Associates, Brookline, Mass. A representative of Evelyn Woods Reading Dynamics, Inc. gave a slightly higher estimate, 250 words per minute.

(19) An estimate of 6.4 minutes per day in 1965 was used as a constant, see A. Szalai et al., The Use of Time (The Hague: Mouton, 1972), p. 577.

(20) A constant of 14.8% is based on the assumption that the percentage of editorial costs to total expenditures for magazines is similar to that of newspapers. The estimate for newspaper editorial costs percentage is the average of data from 1972 to 1976 reported in Sterling and Haight, The Mass Media, (New York: Praeger, 1979), p. 164.

(21) Ibid., pp. 163-164. A constant of 78.65% is our estimate of the ratio of newspaper expenditures to total revenues; the same figure is here used for magazines.

(22) Basebook 1973, p. 121; Basebook 1982, p. 299.

*152* Appendix I  AMERICAN DATA SETS

                          Books

## Equations

1. VS (Volume supplied) = NW X NP X NUS X (P/TH)
2. VC (Volume consumed) = WR X RT X 365 X P
3. PC  (Production costs) = R X S
4. TC (Transmission costs) = S - PC

## Definitions of Symbols

### Equation 1

NW: average number of words per page in books published.(1)
NP: average number of pages per book.(2)
NUS: number of books sold.(3)

### Equation 2

WR: average number of words consumed per minute of reading.(4)
RT: average minutes of book-reading per person per day.(5)

### Equation 3

R: authors' royalties as a percentage of total book sales.(6)
S: total consumer expenditures on books.(7)

### Equation 4

S: total consumer expenditures on books.(7)
PC: production costs of books published, the result of Equation 3.

## Sources

(1) A constant of 395 words per page is based on a sample of 80 books randomly selected from the Boston Public Library stacks in September, 1979.

(2) A constant of 263 for the average number of pages per book is based on a sample study of 225 books randomly selected from the <u>Cumulative Book Index</u> for the years 1960-1961, 1965-66, 1970 and 1977. Averages for books published in each of these periods were first computed and the resulting figures were then averaged to arrive at 263.

(3) U.S. Bureau of the Census, <u>1967 Census of Manufactures</u>, Vol. II, p. 27A-25; <u>1972 Census of Manufactures</u>, Vol. II, p. 27A-31; <u>Statistical Abstract of the United States</u>, p. 565 for 1977 through 1980.

(4) A constant of 240 words per minute was provided by Sanborn Associates of Brookline, Massachusetts. A representative of Evelyn Woods Reading Dynamics estimated the average reading rate to be slightly higher at 250 words per minute.

(5) A constant of 9 minutes per day per person spent reading books is based on the results of a time-use survey, J. Robinson, <u>How Americans Used Time in 1965</u> (Ann Arbor: U. of Michigan, Institute of Social Research, 1977), pp. 148-150, for the categories of book reading (5.5 min.) and study (6.8 min.). The latter category results were adjusted to reflect study time of students, 10-18 years old and college students not included in Robinson's sample population. For study time of the former, see C. West and E. Wood, "Academic Pressures on Public School Students," <u>Educational Leadership</u>, 27 (March, 1970), pp. 585-589. College students were estimated to study on the average, one hour for each hour spent in classes. Study time was converted to normal reading consumption time by assuming that 40% of study time is spent reading books, but the rate for such reading is assumed to be half the normal reading rate. The final estimate is that 7 minutes

## 154 Appendix I  AMERICAN DATA SETS

per person per day or the equivalent of 3.5 minutes of normal reading is spent in reading that is study. Thus 39% of total reading consumption is "study". (6) A constant of 12.9% is the weighted average of royalties as percentage of expenditure in the five principal book publishing sectors in the year 1976. See Sterling and Haight, *The Mass Media*, (New York: Praeger and the Aspen Institute for Humanistic Studies, 1978), pp. 143-148. The royalty percentage in each sector was weighted by unit sales in that sector. (7) J. Dessauer et al., Book Industry Trends 1979 (Darien, Conn: Book Industry Study Group, Inc., 1979), Table 3, for 1974-1978; *Statistical Abstract of the United States, loc. cit.* for 1979-1980. Other years are estimates based of the wholesale volumes reported in the 1962, 1967, and 1972 *Census Of Manufactures*.

### Direct Mail

#### Equations

1. VS (Volume supplied) = [(PLNW X PL X TN) + (PSNW X PS X TN) + PCNW X PCAT X TN)] X (P/TH)
2. VC (Volume consumed) = [(CWR X CPR X TN) + (CWG X CPG X TN)] X (P/TH)
3. PC (Production costs) = PP X REV
4. TC (Transmission costs) = REV - PC

#### Definitions of Symbols

#### Equation 1

PLNW: average number of words per unit of direct mail in letter form.(1)

PL: percentage of letter-form direct mail to the total.(2)
TN: total number of direct mail units.(3)
PSNW: average number of words per unit of direct mail single sheets.(4)
PS: percentage of single-sheet direct mail to the total.(5)
PCNW: average number of words per unit of direct mail catalogs.(6)
PCAT: percentage of catalogs to the direct mail total.(7)

Equation 2

CWR: number of words consumed per unit per reader who is "reading fairly thoroughly."(8)
CPR: percentage "reading-fairly-thoroughly" of total readers.(9)
TN: total number of direct mail units.(3)
CWG: total number of words consumed per unit per reader "glancing" at the material.(10)
CPG: percentage of "glancing" readers in the total.(11)

Equation 3

PP: editorial costs as a percentage of the total costs, assumed to be equal to that of newspapers.
REV: dollar volume of direct mail advertising.(12)

Equation 4

REV: dollar volume of direct mail advertising.(12)
PC: production costs for direct mail, the result of equation 3.

Sources

(1) This constant, 2800 words per unit, was derived from a sample study of 74 letter-size enveloped

direct mail pieces received by seven members of the MIT Political Science Department (faculty, staff, and students) during February, 1980.
(2) This constant, 58 percent, is the percentage of letter-size enveloped direct mail pieces to the total number of direct mail pieces received by seven members of the MIT Political Science Department in February, 1980.
(3) U.S. Postal Service, Annual Report of the Postmaster General (Washington: U.S. Government Printing Office, annual). Data for years 1972 and 1973 were interpolated.
(4) This constant, 780 words per unit, was derived from a sample study of 13 single-sheet direct mail pieces received by seven members of the MIT Political Science Department in February, 1980.
(5) This constant, 10%, is the percentage of self-mailer pieces in direct mail received by seven members of the MIT Political Science Department in February, 1980.
(6) This constant, 24,200 words per unit, was derived from a sample of 41 catalogs (including shopping guides and circulars) received by seven members of the MIT Political Science Department in February, 1980.
(7) This constant, 32%, is the percentage of catalogs in the direct mail received by seven members of the MIT Political Science Department during February, 1980.
(8) This constant, 110 words, was estimated on the basis of reading by a small sample of subjects of the items collected in our February, 1980 sample of direct mail pieces.
(9) A constant of 34% is based on results of an A.C. Nielsen Co. 1963-1964 survey of approximately 1400 direct mail recipients; see R. Hodgson, The Direct Mail and Mail Order Handbook. (Chicago: Dartnell Corp., 1974).
(10) This constant, 25 words, was estimated on the basis of reading by a small sample of subjects of

the items collected in our February, 1980 sample of direct mail pieces.
(11) A constant of 44% is based on the A.C. Nielsen 1964 study finding reported in R. Hodgson, *Direct Mail and Mail Order Handbook*.
(12) Sterling and Haight, *The Mass Media*, pp. 127-129 for 1960-1976; Robert Coen, "Ad Spending is Out-Muscling National Economy in General," *Advertising Age*, vol. 50, no. 2, Jan. 8, 1979, p. 58-8, for 1977 and 1978; *Television Factbook*, 1981-1982 ed., p. 74-a.

## First Class Mail

### Equations

1. $VS$ (Volume suum: $i = 1$ to $5$) $[IP_i \times R_i \times (FCM + DAIR)]$
2. $PC$ (Production costs) $= (Sum: i = 1$ to $5) [EX_i \times R_i \times (FCM + DAIR)]$
3. $TC$ (Transmission costs) $= RVFC + RVDA + \{(TEX - TRV) \times [(RVFC + RVDA)/TRV]\}$, where $(TEX - TRV) \geq 0$.

### Definitions of Symbols

### Equation 1

$IP_i$: average number of words in the i-th type of correspondence for first class and domestic air mail. These types are:
- 1 = personal correspondence
- 2 = government correspondence
- 3 = financial transactions
- 4 = business letters
- 5 = greeting cards (1)

$R_i$: what the i-th type constitutes as a percentage of total first class and domestic air mail.(2)

FCM: total number of pieces of first class mail per year.(3)
DAIR: total number of pieces of domestic air mail per year.(3)

Equation 2

EXi: expense for producing one piece of the i-th type of correspondence.(4)
Ri: percentage that the i-th type of correspondence constitutes of total first class and domestic air mail.(2)
FCM: total number of pieces of first class mail per year.(3)
DAIR: total number of pieces of domestic air mail per year.(3)

Equation 3

RVFC: total revenues for first class mail per year.(3)
RVDA: total revenues for domestic air mail per year.(3)
TEX: total operating expenses for the U.S. Postal Service.(5)
TRV: total operating revenues for the U.S. Postal Service.(5)

Sources

(1) These five constants were estimated from a study conducted in 1976 by the RCA Government Communications System for the U.S. Postal Service. The final report of the study, "EMS (Electronic Message Service) - System Definition and Evaluation," Microfiche cat. no. PB 292 934, does not include these data. As a preliminary part of the study, the RCA researchers sampled the incoming and outgoing mail of RCA as well as the personal mail of a sample of their employees. They counted

the number of characters (including punctuation and
spaces) in each piece of mail studied and derived
the average number of characters per each particular
type of mail. These figures were divided by seven
(the estimated number of characters per word) to
produce the average number of words per each type of
mail. Included in these figures are the words
appearing on the outside of the envelope.
Government correspondence was not studied in the RCA
study. We have assumed that the average number of
words in governmental correspondence is equal to the
average number of words in a piece of business
correspondence. We wish to thank Mr. Peter
Patterson of RCA for sharing these results with us.
(2) A.D. Little, Inc., Toward Postal Excellence:
Report of the President's Commission on Postal
Organization (Washington: U.S. Government
Printing Office, 1976). The percentage figures are
as follows: personal correspondence - 10 %;
government correspondence - 6%; financial
transactions - 65%; business correspondence - 8%;
and greeting cards - 11%.
(3) U.S. Postal Service, Annual Report of the
Postdmaster General (Washington: U.S. Government
Printing Office, annual). Data were available for
all years but 1972 and 1973, which were
interpolated.
(4) No expenses are assumed for the production of
personal correspondence. The expenses for
government correspondence, are assumed to equal
those for business correspondence. Estimates for the
latter are wage trend adjustments of an estimate of
$6.00 in P. Baran, Cabledata Associates Report
R-160, Appendix G "The Costs of Electronic Messages"
(mimeo) (Palo Alto, CA: 1974), p. G-8. Estimates
for production expenses of financial correspondence,
are similarly based on an estimate of $1.00 in 1974
adjusted for wage trends. Estimates of greeting card
expenses, are gross national product deflator
adjustments of an estimate of average greeting card

(retail) cost of $.50 in 1978 made by measuring a random sample in January, 1979.
(5) For years 1960 to 1970, U.S. Bureau of the Census, *Historical Statistics of the United States* (Washington: U.S. Government Printing Office, 1976); for years 1971 to 1973, U.S. Bureau of the Census, *Statistical Abstracts of the United States* (Washington: U.S. Government Printing Office, annual); for years 1974 to 1978, U.S. Postal Service, *op. cit.* The third term in equation 3 adds a pro-rated share of a postal service operating deficit to the transmission costs for first class and domestic air mail. Since our study considers carriers' profits as part of "true" transmission costs, this term would have been ignored for any year in which the postal service had a surplus. However during the 1960-1980 period, except for 1979, the postal service always had a deficit, paid for from the public treasury.

Telephone

Equations

1. VS (Volume supplied) = IP X [(TLCR X RLC X LC) + (TLGR X RLG X LG) + (TLCB X BLC X LC) + (TLGB X BLG X LG)]
2. PC (Production costs) = HP X [(TLCB X BLC X LC) + (TLGB X BLG X LG)]/60
3. TC (Transmission costs) = LCRV + LGRV

Definitions of Symbols

Equation 1

IP: average number of words per minute of a telephone call.(1)

TLCR: average holding time per residence phone call, in minutes.(2)
RLC: number of local residence phone calls as a percentage of total local calls.(3)
LC: total number of local telephone calls per year.(4)
TLGR: average holding time per long distance residence telephone call, in minutes.(5)
RLG: number of long distance residence calls as a percentage of long distance calls.(6)
LG: total number of long distance telephone calls.(4)
TLCB: average holding time per local business telephone call, in minutes.(7)
BLC: number of local business calls as a percentage of total local calls.(8)
LC: total number of local telephone calls.(4)
TLGB: average holding time per long distance business telephone call.(9)
BLG: number of long distance business telephone calls as a percentage of total long distance calls.(10)
LG: total number of toll telephone calls.(4)

Equation 2

HP: average hourly salary of persons age 14 and over.(11)
TLCB: average holding time per local business telephone call, in minutes.(7)
BLC: number of local business calls as a percentage of total local calls.(8)
LC: total number of local telephone calls.(4)
TLGB: average holding time per long distance business telephone call.(9)
BLG: number of long distance business telephone calls as a percentage of total long distance calls.(10)
LG: total number of toll telephone calls.(4)

### Equation 3

LCRV: total revenues for local telephone calls.(4)
LGRV: total revenues for toll telephone calls.(4)

### Sources

(1) The rate of speech is ordinarily 120 to 150 words per minute, but a telephone rate faster than 125 words per minute can create comprehension problems. A rate of 120 words per minute, was used here. Cf. Roger Wilcox, <u>Oral Reporting in Business and Industry</u> (Englewood Cliffs, NJ: Prentice Hall, 1967), p. 293, and Arthur Sager, <u>Speak Your Way to Success</u> (New York: McGraw Hill, 1968), p. 145.
(2) Martin Mayer, "The Telephone and the Uses of Time," in Ithiel de Sola Pool, ed., <u>The Social Impact of the Telephone</u> (Cambridge, Massachusetts: MIT Press, 1977), p. 235. Mayer reports a holding time of 4.15 minutes. This figure was used as a constant.
(3) John R. Meyer, et al., <u>The Economics of Competition in the Telecommunications Industries</u> (Cambridge, MA: Charles River Associates, 1979), p. 143. For 1975, this percentage was 44.2% which was treated as a constant.
(4) Federal Communications Commission, <u>Statistics of Common Carriers</u> (Washington: U.S. Government Printing Office, annual.
(5) Personal communication from Mr. A.C. Barry of New England Telephone who estimates this figure to be 6.55 minutes, which was treated here as a constant.
(6) Personal communication from Delbert Staley of AT&T, whose estimate of 55% was treated as a constant.
(7) Martin Mayer, "The Telephone and the Uses of Time," in Pool, ed., <u>The Social Impact of the Telephone</u>, p. 235. This time was estimated by

Mayer to be 3.48 minutes, which was used as a constant.
(8) John R. Meyer, et al., The Economics of Competition in the Telecommunications Industry p. 143. For 1975, Meyer et al. found this percentage to be 55.8%, which was used as a constant.
(9) Personal communication from A.C. Barry of New England Telephone, whose estimate of four minutes, was used as a constant.
(10) Personal communication from Mr. Delbert Staley of AT&T, who estimates this percentage to be 45%, which was treated as a constant.
(11) Dept. of Health, Education, and Welfare, Digest of Educational Statistics (Washington: U.S. Government Printing Office, 1971).

## Telex

### Equations

1. VSD (Volume supplied, domestic) = IPD X NTD
2. PCD (Production costs, domestic) = CW X NTD
3. TCD (Transmission costs, domestic) = DTRV
4. VSI (Volume supplied, international) = IPI X NTI
5. PCI (Production costs, international) = CW X NTI
6. TCI (Transmission costs, international) = OTRV

### Definitions of Symbols

### Equation 1

IPD: average number of words per domestic telex message.(1)
NTD: total number of domestic messages for Telex, TCCS, TWX, Tel(t)ex.(2)

## Appendix I  AMERICAN DATA SETS

### Equation 2

CW: cost of producing one telex message, in dollars.(3)
NTD: total number of domestic message for Telex, TCCS, TWX, Tel(t)ex.(2)

### Equation 3

DTRV: total revenues from domestic telex messages.(2)

### Equation 4

IPI: average number of words per overseas telex message terminating in the U.S. (4)
NTI: total number of overseas telex messages terminating in the U.S. (5)

### Equation 5

CW: cost of producing one telex message, in dollars.(3)
NTI: total number of overseas telex messages terminating in the U.S.(5)

### Equation 6

OTRV: total revenues from overseas telex messages terminating in the U.S.(2)

### Sources

(1) The average number of words per domestic telex message was estimated at a constant value of 50.
(2) Federal Communications Commission, *Statistics of Communications Common Carriers* (Washington, D.C.: annual). The data for 1960, 1961 and 1962 are extrapolations.

(3) The data are wage index pegged adjustments of an estimate of $2.90 in 1974 in P. Baran, Cabledata Associates Report R-160 (mimeo) Appendix G "The Costs of Electronic Messages" (Palo Alto, CA: 1974), p. G-14.
(4) The average number of words per international telex message was estimated as a constant of 50.
(5) Federal Communications Commission, op. cit. Data for 1960-1966 are extrapolations. Since the purpose of the present study is to estimate information flows in the U.S., the decision was made to count only international messages received in the U.S., not ones reaching foreign recipients.

## Telegraph

### Equations

1. VSD (Volume supplid, domestic) = IPD X DM
2. PCD (Production costs, domestic) = CW X DM
3. TCD (Transmission costs, domestic) = DMRV
4. VSI (Volume supplied, foreign) = WTT
5. PCI (Production costs, foreign) = CW X TM
6. TCI Transmission costs, foreign) = OTRV

### Definitions of Symbols

### Equation 1

IPD: average number of words per domestic telegram.(1)
DM: total number of domestic telegraph messages sent, excluding money order messages, Tel(t)ex, TCCS message service, mailgrams and telex messages.(2)

*166* Appendix I  AMERICAN DATA SETS

Equation 2

CW: cost of producing a telegram.(3)
DM: total number of domestic telegraph messages sent in the U.S., excluding money orders, Tel(t)ex, TCCS message service, mailgrams and telex messages.(2)

Equation 3

DMRV: total revenues for domestic telegraph messages excluding money order messages, Tel(t)ex, TCCS message service, mailgrams and telex messages.(2)

Equation 4

WTT: total number of words in international messages terminating in the U.S.(2) Since the purpose of the present study is to estimate information flows in the U.S, the decision was made count only international messages received in the U.S., not ones reaching foreign recipients.

Equation 5

CW: cost of preparing one telegram.(3)
TM: total number of international telegraph messages terminating in the U.S.(2)

Equation 6

OTRV: total revenues for international telegraph messages terminating in the U.S.(2)


Sources

(1) A constant of 50 was estimated to be the average number of words per telegram. This includes the address and signature.

(2) Federal Communications Commission, Statistics of Common Carriers (Washington: U.S. Government Printing Office, annual).
(3) These values are adjustments pegged to the wage index of an estimated value of $2.00 for 1974 reported in Paul Baran, Cabledata Associates Report-160, Appendix G, "The Costs of Electronic Messages" (mimeo) (Palo Alto, CA: 1974), p. G-9. We assume foreign costs to be equal to domestic costs.

Mailgram

Equations

1. VS (Volume supplied) = IP X NM
2. PC (Production costs) = PCM X NM
3. TC (Transmission costs) = TCM

Definition of Symbols

Equation 1

IP is the average number of words per mailgram.(1)
NM is the total number of mailgram messages.(2)

Equation 2

PCM is the cost of producing one mailgram message.(3)
NM is the total number of mailgram messages.(2)

Equation 3

TCM are the total transmission revenues for mailgrams in dollars.(4)

## Sources

(1) A constant of 100 is the estimated average number of words per mailgram for the years 1972 (when mailgrams were introduced) to 1978.
(2) Federal Communications Commission, <u>Statistics of Common Carriers</u> (Washington: U.S. Government Printing Office, annual).
(3) These data are wage index based adjustments of the estimate of a 1974 cost of $2.00, reported in Paul Baran, Cabledata Associates Report R-160, Appendix G, "The Costs of Electronic Messages" (mimeo) (Palo Alto, California, 1974), p. G-9.

## Facsimile

## Equations

1. VS (Volume supplied) = IP X NP
2. PC (Production costs) = (EX X NP) + EQR
3. TC (Transmission costs) = TCPM X NP

## Definitions of Symbols

### Equation 1

IP: average number of words per page of facsimile.(1)
NP: total number of facsimile pages sent.(2)

### Equation 2

EX: expense for producing one piece of business correspondence.(3)
NP: total number of facsimile pages sent.(2)
EQR: total equipment sales for facsimile.(4)

Equation 3

TCP : average cost of transmitting one page of facsimile.(5)
NP: total number of facsimile pages sent.(2)


Sources

(1) This constant is the estimate presented in Howard Anderson, "Memo Tells How the Decision Was Made," Communication News (December 1976): 33.
(2) Personal communication from Mr. David Mack of the Yankee Group (Cambridge, MA), February 7, 1980.
(3) These values are adjustments pegged to the wage index of an estimated cost of $6.00 in 1974 for preparing a piece of business correspondence. This estimate is found in Paul Baran, Cabledata Associates Report R-160, Appendix G, "The Costs of Electronic Messages" (mimeo) (Palo Alto, California: 1974), p. G-8.
(4) Predicast, Forecast Abstract (Cleveland, Ohio: Predicast, Inc.) 1968, 1969, 1970, 1972, 1973, 1974, 1975, 1976, 1977, 1978, 1979). Values for 1960-1962 are extrapolations and those for 1964-1966 are interpolations.
(5) International Data Corporation, "Information Processing and Tomorrow's Office (advertisement)," Fortune (October 8, 1979): 54. This advertisement presents data for years 1969 and 1978. Other years represent extrapolations or interpolations.


Data Transmission


Five separate estimates of traffic projections were collected from which five estimates of the 1960 to 1980 volume of traffic were derived. We projected either forward or backward for years not covered in each, using the same growth rate as the analyst established in the years he reported. Three projection were presented in terms of bits per year.(1) The others were in terms of transactions per year.(2) An estimate of the average number of bits per transaction (7300) was used (3) in order to calculate the growth rates in bits per year estimated by those projections.

We received a verbal report of another study (4) from representatives of the American Telephone and Telegraph (AT&T) which proved useful for our purposes. This study, conducted by AT&T in 1976, projected U.S. domestic data communication traffic, providing estimates for the total volume of traffic in bits per year for years 1975, 1980, and 1985. The data points for years 1975 to 1980 corresponded closely to our earlier estimates. The AT&T study estimated the 1975 to 1980 growth rate to be 27 percent. In light of the plausibility of these results and considering that the bulk of data communciation transmissions are handled by AT&T, we chose the AT&T study as the most likely basis for an estimate of traffic trends in this medium.

Production costs for data transmission are considered by this study to be those for the equipment, such as terminals, modems, data concentrators, needed to produce the message in a form suitable for transmission and also the costs of the requisite software. Unfortunately we have so far failed to find a set of data that would indicate the yearly costs for the period under examination or which would allow us to estimate what percent of each year's expenditures for computer hardware and software was devoted to equipment for data transmission purposes.

Transmission costs are defined as the revenues of common carriers for transmitting the bits. Again

we experienced difficulty in estimating for the
relevant period how much of telephone revenues was
for calls that were data transmissions. However on
the basis of several sources (5) we compiled a time
series which reflects the growth of data
transmission costs and which we believe reasonably
approximates the values.

Sources

(1) Two studies which provided three of our
estimates, reported growth rates in bits. One study
was Peter Stanek, Elliott Hurwitz, and Ray
Oleszewski, Cost, Quality, and Availability of
Service, A Report Submitted to the Office of
Technology Assessment, OTA Task 10, KFR 259-80, 19
February 1979. Two estimates were derived from the
optimistic and pessimistic projections of Herbert S.
Dordick, H. Bradley and B. Nanus, The Emerging
Network Marketplace (Norwood, NJ: Ablex, 1981).
Professor Dordick of the Annenberg School of
Communications, University of Southern California
provided this information to us.
(2) James A. Stone and James Clark, "Integrated
Business Systems," Infosystems, 19 (July 1972):
26-30; Anonymous, "Manufacturing Set to Tap Surging
Data Transmissions," Industry Week, (December
28, 1970): 47. The latter article reports the
results of a study conducted by the Data
Transmission Company (Datran) of Vienna, Virginia.
(3) This is the estimate presented in Stone and
Clark.
(4) The study is considered proprietary.
(5) EDP Reports, Nov. 16, 1979, p. 1.24, for 1962,
1965, 1968. (Values are for AT&T data service
revenue.) Predicasts', Forecast Abstracts 1972,
p. 423 for 1970. The same source also reports an
estimate of 550 million for 1970. This appeared too
low to us. Telephony, February 26, 1973, for
1972. Predicasts, op. cit. has a report of $900

million. Predicasts', Basebook 1977, p. 533,
and for 1973, and 1974. Datamation, June, 1976,
p. 112; June 1980, p. 12; August 1980, p. 107,
for 1975, 1978 and 1979. Other values are
interpolations or extrapolations.

## Aggregate Data

Definition of symbols:

tt.: grand total of all media
mm.: mass media
pt.: point-to-point media
el.: electronic media
vs : volume supplied
vc : volume consumed

---

In the columns that follow:

- means missing value.
* on left means that in that column there is a mix
  of actual measures and estimates. The * marks an
  actual observation; in those columns values
  without * are interpolations or extrapolations.
  The unit symbols are, U=units, C=hundreds,
  K=thousands, M=millions.

## FREQUENTLY USED VARIABLES

```
FREQUENTLY USED VARIABLES   RADIO DATA
unit   M      M                U     U     U     U      U     U    M    %     M
yr     p      th    gdpde  !  amst  fmst  tst    st    amth  fmth  riu  pam  riufm
60  140828  52.60  0.69   !  3456   850  4306  10.60  16.8  19.8  156  99    1.6
61  143274  53.50  0.69   !  3547   990  4537  11.10  16.8  19.8  168  96    6.8
62  145661  54.70  0.71   !  3618  1154  4772  11.70  16.8  19.8  184  92   14.7
63  148145  55.20  0.72   !  3760  1290  5050  12.30  16.8  19.8  200  89   22.0
64  150740  56.00  0.73   !  3854  1383  5237  12.80  16.8  19.8  214  86   29.9
65  153324  57.40  0.74   !  4044  1525  5569  13.70  16.8  19.8  228  83   38.8
66  155795  58.40  0.77   !  4065  1714  5779  14.20  16.8  19.8  242  79   50.8
67  158361  59.20  0.79   !  4121  1939  6060  14.90  16.8  19.8  258  76   61.9
68  161072  60.80' 0.83   !  4190  2079  6269  15.30  16.8  19.8  267  73   72.1
69  163766  62.20  0.87   !  4265  2300  6565  16.10  16.8  19.8  300  71   87.0
70  166899  63.40  0.91   !  4292  2597  6889 *16.90 *15.4 *18.4  321  68  102.6
71  170188  64.80  0.96   !  4343  2668  7011  17.10  16.8  19.8  336  64  121.0
72  173366  66.70  1.00   !  4374  2815  7189  17.60  16.8  19.8  354  59  144.9
73  176277  68.30  1.06   !  4395  2984  7379  18.10  16.8  19.8  369  56  162.2
74  179050  69.90  1.15   !  4407  3154  7561  18.50  16.8  19.8  383  52  183.5
75  181750  71.10  1.26   !  4432  3353  7785 *18.39 *16.7 *21.3  402  49  204.8
76  184275  72.90  1.32   !  4463  3571  8034  19.20  16.8  19.8  413  47  218.9
77  186666  74.14  1.40   !  4497  3676  8173  19.30  16.8  19.8  425  44  238.0
78  189060  76.03  1.50   !  4513  3927  8440 *20.57  16.8  19.8  444  41  262.0
79  191557  77.33  1.63   !  4551  4097  8648 *21.10  16.8  19.8  450  38  279.0
80  194113  79.11  1.79   !  4590  4276  8866 *21.60  16.8  19.8  453  35  294.0

           Constants: ipam=87  ipfm=48  ra=0.65
```

```
unit  U    U     %      %      $M      $M    $M       M             M            $M
yr    ic   ly   pgccr  pgcpr   rvcr    rvpr  cexpr    vs            vc           pc
60    87  108   33.0  *33.0   597.7    1.2   344   114212830000  313933910     197.6
61    85  100   31.3   31.3   583.6    1.5   324   126118620000  288929920     193.1
62    84   93   31.3   31.3   626.8    1.9   388   141278110000  269967650     196.9
63    83   96   31.3   31.3   669.7    2.4   385   161205920000  280054490     210.4
64    82  116   31.3   31.3   719.2    2.9   472   179425630000  340178270     226.0
65    81  140   31.3   31.3   776.8    3.7   576   202021160000  412505180     244.3
66    80  139   31.3   31.3   852.7    4.6   613   218291470000  411021480     268.3
67    79 *138   31.3   31.3   884.7    5.7   592   240274800000  408413390     278.7
68    79 *165   31.3   31.3   994.7    7.2   701   251699390000  497520020     313.6
69    78 *162   31.3   31.3  1040.3    9.0   738   291338190000  491255660     328.4
70    78 *148   31.0  *31.0  1077.4  *11.2   651   294126600000  456178740     337.5
71    77 *166   31.3   31.3  1176.3  *14.1   802   342234740000  514545600     372.6
72    76 *184   31.3   31.3  1292.1  *17.7   983   368972740000  574864460     410.0
73    75 *187   31.3   31.3  1356.9  *21.8   963   392048350000  584981270     431.5
74    75 *183   31.3   31.3  1409.7  *26.0   929   414467080000  582714060     449.4
75    74 *190   31.3  *31.0  1479.7  *31.3   724   434714590000  604993460     438.8
76    73 *181   31.3   31.3  1686.9  *41.3   895   454808780000  577024050     540.9
77    73 *189   31.3   31.3  1846.0   52.2  1043   471990620000  611667520     594.1
78    72 *192   31.3   31.3  2064.8   65.2  1067   518494970000  620068380     666.7
79    72 *194   31.3   31.3  2873.6  *81.5  1063   539987710000  634802260     925.0
80    72 *196   31.3   31.3  3173.4 *106.3  1248   554279590000  649904290    1026.6
```

## Appendix I  AMERICAN DATA SETS

### TELEVISION

| unit yr | $M tc | $M cc | U coms | U eds | U ts | U st | U comm | U edm | K ttv | U wy | M tvh |
|---|---|---|---|---|---|---|---|---|---|---|---|
| 60 | 401.3 | 344 | 515 | 44 | 559 | 3.68 | 15.31 | 5.42 | 56080 | *1092 | 45.20 |
| 61 | 402.0 | 324 | 527 | 52 | 579 | 4.04 | 15.47 | *5.57 | 58740 | 1112 | 46.90 |
| 62 | 431.9 | 388 | 541 | 62 | 603 | 4.40 | 15.62 | 5.73 | 61380 | 1131 | 49.00 |
| 63 | 461.7 | 385 | 557 | 68 | 625 | 4.76 | 15.78 | 5.89 | 64310 | 1151 | 51.30 |
| 64 | 496.1 | 472 | 564 | 85 | 649 | *5.12 | 15.93 | *6.04 | 67350 | 1170 | 52.60 |
| 65 | 536.2 | 576 | 569 | 99 | 668 | 5.48 | 16.09 | 6.56 | 70590 | *1190 | 53.80 |
| 66 | 589.0 | 613 | 585 | 114 | 699 | 5.84 | 16.25 | *7.07 | 74470 | 1233 | 54.90 |
| 67 | 612.0 | 592 | 610 | 127 | 737 | 6.20 | 16.40 | 7.54 | 79250 | 1267 | 56.00 |
| 68 | 688.3 | 701 | 635 | 150 | 785 | *6.56 | 16.56 | *8.01 | 83560 | 1301 | 57.00 |
| 69 | 720.9 | 738 | 662 | 175 | 837 | 6.59 | 16.71 | 8.76 | 88020 | 1335 | 58.50 |
| 70 | 751.1 | 651 | 677 | 185 | 862 | *6.62 | *16.87 | *9.33 | 92380 | 1369 | 60.10 |
| 71 | 817.8 | 802 | 682 | 199 | 881 | 6.80 | 17.03 | 9.73 | 96900 | 1403 | 62.10 |
| 72 | 899.8 | 983 | 693 | 213 | 906 | *6.97 | 17.18 | *10.13 | 05290 | *1478 | 64.80 |
| 73 | 947.2 | 963 | 697 | 230 | 927 | 7.06 | 17.34 | 10.83 | 12730 | *1466 | 66.20 |
| 74 | 986.3 | 929 | 697 | 241 | 938 | 7.16 | 17.49 | *11.53 | 20150 | *1514 | 68.50 |
| 75 | 1072.2 | 724 | 706 | 247 | 953 | 7.25 | *17.65 | 12.26 | 25060 | *1560 | 69.60 |
| 76 | 1187.3 | 895 | 701 | 259 | 960 | *7.34 | 17.74 | *12.99 | 29400 | *1541 | 71.20 |
| 77 | 1304.0 | 1043 | 711 | 261 | 972 | 7.43 | *17.83 | 13.32 | 34120 | *1654 | 72.90 |
| 78 | 1463.3 | 1067 | 727 | 259 | 986 | *8.00 | *17.92 | *13.65 | 38200 | *1731 | 74.50 |
| 79 | 2030.2 | 1063 | 741 | 267 | 1008 | *8.58 | *18.01 | 13.95 | 46800 | *1759 | 76.32 |
| 80 | 2253.2 | 1248 | 753 | 268 | 1021 | *8.91 | *18.10 | *14.25 | 55800 | *1808 | 77.84 |

Constants: ip=153  ra=0.65  pgccm=36.5

| unit yr | % pgcd | M rved | $M rvcm | $K cexpt | $M cexrt | M vs | M vc | $M pc | $M tc |
|---|---|---|---|---|---|---|---|---|---|
| 60 | 14 | 8.8 | 1268.6 | 797091 | 774 | 26902689000 | 683396040 | 470.61 | 806.79 |
| 61 | 14 | 11.7 | 1318.3 | 813500 | 825 | 31049190000 | 722269630 | 482.82 | 847.18 |
| 62 | 14 | 15.5 | 1486.2 | 1005000 | 862 | 35188803000 | 763172600 | 544.63 | 957.07 |
| 63 | 14 | 18.7 | 1597.2 | 1099000 | 904 | 40475302000 | 819499570 | 585.60 | 1030.30 |
| 64 | 14 | 25.5 | 1793.3 | 1384000 | 930 | 45516791000 | 856683110 | 658.12 | 1160.68 |
| 65 | 14 | 32.2 | 1964.8 | 1869000 | 933 | 50815983000 | 884373260 | 721.66 | 1275.34 |
| 66 | 14 | *40.0 | 2203.0 | 2617000 | 946 | 57350680000 | 933865240 | 809.69 | 1433.30 |
| 67 | 14 | 55.0 | 2275.4 | 2570000 | 999 | 65501722000 | 981520310 | 838.22 | 1492.18 |
| 68 | 14 | *70.0 | 2520.9 | 2677000 | 1057 | 72627304000 | 1015960300 | 929.93 | 1660.97 |
| 69 | 14 | 87.5 | 2796.2 | 2585000 | 1082 | 76908279000 | 1063355800 | 1032.86 | 1850.84 |
| 70 | 16 | *105.5 | 2808.2 | 2202000 | 1279 | 82271447000 | 1120083800 | 1027.83 | 1885.87 |
| 71 | 15 | *149.2 | 2750.3 | 2976000 | 1420 | 89189291000 | 1183344800 | 1026.24 | 1873.26 |
| 72 | 14 | *168.3 | 3179.4 | 3474000 | 1609 | 99207035000 | 1287347100 | 1184.04 | 2163.66 |
| 73 | 14 | *190.4 | 3464.8 | 3657000 | 1782 | 108229760000 | 1295313900 | 1291.31 | 2363.89 |
| 74 | 11 | *220.7 | 3781.5 | 3201000 | 1937 | 117832400000 | 1373794300 | 1404.52 | 2597.68 |
| 75 | 14 | *277.1 | 4094.1 | 2492000 | 2246 | 126221260000 | 1435313500 | 1533.14 | 2838.06 |
| 76 | 14 | *322.2 | 5198.5 | 3380000 | 2415 | 132403940000 | 1434265800 | 1942.56 | 3578.14 |
| 77 | 14 | 377.0 | 5889.0 | 3811000 | 2626 | 139716720000 | 1569942600 | 2202.26 | 4063.73 |
| 78 | 14 | 445.0 | 6949.8 | 4308000 | 2823 | 154751710000 | 1658349700 | 2598.98 | 4795.82 |
| 79 | 14 | *521.5 | 7875.1 | 4180000 | 2975 | 177040190000 | 1719738200 | 2947.42 | 5449.18 |
| 80 | 14 | *571.4 | 8807.7 | 4938000 | 3343 | 195033150000 | 1785799200 | 3294.81 | 6084.29 |

FREQUENTLY USED VARIABLES  175

CABLE

| unit $M | | U | U | K | U | U | U | U | $M |
|---|---|---|---|---|---|---|---|---|---|
| yr | cc | aw | sw | sr | paysr | paybw | av | payv | rev |
| 60 | 1571 | 27.2 | 0.35 | 650 | 0 | 0 | 0 | 0 | - |
| 61 | 1639 | 30.4 | 0.43 | 725 | 0 | 0 | 0 | 0 | 35 |
| 62 | 1867 | 33.0 | 0.53 | 850 | 0 | 0 | 3 | 0 | 51 |
| 63 | 2003 | 37.9 | 0.64 | 950 | 0 | 0 | 3 | 0 | 71 |
| 64 | 2314 | 42.3 | 0.79 | 1086 | 0 | 0 | 3 | 0 | 100 |
| 65 | 2802 | 47.2 | 0.96 | 1275 | 0 | 0 | 3 | 0 | 125 |
| 66 | 3563 | 52.7 | 1.17 | 1575 | 0 | 0 | 3 | 0 | - |
| 67 | 3569 | *58.8 | *1.43 | 2100 | 0 | 0 | 3 | 0 | - |
| 68 | 3734 | 65.6 | 1.75 | 2800 | 0 | 0 | 3 | 0 | - |
| 69 | 3667 | 73.3 | 2.14 | 3600 | 0 | 0 | 3 | 0 | - |
| 70 | 3481 | *81.8 | *2.62 | 4500 | 0 | 0 | 3 | 0 | - |
| 71 | 4396 | 88.9 | 3.11 | 5300 | 0 | 0 | 3 | 0 | 449 |
| 72 | 5083 | 96.7 | 3.70 | 6000 | 4900 | 64 | 3 | 244 | - |
| 73 | 5439 | 105.1 | 4.40 | 7300 | 18400 | 64 | 3 | 244 | - |
| 74 | 5138 | 114.2 | 5.23 | 8700 | 66900 | 64 | 3 | 244 | 765 |
| 75 | 4738 | *124.2 | *6.22 | 9800 | 264575 | 64 | 3 | 244 | 895 |
| 76 | 5795 | 131.0 | 8.38 | 10800 | 977809 | 64 | 3 | 244 | 1000 |
| 77 | 6437 | 138.1 | 11.30 | 11900 | 1433654 | 64 | 3 | 244 | 1200 |
| 78 | 7131 | *145.6 | *15.23 | 12800 | 3800000 | 64 | 3 | 244 | 1511 |
| 79 | 7155 | *167.0 | *15.44 | 14100 | 5600000 | 64 | 3 | 244 | 1817 |
| 80 | 8281 | *167.0 | *15.65 | 15800 | 8000000 | 70 | 3 | 244 | 2238 |

Constants: ip=153 sv=5 ra=0 prog=17

RECORDS AND TAPES

| unit | M | M | $M | $M | M | M | M | $M | $M | $M |
|---|---|---|---|---|---|---|---|---|---|---|
| yr | vs | vc | pc | tc | ndl | nt | nds | asri | cph | ctr |
| 60 | 22886756 | 34683.20 | 4.1 | 19.9 | - | - | - | - | 359 | 15 |
| 61 | 28574007 | 38639.00 | 6.0 | 29.1 | - | - | - | - | 304 | 54 |
| 62 | 37201284 | 80215.82 | 8.7 | 42.3 | - | - | - | - | 389 | 58 |
| 63 | 46906092 | 90351.85 | 12.1 | 58.9 | - | - | - | - | 421 | 79 |
| 64 | 60130223 | 103539.19 | 17.0 | 83.0 | - | - | - | - | 440 | 97 |
| 65 | 78296243 | 120661.66 | 21.3 | 103.8 | - | - | - | - | 505 | 122 |
| 66 | 108047370 | 148857.33 | 26.4 | 128.7 | 198 | 11 | 279 | 1009 | 528 | 113 |
| 67 | 161525370 | 198996.08 | 32.5 | 158.5 | 214 | 27 | 272 | 1173 | 480 | 129 |
| 68 | 238483380 | 262768.44 | 40.3 | 196.7 | 224 | 50 | 258 | 1358 | 503 | 160 |
| 69 | 341337140 | 335764.33 | 49.8 | 243.2 | 223 | 83 | 245 | 1586 | 490 | 198 |
| 70 | 477384530 | 438017.19 | 61.5 | 300.5 | 217 | 91 | 220 | 1660 | 376 | 244 |
| 71 | 611379460 | 452686.32 | 76.3 | 372.7 | 269 | 87 | 204 | 1790 | 425 | 393 |
| 72 | 747816590 | 551510.87 | 91.1 | 444.9 | 279 | 101 | 216 | 1924 | 649 | 445 |
| 73 | 986273290 | 734679.26 | 109.0 | 532.0 | 280 | 109 | 228 | 2017 | 614 | - |
| 74 | 1275738800 | 1017918.40 | 130.1 | 635.0 | 276 | 114 | 204 | 2200 | 554 | - |
| 75 | 1580290600 | 1753641.50 | 152.2 | 742.9 | 257 | 112 | 164 | 2389 | 400 | - |
| 76 | 1891902600 | 4099823.50 | 170.0 | 830.0 | 273 | 129 | 190 | 2737 | 491 | 1055 |
| 77 | 2247038800 | 5615998.40 | 204.0 | 996.0 | 344 | 164 | 190 | 3501 | 602 | 1229 |
| 78 | 2732327800 | 13050811.00 | 256.9 | 1254.1 | 341 | 195 | 190 | 4131 | 810 | 1676 |
| 79 | 3465634900 | 18741227.00 | 308.9 | 1508.1 | 290 | 181 | 212 | 3677 | 725 | 1766 |
| 80 | 4036157900 | 26142497.00 | 380.5 | 1857.5 | 308 | 184 | 157 | 3679 | 801 | 1838 |

Constants: ip=41 tdl=tt=45.5

176 Appendix I   AMERICAN DATA SETS

|      |         |         |     |      |      | MOVIES |          |      |           |      |
|------|---------|---------|-----|------|------|--------|----------|------|-----------|------|
| unit | M       | M       | $M  | $M   | $M   | U      | U        | $M   | M         | M    |
| yr   | vs      | vc      | pc  | tc   | cc   | min    | mdr      | mrv  | vs        | n    |
| 60   | -       | 2107491 | -   | -    | 374  | 6745723 | 1514131 | 954  | 191292060 | -    |
| 61   | -       | 2144095 | -   | -    | 358  | 6624690 | 1558797 | 956  | 192153190 | -    |
| 62   | -       | 2179817 | -   | -    | 447  | 6505829 | 1604782 | 955  | 193125610 | -    |
| 63   | -       | 2216990 | -   | -    | 500  | 6389100 | *1652200 | 945  | 194215530 | -    |
| 64   | -       | 2255824 | -   | -    | 537  | 5944219 | 1585873 | 942  | 183603830 | -    |
| 65   | -       | 2294494 | -   | -    | 627  | 5530484 | 1522229 | 951  | 173617880 | -    |
| 66   | 1253730 | 2331472 | 141 | 868  | 641  | 5145545 | 1461139 | 1067 | 164214850 | 975  |
| 67   | 1411471 | 2369872 | 164 | 1009 | 609  | 4787400 | *1402500 | 1110 | 155358670 | 927  |
| 68   | 1550299 | 2410442 | 190 | 1168 | 663  | 5019110 | 1493705 | 1282 | 164272070 | 979  |
| 69   | 1688101 | 2450758 | 222 | 1364 | 688  | 5262035 | 1590840 | 1294 | 173707460 | 912  |
| 70   | 1678767 | 2497644 | 232 | 1428 | 620  | 5516717 | 1694292 | 1429 | 183696090 | 921  |
| 71   | 1897980 | 2546863 | 251 | 1539 | 818  | 5783727 | 1804472 | 1350 | 194271040 | 820  |
| 72   | 2003669 | 2594422 | 269 | 1655 | 1094 | 6063800 | *1921900 | 1583 | 205474380 | 934  |
| 73   | 2041808 | 2637985 | 282 | 1735 | 1166 | 5922889 | 1870283 | 1524 | 200283810 | 865  |
| 74   | 2013590 | 2679483 | 308 | 1892 | 1238 | 5875484 | 1820050 | 1909 | 196573150 | 1011 |
| 75   | 1879969 | 2719889 | 334 | 2055 | 1248 | 5651266 | 1771166 | 2115 | 190301150 | 1033 |
| 76   | 2033499 | 2757675 | 383 | 2354 | 1546 | 5520162 | 1723595 | 2036 | 185498950 | 957  |
| 77   | 2523299 | 2793457 | 490 | 3011 | 1831 | 5392100 | *1677301 | 2372 | 180818530 | 1063 |
| 78   | 2622018 | 2829283 | 578 | 3553 | 2486 | 5267000 | 1632200 | 2811 | 176253660 | 1133 |
| 79   | 2327257 | 2866651 | 515 | 3162 | 2491 | 5145000 | 1588400 | 2946 | 171812880 | 1121 |
| 80   | 2362641 | 2904901 | 515 | 3164 | 2639 | 5026000 | 1545700 | 2899 | 167482670 | 1022 |

tds=7  trt=1  r=14                    Constants: ip=110  ms=135  ns=19.35

## FREQUENTLY USED VARIABLES

### EDUCATION

| unit<br>yr | M<br>vc | $M<br>pc | $M<br>tc | | K<br>cl | M<br>stt | M<br>stt10 | U<br>st | K<br>tf | M<br>hst | U<br>sta | M<br>pex |
|---|---|---|---|---|---|---|---|---|---|---|---|---|
| 60 | 17493300 | 328 | 626 | ! | 1600 | 42.18 | 13.4 | 179 | 276 | 3.58 | 162.0 | 15200000 |
| 61 | 16617150 | 329 | 627 | ! | 1668 | 43.40 | 13.8 | *179 | 292 | 3.90 | *162.4 | 16600000 |
| 62 | 15087600 | 325 | 626 | ! | 1727 | 44.80 | 13.9 | 179 | 312 | 4.20 | 162.8 | 18100000 |
| 63 | 15087600 | 325 | 620 | ! | 1806 | 46.49 | 14.1 | *179 | 331 | 4.49 | *163.2 | *19500000 |
| 64 | 14137200 | 324 | 618 | ! | 1882 | 47.70 | 14.3 | 179 | 367 | 5.00 | 163.2 | 21000000 |
| 65 | 14627250 | 327 | 624 | ! | 1951 | 48.47 | 14.4 | 179 | 412 | 5.53 | 163.2 | *22400000 |
| 66 | 14478750 | 367 | 700 | ! | 2028 | 49.20 | 14.6 | 179 | 445 | 5.90 | 163.2 | 25300000 |
| 67 | 13765950 | 382 | 728 | ! | 2087 | 49.89 | 14.6 | *179 | 484 | 6.41 | *163.2 | *28100000 |
| 68 | 14538150 | 441 | 841 | ! | 2162 | 50.74 | 14.6 | 179 | 523 | 6.93 | 162.8 | *33000000 |
| 69 | 13543200 | 445 | 849 | ! | 2251 | 51.12 | 14.6 | 179 | 546 | 7.48 | 162.5 | *35200000 |
| 70 | 13676850 | 492 | 937 | ! | 2312 | 51.31 | 14.4 | 179 | 574 | 8.58 | 162.1 | *40800000 |
| 71 | 12177000 | 464 | 886 | ! | 2322 | 51.18 | 14.2 | *179 | 580 | 8.95 | *161.7 | *46000000 |
| 72 | 13869900 | 545 | 1038 | ! | 2329 | 50.74 | 13.9 | 179 | 592 | 9.21 | 160.6 | *48100000 |
| 73 | 12845250 | 524 | 1000 | ! | 2377 | 50.33 | 13.6 | *179 | 600 | 9.60 | *159.5 | *50600000 |
| 74 | 15013350 | 657 | 1252 | ! | 2408 | 50.05 | 13.3 | 179 | 633 | 10.22 | 160.0 | *57000000 |
| 75 | 15340050 | 728 | 1387 | ! | 2484 | 49.79 | 13.6 | 179 | 654 | 11.18 | 160.6 | *64800000 |
| 76 | 14211450 | 700 | 1336 | ! | 2460 | 49.33 | 13.9 | *178 | 677 | 11.51 | *161.1 | *70400000 |
| 77 | 15785550 | 816 | 1556 | ! | 2440 | 48.69 | 13.9 | 179 | 699 | 11.29 | 162.6 | *75000000 |
| 78 | 16825050 | 967 | 1844 | ! | 2480 | 47.64 | 15.7 | 179 | 647 | 11.26 | *164.0 | *80800000 |
| 79 | 16646850 | 1013 | 1933 | ! | 2471 | 46.68 | 13.3 | 179 | 657 | 11.57 | *164.0 | *87100000 |
| 80 | 15176700 | 997 | 1902 | ! | 2485 | 46.09 | 12.9 | 179 | 678 | 12.10 | *164.0 | *94700000 |

prh=34.4                    Constants: ip=120 htw=556.5 nwy=30 hsw=15 ptd=5

| unit<br>yr | %<br>pptc | $M<br>npex | $K<br>hex | $K<br>htc | $U<br>rbtp | $U<br>rbtn | K<br>nps | $K<br>ps | $U<br>i | M<br>vs |
|---|---|---|---|---|---|---|---|---|---|---|
| 60 | *54.6 | 1.4 | 6172622 | 1913672 | *651 | * 760 | *1467 | *2116 | 2664 | 182220850 |
| 61 | *54.5 | 1.7 | * 7190077 | * 2215992 | 665 | 770 | 1545 | 2433 | *2768 | 188217040 |
| 62 | 54.8 | 2.0 | 8207533 | 2518312 | *679 | 780 | 1622 | 2749 | 2846 | 196798030 |
| 63 | *55.1 | 2.3 | * 9224988 | * 2820631 | 695 | 790 | *1700 | *3066 | 2924 | 206571060 |
| 64 | *55.1 | 2.6 | 10689434 | 3300670 | *707 | * 799 | 1826 | 3518 | *3059 | 214211230 |
| 65 | *55.0 | *2.9 | *12569943 | * 3780709 | *726 | * 851 | *1951 | *3970 | 3224 | 219900510 |
| 66 | 55.4 | 3.2 | 14900179 | 4473623 | *751 | 891 | 2024 | 4393 | *3496 | 224241400 |
| 67 | *55.7 | *3.5 | *16565909 | * 5166537 | *780 | * 908 | *2096 | *4816 | 3510 | 229750690 |
| 68 | 56.5 | *4.0 | *18578772 | * 5973493 | 828 | 958 | *2082 | *5431 | *3674 | 236708460 |
| 69 | *57.2 | *4.0 | 21216296 | 6797986 | 880 | 1011 | *2108 | *5897 | 4060 | 240743280 |
| 70 | 57.9 | *4.6 | 23321668 | 7615480 | *936 | 1066 | *2153 | *6428 | 4258 | 244480990 |
| 71 | *58.6 | *5.3 | *25559560 | * 8443261 | 985 | 1125 | *2144 | *6804 | 4479 | 245911420 |
| 72 | 57.9 | *5.4 | *27955624 | * 9263641 | *1036 | *1188 | *2144 | *7070 | *4837 | 245167600 |
| 73 | *57.2 | *5.8 | 29301260 | 10334000 | 1080 | 1230 | *2183 | *7420 | 5190 | 244992920 |
| 74 | 56.9 | *6.4 | *30713581 | *11574145 | *1131 | *1286 | *2235 | *7988 | 5466 | 247096440 |
| 75 | 56.5 | *7.1 | *35051563 | *11797823 | *1233 | *1391 | *2350 | *8835 | 5870 | 246076890 |
| 76 | *56.2 | *8.0 | *38903177 | *13094943 | *1316 | *1478 | *2859 | *8653 | 6192 | 241948630 |
| 77 | 56.0 | *8.8 | *42599810 | *14031145 | *1381 | *1570 | 2443 | 8847 | *6708 | 241567820 |
| 78 | 55.8 | *9.6 | *45970790 | *15336229 | *1455 | *1684 | 2476 | 8784 | *7583 | 237792200 |
| 79 | 55.6 | 10.5 | *50720984 | *16662820 | *1582 | *1782 | 2533 | 9037 | *8530 | 235379460 |
| 80 | *55.5 | 11.7 | *56913588 | *18496717 | *1738 | *1970 | 2643 | 9457 | 9365 | 235970250 |

psd=4.6

*178* Appendix I  AMERICAN DATA SETS

## NEWSPAPER

| unit | M | $M | $M | $M | U | $M | $M | M |
|---|---|---|---|---|---|---|---|---|
| yr | vc | pc | tc | cc | cw | nrv | adex | vs |
| 60 | 166016560 | 9401 | 8098 | 12029 | *22277475 | 3920 * | 34 | 9498335400 |
| 61 | 171845160 | 10653 | 9018 | 13331 | 23127895 | 3955 | 63 | 9842699100 |
| 62 | 180218820 | 11956 | 10116 | 15085 | 23978315 | 4089 | 91 | 10296534000 |
| 63 | 189621500 | 13224 | 11189 | 16602 | 24828735 | 4255 | 120 | 10418451000 |
| 64 | 196733140 | 14808 | 12406 | 19241 | 25679155 | 4620 | 148 | 11164406000 |
| 65 | 202071810 | 16792 | 13562 | 22371 | *26529575 | 4886 | 177 | 11359028000 |
| 66 | 206135360 | 19366 | 15577 | 25279 | 28481130 | 5256 | 206 | 11463958000 |
| 67 | 211517340 | 21302 | 17617 | 28159 | 30432685 | 5550 | 234 | 11292943000 |
| 68 | 217317760 | 24069 | 20863 | 31952 | 32384241 | 5938 | 263 | 11095878000 |
| 69 | 220785830 | 26404 | 22816 | 37689 | 34335796 | 6538 | 291 | 10887651000 |
| 70 | 223821430 | 29455 | 26525 | 42035 | 36287351 | 6636 | 320 | 10637571000 |
| 71 | 224355330 | 32462 | 30164 | 45483 | 38716347 | 7037 | 428 | 11545225000 |
| 72 | 222717010 | 35045 | 31754 | 49825 | 41145343 | 7908 | 535 | 12331375000 |
| 73 | 221636160 | 36584 | 33877 | 54917 | 43574339 | 8496 | 643 | 13439634000 |
| 74 | 223970400 | 39204 | 38062 | 61212 | 46003335 | 9187 * | 750 | 13493649000 |
| 75 | 224022410 | 45987 | 41325 | 71278 | 48432330 | 10020 | 793 | 12646947000 |
| 76 | 221765440 | 50478 | 44749 | 78152 | 50861326 | 11240 * | 838 | 12255894000 |
| 77 | 222671000 | 54921 | 47570 | 89170 | 53290322 | 12470 | *1086 | 12240560000 |
| 78 | 220930810 | 59107 | 51281 | 102562 | *55719318 | 13800 | *1390 | 13608532000 |
| 79 | 218796270 | 65052 | 55475 | 117502 | *60059354 | 15530 | *1777 | 14500940000 |
| 80 | 219481460 | 72519 | 61029 | 134950 | *64737441 | 17150 | *2032 | 14735322000 |

Constants: wd=3048 pw=36 ww=1295

## MAGAZINE

| unit | M | M | $M | $M | U | U | C | U | M | M | M |
|---|---|---|---|---|---|---|---|---|---|---|---|
| yr | vc1 | vc2 | pc | tc | pd | ps | cd | cs | cwg | cwt | cwa |
| 60 | 358374570 | 311826990 | 461 | 3476 | *43 | *142 | 58882 | 47699 | *4287 | *1327 | *365 |
| 61 | 354912610 | 317243020 | 470 | 3516 | 44 | 147 | 59261 | 48216 | *4441 | 1347 | 364 |
| 62 | 349883530 | 322528410 | 489 | 3645 | 46 | 151 | 59849 | 48888 | *4519 | 1367 | 363 |
| 63 | 346947280 | 328028580 | 513 | 3802 | 47 | 157 | 58905 | 46830 | *4642 | 1388 | 361 |
| 64 | 342833390 | 333774540 | 560 | 4135 | 49 | 162 | 60412 | 48383 | *4781 | 1408 | 360 |
| 65 | 339496120 | 339496130 | 595 | 4380 | *50 | *167 | 60358 | 48600 | *4847 | *1428 | 359 |
| 66 | 335604840 | 344967520 | 642 | 4717 | 50 | 163 | 61397 | 49282 | *5117 | 1625 | 358 |
| 67 | 332805130 | 350649260 | 681 | 4986 | 49 | 159 | 61561 | 49224 | *5253 | 1822 | 357 |
| 68 | 328822670 | 356652060 | 730 | 5340 | 48 | 154 | 62535 | 49693 | *5391 | 2020 | 355 |
| 69 | 325710910 | 362617220 | 804 | 5880 | 48 | 149 | 62060 | 49675 | *5457 | 2217 | 354 |
| 70 | 323165850 | 369554440 | 820 | 5976 | *47 | *145 | 62108 | 49217 | *5524 | *2414 | *353 |
| 71 | 321863610 | 376837070 | 882 | 6368 | *51 | 156 | 62231 | 49665 | *5391 | 2435 | 345 |
| 72 | 318757650 | 383873930 | 1000 | 7176 | *55 | 168 | 62510 | 49339 | *5475 | 2455 | 337 |
| 73 | 316164770 | 390319580 | 1084 | 7733 | *59 | *182 | 63147 | 51717 | *5423 | 2476 | 329 |
| 74 | 313068190 | 396459670 | 1180 | 8381 | *60 | *188 | 61887 | 51679 | *5928 | 2496 | 322 |
| 75 | 310962600 | 402438120 | 1284 | 9133 | *57 | *180 | 60655 | 51096 | *5731 | *2517 | 314 |
| 76 | 306977070 | 408029070 | 1432 | 10227 | *55 | *177 | 60977 | 51565 | 5930 | 2905 | 306 |
| 77 | 303948980 | 413323320 | 1612 | 11401 | *54 | *177 | 61495 | 52429 | 6137 | 3293 | 298 |
| 78 | 300746050 | 418624210 | 1812 | 12683 | *60 | *196 | 61990 | 53990 | 6351 | *3682 | *290 |
| 79 | 297523260 | 424153170 | 2071 | 14348 | *64 | *207 | 62200 | 54400 | 6573 | 3901 | 287 |
| 80 | 294202310 | 429812770 | 2297 | 15869 | *66 | *208 | 62200 | 54700 | 6803 | 4133 | 283 |

ic=240 snt=45 dnt=22 nec=14.8 nex=78.65 adexp=50 ecp=14.8

## FREQUENTLY USED VARIABLES

```
                                                                    BOOKS
unit  M      M     M     M     $M     M           M         $M    $M  !   M     $M
 yr  cwr    cwc   cwf   cwm   rvmg    vs          vc        pc    tc  !  nus     s
 60  *3401  *257  *252  *320  1897   1506083600   78953807  221   1676 !  875   1421
 61   3450   268   261   331  1978   1549603100   80325133  230   1748 !  906   1547
 62   3498   278   269   342  2006   1567177000   81663381  234   1773 !  937   1674
 63   3547   289   278   353  2043   1616040900   83056011  238   1805 !  668   1801
 64   3595   300   287   364  2170   1660886000   84510871  253   1917 ! 1025   1980
 65   3644   311   296   375  2300   1672219500   85959565  268   2032 ! 1082   2158
 66   3693   321   304   386  2405   1765459300   87344907  280   2125 ! 1139   2337
 67   3741   332   313   397  2668   1837126100   88783509  311   2357 ! 1196   2515
 68   3790   343   322   408  2802   1886153600   90303404  326   2476 ! 1208   2676
 69   3838   353   330   419  2897   1925281400   91813768  337   2560 ! 1220   2837
 70  *3887  *364  *339  *430  2837   1976173500   93570253  330   2507 ! 1232   2997
 71   3625   351   339   431  2922   1925744900   95414198  340   2582 ! 1244   2158
 72   3364   338   340   431  3198   1905818600   97195912  372   2826 ! 1256   3319
 73   3102   325   340   432  3412   1864243600   98827935  397   3015 ! 1311   3665
 74   2840   312   341   432  3574   1937229700  100382590  416   3158 ! 1367  *4012
 75   2578   299   341   433  3773   1875445100  101896320  439   3334 ! 1422  *4497
 76   2317   286   341   433  4455   1932362700  103311930  519   3936 ! 1392  *5022
 77   2055   273   342   434  5529   2003942800  104652420  644   4885 ! 1529  *5762
 78  *1793  *260  *342  *434  6519   2058822500  105994600  759   5760 ! 1609  *6612
 79   1782   267   340   415  7434   2124358300  107394510  865   6569 ! 1644  *7309
 80   1771   274   338   397  8419   2180461400  108827510  980   7439 ! 1693  *8224
     Constants: pwg=185  nwg=436  pwt=70  nwt=836  pwa=45  ic=240  rd=6.4
                pe=14.8  px=78.65
```

```
                                         DIRECT MAIL
         M           M          $M    $M  !    K        $M       M           M
 yr      vs          vc         pc    tc  !    tn       rev      vs          vc
 60   243368390   111028790    183.3  1237 ! 17910207   1830   452951610   2320862
 61   252054610   112957220    199.6  1347 ! 17568833   1850   444431110   2277204
 62   259208000   114839130    216.0  1458 ! 17836510   1933   448656310   2298853
 63   269883370   116797520    232.3  1569 ! 18407051   2078   466637970   2390989
 64   286627060   118843420    255.4  1725 ! 18598504   2184   472896860   2423058
 65   300246770   120880640    278.4  1880 ! 19453842   2324   490853130   2515064
 66   315658310   122828780    301.5  2036 ! 20305155   2461   511675840   2621756
 67   332361380   124851810    324.4  2191 ! 20985049   2488   530254610   2716951
 68   332457580   126989160    345.2  2331 ! 20664523   2612   517118160   2649642
 69   333692180   129113110    366.0  2471 ! 19621593   2680   487995200   2500420
 70   336920960   131583170    386.6  2610 ! 19974208   2766   496686070   2544951
 71   339411960   134176220    407.4  2751 ! 20532160   3067   509373680   2609960
 72   339141220   136681750    428.2  2891 ! 21907627   3420   537875020   2755997
 73   351504160   138976790    472.8  3192 ! 22689120   3698   553146960   2834249
 74   363762980   141163020    517.5  3494 ! 22537096   4054   545309470   2794090
 75   377621970   143291700    580.1  3917 ! 21867253   4124   528015870   2705480
 76   365536690   145282410    647.9  4374 ! 22513993   4786   537575360   2754461
 77   399919850   147167470    743.3  5019 ! 24049663   5164   571965150   2930671
 78   415645950   149054900    853.0  5759 ! 26329813   5987   618458220   3168895
 79   423062640   151023540    942.9  6366 ! 27513000   6653   643777660   3298628
 80   431551900   153038690   1060.9  7163 ! 30381000   7655   704163060   3608034
     Constants: nw=395  np=263  rt=9  r=12.9    Constants: plnw=2800  pl=58  psnw=780
                                                          pp=14.8  pcnw=24200  pcat=32  ps=10
```

180 Appendix I  AMERICAN DATA SETS

## MAIL

| unit | $M | $M | K | K | $K | $K | $U | $U | $U | $U |
|------|-----|-----|-----|-----|-----|-----|-----|-----|-----|-----|
| yr | pc | tc | fcm | dair | rvfc | rvda | ex2 | ex3 | ex4 | ex5 |
| 60 | 270.9 | 1559.3 | 33234810 | 1355728 | 1510113 | 157256 | 3.20 | 0.53 | 3.20 | 0.20 |
| 61 | 273.8 | 1576.2 | 34288943 | 1452687 | 1558072 | 170801 | 3.24 | 0.54 | 3.24 | 0.20 |
| 62 | 286.1 | 1646.9 | 35332707 | 1544735 | 1614628 | 184574 | 3.30 | 0.55 | 3.30 | 0.20 |
| 63 | 307.5 | 1770.5 | 35833487 | 1545349 | 1824335 | 200038 | 3.36 | 0.56 | 3.36 | 0.21 |
| 64 | 323.2 | 1860.8 | 36943064 | 1504683 | 2109398 | 216054 | 3.40 | 0.57 | 3.40 | 0.21 |
| 65 | 344.0 | 1980.1 | 38067778 | 1629248 | 2192790 | 242987 | 3.48 | 0.58 | 3.48 | 0.22 |
| 66 | 364.2 | 2096.8 | 40421755 | 1828166 | 2333875 | 276981 | 3.64 | 0.61 | 3.64 | 0.22 |
| 67 | 368.2 | 2119.8 | 41998337 | 2110606 | 2441875 | 329343 | 3.81 | 0.64 | 3.81 | 0.24 |
| 68 | 386.6 | 2225.4 | 43182828 | 1948890 | 2721819 | 224999 | 4.05 | 0.68 | 4.05 | 0.25 |
| 69 | 396.6 | 2283.4 | 46411115 | 1657103 | 3135403 | 215678 | 4.32 | 0.72 | 4.32 | 0.27 |
| 70 | 409.4 | 2356.6 | 48640276 | 1533191 | 3290755 | 201287 | 4.58 | 0.76 | 4.58 | 0.28 |
| 71 | 453.9 | 2613.1 | 50035754 | 1457405 | 3506137 | 197879 | 4.89 | 0.82 | 4.89 | 0.30 |
| 72 | 506.2 | 2913.8 | 48933443 | 1359525 | 4379050 | 209914 | 5.22 | 0.87 | 5.22 | 0.32 |
| 73 | 547.3 | 3150.7 | 50964631 | 1326629 | 4578252 | 212772 | 5.57 | 0.93 | 5.57 | 0.34 |
| 74 | 600.0 | 3454.0 | 51594460 | 1334733 | 5018656 | 230764 | 6.00 | 1.00 | 6.00 | 0.37 |
| 75 | 610.4 | 3513.7 | 51372664 | 1109182 | 5797840 | 218781 | 6.45 | 1.08 | 6.45 | 0.40 |
| 76 | 708.3 | 4077.7 | 52107941 | 351596 | 6733967 | 83469 | 6.92 | 1.15 | 6.92 | 0.43 |
| 77 | 764.3 | 4399.7 | 53654108 | 13360 | 7831430 | 5800 | 7.45 | 1.24 | 7.45 | 0.46 |
| 78 | 886.1 | 5100.9 | 56020000 | 0 | 8575000 | 0 | 8.09 | 1.35 | 8.09 | 0.50 |
| 79 | 984.6 | 5668.4 | 57976000 | 0 | 9733000 | 0 | 8.76 | 1.46 | 8.76 | 0.54 |
| 80 | 1132.9 | 6522.1 | 60332000 | 0 | 10146000 | 0 | 9.47 | 1.58 | 9.47 | 0.59 |

cwr=110 cpr=34  Constants: ip1=1052 r1=10 ip2=ip4=453 r2=6 ip3=332 r3=65
cwg=25 cpg=44

## TELEPHONE

| unit | $K | $K | M | $M | $M | K | K |
|------|-----|-----|-----|-----|-----|-----|-----|
| yr | trv | tex | vs | pc | tc | lc | lg |
| 60 | 3276588 | 3873953 | 13654961 | 28232.10 | 1971.35 | 101300804 | 3942466 |
| 61 | 3423059 | 4249414 | 14109366 | 29560.56 | 2146.24 | 103923711 | 4174561 |
| 62 | 3557041 | 4331617 | 14557739 | 31035.03 | 2190.99 | 108024089 | 4531551 |
| 63 | 3879128 | 4698528 | 14755669 | 31999.35 | 2451.99 | 112035199 | 4851651 |
| 64 | 4276123 | 4927825 | 15177632 | 33332.83 | 2679.86 | 117916030 | 5309652 |
| 65 | 4483390 | 5275840 | 15670798 | 35279.91 | 2866.31 | 125789672 | 5921498 |
| 66 | 4784186 | 5726523 | 16678579 | 39234.60 | 3125.11 | 134494250 | 6655464 |
| 67 | 5101982 | 6249027 | 17412446 | 42880.99 | 3394.25 | 141912636 | 7327186 |
| 68 | 6423515 | 6543920 | 17816197 | 46658.43 | 3002.05 | 150197914 | 8264475 |
| 69 | 7025898 | 7168489 | 18975410 | 53007.22 | 3419.09 | 159983936 | 9594276 |
| 70 | 7701695 | 7867269 | 19806478 | 58604.83 | 3567.12 | 169672916 | 10623265 |
| 71 | 8751000 | 8955000 | 20327439 | 64255.66 | 3790.36 | 179130966 | 11184161 |
| 72 | 9347000 | 9522000 | 19853652 | 66954.03 | 4674.88 | 189477358 | 12383746 |
| 73 | 9913000 | 9926000 | 20642498 | 74356.44 | 4797.31 | 200092236 | 13351593 |
| 74 | 10857000 | 11295000 | 20894328 | 81023.52 | 5461.20 | 211186082 | 14359475 |
| 75 | 11590000 | 12578000 | 20717733 | 86430.76 | 6529.51 | 217020890 | 17914776 |
| 76 | 12747000 | 13923000 | 20708927 | 92673.76 | 7446.39 | 228003816 | 20424065 |
| 77 | 14622000 | 15310169 | 21185769 | 102010.71 | 8206.08 | 242764642 | 23119446 |
| 78 | 15841000 | 16219619 | 22114455 | 115626.87 | 8779.95 | 256416228 | 26575045 |
| 79 | 17999000 | 17529000 | 22886606 | 129548.49 | 9478.85 | 268772216 | 29855662 |
| 80 | 19106000 | 19412000 | 23816660 | 145755.63 | 10308.50 | 279485056 | 31704010 |

ip5=94 r5=11 ex1=0

## FREQUENTLY USED VARIABLES

| unit | $ | $K | $K | M | $M | $M | TELEX U | U |
|---|---|---|---|---|---|---|---|---|
| yr | hp | lcrv | lgrv | vs | pc | tc | ntd | nti |
| 60 | 2.25 | 4760557 | 2940627 | 48459021 | 7643 | 7701 | 1032759 | 506890 |
| 61 | 2.28 | 5023771 | 3151581 | 49798024 | 7954 | 8175 | 1371356 | 672269 |
| 62 | 2.32 | 5326762 | 3390953 | 51887493 | 8426 | 8718 | 1709953 | 817085 |
| 63 | 2.36 | 5642137 | 3674786 | 53912595 | 8901 | 9317 | *1727226 | 920102 |
| 64 | 2.39 | 5954914 | 4090824 | 56874338 | 9502 | 10046 | *2715395 | 1354841 |
| 65 | 2.45 | 6300964 | 4504795 | 60838834 | 10409 | 10806 | *2897351 | * 2164360 |
| 66 | 2.56 | 6734795 | 5161598 | 65259029 | 11654 | 11896 | *3317742 | * 2944964 |
| 67 | 2.68 | 7142003 | 5639248 | 69056050 | 12898 | 12781 | *3263749 | 3938177 |
| 68 | 2.85 | 7634655 | 6269982 | 73418059 | 14560 | 13905 | *3321427 | * 4766284 |
| 69 | 3.04 | 8284562 | 7200550 | 78714575 | 16615 | 15485 | *3561033 | * 6268513 |
| 70 | 3.22 | 9020960 | 7744772 | 83772103 | 18708 | 16766 | *5250158 | * 7663913 |
| 71 | 3.44 | 9815920 | 8680854 | 88421519 | 21097 | 18497 | *4572341 | * 9337222 |
| 72 | 3.67 | 11090444 | 9901298 | 93887543 | 23869 | 20992 | *4589831 | *11939748 |
| 73 | 3.92 | 12247452 | 11525709 | 99324989 | 26955 | 23773 | *3965292 | *15433168 |
| 74 | 4.22 | 13691293 | 12778112 | 105005430 | 30661 | 26469 | *3366229 | *19179099 |
| 75 | 4.54 | 14937820 | 13808225 | 109954300 | 34327 | 28746 | *2647619 | *21910258 |
| 76 | 4.87 | 16704532 | 16629018 | 116557840 | 38920 | 33334 | *1946476 | *25970820 |
| 77 | 5.24 | 18477662 | 19055663 | 124993930 | 44804 | 37533 | *1787809 | *31322483 |
| 78 | 5.69 | 20265655 | 21956597 | 133420230 | 51756 | 42222 | *1650556 | *37230252 |
| 79 | 6.16 | 21763105 | 24551794 | 141146000 | 59100 | 46315 | *1469592 | *44185418 |
| 80 | 6.66 | 24022014 | 27648301 | 147198670 | 66576 | 51670 | *1328762 | *50720660 |

Constants: ip=120 tlcr=4.15 rlc=44.2 tlcb=3.48
blc=55.8 tlgr=6.55 rlg=55 tlgb=4 blg=45

| unit | $U | $U | $U | M | M | $M | $M | $M | $M |
|---|---|---|---|---|---|---|---|---|---|
| | dtrv | otrv | cw | vsd | vsi | pcd | pci | tcd | tci |
| 60 | 737685 | 4224080 | 1.55 | 51.6 | 25.3 | 1.6 | 0.9 | 0.7 | 4.2 |
| 61 | 979540 | 5602240 | 1.57 | 68.6 | 33.6 | 2.2 | 1.1 | 1.0 | 5.6 |
| 62 | 1221395 | 6809040 | 1.59 | 85.5 | 40.9 | 2.7 | 1.3 | 1.2 | 6.8 |
| 63 | 1233344 | 7667520 | 1.62 | 86.4 | 46.0 | 2.8 | 1.5 | 1.2 | 7.7 |
| 64 | 1974720 | 9784721 | 1.64 | 135.8 | 67.7 | 4.5 | 2.2 | 2.0 | 9.8 |
| 65 | 2174479 | 13321365 | 1.68 | 144.9 | 108.2 | 4.9 | 3.6 | 2.2 | 13.3 |
| 66 | 3088101 | 17173219 | 1.76 | 165.9 | 147.3 | 5.8 | 5.2 | 3.1 | 17.2 |
| 67 | 3650081 | 21143518 | 1.84 | 163.2 | 196.9 | 6.0 | 7.3 | 3.7 | 21.1 |
| 68 | 4574172 | 25954015 | 1.96 | 166.1 | 238.3 | 6.5 | 9.3 | 4.6 | 26.0 |
| 69 | 5878136 | 32682324 | 2.09 | 178.1 | 313.4 | 7.4 | 13.1 | 5.9 | 32.0 |
| 70 | 11535294 | 34478312 | 2.21 | 262.5 | 383.2 | 11.6 | 17.0 | 11.5 | 34.5 |
| 71 | 12477028 | 39993376 | 2.36 | 228.6 | 466.9 | 10.8 | 22.1 | 12.5 | 40.0 |
| 72 | 14223060 | 48419215 | 2.52 | 229.5 | 597.0 | 11.6 | 30.1 | 14.2 | 48.4 |
| 73 | 15950325 | 63594086 | 2.69 | 198.3 | 771.7 | 10.7 | 41.6 | 16.0 | 63.6 |
| 74 | 16521298 | 80494903 | 2.90 | 168.3 | 959.0 | 9.8 | 55.6 | 16.5 | 80.5 |
| 75 | 13370771 | 91484567 | 3.12 | 132.4 | 1095.5 | 8.3 | 68.4 | 13.4 | 91.5 |
| 76 | 10247416 | 107214482 | 3.35 | 97.3 | 1298.5 | 6.5 | 86.9 | 10.3 | 107.2 |
| 77 | 9780386 | 122026518 | 3.60 | 89.4 | 1566.1 | 6.4 | 80.6 | 9.8 | 122.0 |
| 78 | 9261122 | 140460760 | 3.91 | 82.5 | 1861.5 | 6.5 | 145.6 | 9.3 | 140.5 |
| 79 | 8992463 | 163405158 | 4.23 | 73.5 | 2209.3 | 6.2 | 187.0 | 9.0 | 163.4 |
| 80 | 8518726 | 185498512 | 4.58 | 66.4 | 2536.0 | 6.1 | 232.1 | 9.5 | 185.5 |

Constants: ipd=ipi=50

182  Appendix I  AMERICAN DATA SETS

### TELEGRAMS

| unit<br>yr | U<br>dm | U<br>wtt | $U<br>cw | $U<br>dmrv | $U<br>otrv | M<br>vsd | M<br>vs | $M<br>psd | $M<br>tcd |
|---|---|---|---|---|---|---|---|---|---|
| 60 | 106476579 | 307675116 | 1.07 | 168923878 | 25387038 | 5324 | 308 | 164.79 | 168.92 |
| 61 | 99433959 | 309516464 | 1.08 | 166749182 | 25477167 | 4972 | 310 | 154.60 | 166.75 |
| 62 | 93710923 | 315683208 | 1.10 | 159440214 | 25319648 | 4686 | 316 | 145.53 | 159.44 |
| 63 | 83576794 | 325398176 | 1.12 | 152654088 | 25730170 | 4179 | 325 | 130.19 | 152.65 |
| 64 | 76360618 | 318021812 | 1.13 | 150835882 | 25413908 | 3818 | 318 | 118.48 | 150.84 |
| 65 | 72446436 | 314957064 | 1.16 | 147504104 | 24516748 | 3622 | 315 | 112.91 | 147.50 |
| 66 | 69685298 | 320204400 | 1.21 | 146192164 | 23413853 | 3484 | 320 | 109.94 | 146.19 |
| 67 | 65554092 | 319715400 | 1.27 | 138367008 | 22590596 | 3278 | 320 | 105.00 | 138.37 |
| 68 | 61317652 | 264397786 | 1.35 | 137232806 | 18988639 | 3066 | 264 | 100.27 | 137.23 |
| 69 | 51959582 | 271989192 | 1.44 | 137906504 | 19291417 | 2598 | 272 | 86.15 | 137.91 |
| 70 | 42888348 | 263024734 | 1.53 | 125198507 | 18795091 | 2144 | 263 | 71.69 | 125.20 |
| 71 | 23928672 | 241496318 | 1.63 | 80758697 | 17429458 | 1196 | 242 | 40.64 | 80.76 |
| 72 | 18184011 | 219380974 | 1.74 | 71173533 | 16479269 | 909 | 219 | 31.63 | 71.17 |
| 73 | 12908955 | 235764372 | 1.86 | 52689551 | 17938257 | 645 | 236 | 22.63 | 52.69 |
| 74 | 9296526 | 235518650 | 2.00 | 43554624 | 20772495 | 465 | 236 | 16.17 | 43.55 |
| 75 | 7371524 | 208651502 | 2.15 | 37462571 | 16011543 | 369 | 209 | 12.59 | 37.46 |
| 76 | 5879750 | 202986808 | 2.31 | 32106308 | 13993252 | 294 | 203 | 10.28 | 32.11 |
| 77 | 5232758 | 200254104 | 2.48 | 29745681 | 14511037 | 262 | 200 | 9.28 | 29.75 |
| 78 | 5418603 | 197193338 | 2.70 | 30765728 | 14564265 | 271 | 197 | 9.74 | 30.77 |
| 79 | 5145529 | 191420070 | 2.92 | 31289884 | 14347749 | 257 | 191 | 9.22 | 31.29 |
| 80 | 4802229 | 184167622 | 3.16 | 32533247 | 13985397 | 240 | 184 | 8.47 | 32.53 |

Constants: ipd=50

### MAILGRAM

| unit<br>yr | $M<br>tci | $M<br>pci | U<br>tm | U<br>nm | $U<br>pcm | $U<br>tcm | M<br>vs | $M<br>pc | $M<br>tc |
|---|---|---|---|---|---|---|---|---|---|
| 60 | 25.39 | 12.56 | 11900892 | 0 | 1.07 | 0 | 0 | 0 | 0 |
| 61 | 25.48 | 13.04 | 11944010 | 0 | 1.08 | 0 | 0 | 0 | 0 |
| 62 | 25.32 | 13.79 | 11949028 | 0 | 1.10 | 0 | 0 | 0 | 0 |
| 63 | 25.73 | 14.46 | 12091479 | 0 | 1.12 | 0 | 0 | 0 | 0 |
| 64 | 25.41 | 14.58 | 12290365 | 0 | 1.13 | 0 | 0 | 0 | 0 |
| 65 | 24.52 | 14.75 | 12313150 | 0 | 1.16 | 0 | 0 | 0 | 0 |
| 66 | 23.41 | 15.81 | 12652562 | 0 | 1.21 | 0 | 0 | 0 | 0 |
| 67 | 22.59 | 16.50 | 12743550 | 0 | 1.27 | 0 | 0 | 0 | 0 |
| 68 | 18.99 | 13.84 | 10254188 | 0 | 1.35 | 0 | 0 | 0 | 0 |
| 69 | 19.29 | 14.67 | 10552714 | 0 | 1.44 | 0 | 0 | 0 | 0 |
| 70 | 18.80 | 14.51 | 10232836 | 0 | 1.53 | 0 | 0 | 0 | 0 |
| 71 | 17.43 | 13.73 | 8774867 | 0 | 1.63 | 0 | 0 | 0 | 0 |
| 72 | 16.48 | 13.36 | 8433703 | 1391214 | 1.74 | 1802731 | 139 | 2.42 | 2 |
| 73 | 17.94 | 14.55 | 8631325 | 5350769 | 1.86 | 7211010 | 535 | 9.94 | 7 |
| 74 | 20.77 | 14.90 | 8641878 | 14313745 | 2.00 | 17222320 | 1431 | 28.63 | 17 |
| 75 | 16.01 | 13.55 | 7935339 | 17826194 | 2.15 | 26150400 | 1783 | 38.36 | 26 |
| 76 | 13.99 | 13.94 | 7501236 | 20940153 | 2.31 | 34391582 | 2094 | 48.33 | 34 |
| 77 | 14.51 | 14.39 | 7289654 | 24357086 | 2.48 | 41876574 | 2436 | 60.49 | 42 |
| 78 | 14.56 | 14.47 | 7303450 | 28607491 | 2.70 | 52053676 | 2861 | 77.15 | 52 |
| 78 | 14.35 | 15.25 | 7089630 | 33464750 | 2.92 | 63609924 | 3346 | 97.70 | 64 |
| 80 | 13.99 | 16.00 | 6821020 | 34792420 | 3.16 | 75277187 | 3479 | 109.82 | 75 |

Constants: ip=100

## FREQUENTLY USED VARIABLES

| | FACSIMILE | | | | | | | | DATA TRANSMISSION | |
|---|---|---|---|---|---|---|---|---|---|---|
| unit | M | $U | $M | $U | M | $M | $M | | M | $M |
| yr | np | ex | eqr | tcpm | vs | pc | tc | | vs | tc |
| 60 | 0.00 | 3.20 | 0.00 | 4.24 | 0.00 | 0.00 | 0.00 | : | 140000 | 124 |
| 61 | 1.32 | 3.24 | 3.40 | 3.99 | 396.00 | 7.68 | 5.27 | : | 200000 | 136 |
| 62 | 2.64 | 3.30 | 6.90 | 3.75 | 792.00 | 15.61 | 9.90 | : | 260000 | 150 |
| 63 | 3.96 | 3.36 | 10.30 | 3.52 | 1188.00 | 23.59 | 13.94 | : | 320000 | 165 |
| 64 | 5.94 | 3.40 | 13.80 | 3.31 | 1782.00 | 33.98 | 19.66 | : | 420000 | 182 |
| 65 | 9.24 | 3.48 | 17.30 | 3.11 | 2772.00 | 49.49 | 28.74 | : | 530000 | 200 |
| 66 | 12.32 | 3.64 | 20.80 | 2.92 | 3696.00 | 65.64 | 35.97 | : | 680000 | 250 |
| 67 | 17.60 | 3.81 | 24.30 | 2.74 | 5280.00 | 91.36 | 48.22 | : | 860000 | 296 |
| 68 | 21.11 | 4.05 | 26.20 | 2.58 | 6333.00 | 111.74 | 54.46 | : | 1090000 | 350 |
| 69 | 24.64 | 4.32 | 31.70 | 2.42 | 7392.00 | 138.20 | 59.63 | : | 1380000 | 500 |
| 70 | 31.68 | 4.58 | 35.00 | 2.27 | 9504.00 | 180.04 | 71.91 | : | 1760000 | 700 |
| 71 | 36.63 | 4.89 | 39.90 | 2.14 | 10989.00 | 219.06 | 78.39 | : | 2240000 | 857 |
| 72 | 47.30 | 5.22 | 53.70 | 2.01 | 14190.00 | 300.51 | 95.07 | : | 2860000 | 1048 |
| 73 | 55.00 | 5.57 | 64.00 | 1.89 | 16500.00 | 370.54 | 103.95 | : | 3640000 | 1220 |
| 74 | 76.56 | 6.00 | 74.10 | 1.77 | 22968.00 | 533.46 | 135.51 | : | 4640000 | 1568 |
| 75 | 91.08 | 6.45 | 90.00 | 1.66 | 27324.00 | 677.92 | 151.19 | : | 5900000 | 1700 |
| 76 | 124.41 | 6.92 | 98.00 | 1.56 | 37323.00 | 959.44 | 194.08 | : | 7500000 | 1844 |
| 77 | 155.94 | 7.45 | 126.00 | 1.47 | 46782.00 | 1287.79 | 229.23 | : | 9560000 | 2000 |
| 78 | 235.65 | 8.09 | 151.50 | 1.39 | 70695.00 | 2057.92 | 327.55 | : | 12160000 | 2500 |
| 79 | 285.00 | 8.76 | 180.00 | 1.30 | 85500.00 | 2676.11 | 370.50 | : | 15480000 | 3980 |
| 80 | 345.00 | 9.47 | 207.30 | 1.22 | 103500.00 | 3474.17 | 420.90 | : | 19700000 | - |

Constants: ip=30

### AGGREGATE DATA

| unit | M | M | M | M | M | M |
|---|---|---|---|---|---|---|
| yr | tt.vs | tt.vc | mm.vs | mm.vc | el.vs | el.vc |
| 60 | 153274910000 | 1795919700 | 153212650000 | 1733660000 | 141187000000 | 1048076800 |
| 61 | 169729650000 | 1816429900 | 169665540000 | 1752316700 | 157246390000 | 1063386100 |
| 62 | 189532320000 | 1846874900 | 189465610000 | 1855762200 | 176556270000 | 1087553700 |
| 63 | 214968920000 | 1924756300 | 214899930000 | 1958601800 | 201782370000 | 1156099800 |
| 64 | 239057660000 | 2031179900 | 238985180000 | 2064844000 | 225059850000 | 1256521200 |
| 65 | 267208340000 | 2141890600 | 267131300000 | 2116381400 | 252976810000 | 1360669400 |
| 66 | 290279270000 | 2199006800 | 290196650000 | 2166943200 | 275817390000 | 1413313900 |
| 67 | 320404570000 | 2254281000 | 320317240000 | 2166943200 | 306009370000 | 1462427800 |
| 68 | 338891640000 | 2389108600 | 338799310000 | 2296774300 | 324641240000 | 1590671600 |
| 69 | 382737640000 | 2439946000 | 390752630000 | 2340865200 | 368669590000 | 1637503300 |
| 70 | 390857980000 | 2472911800 | 390752630000 | 2367560600 | 376962650000 | 1664627800 |
| 71 | 446908240000 | 2602488300 | 446797240000 | 2491486200 | 432127980000 | 1791564600 |
| 72 | 484611060000 | 2773953100 | 484494440000 | 2657335600 | 469026350000 | 1962121300 |
| 73 | 518043850000 | 2798579300 | 517920230000 | 2674952900 | 501369410000 | 1986651700 |
| 74 | 550491410000 | 2887163300 | 550360840000 | 2756597400 | 533686900000 | 2069877400 |
| 75 | 578522570000 | 2982793400 | 578355790000 | 2846190500 | 562633890000 | 2160665700 |
| 76 | 604777350000 | 2963660900 | 604632550000 | 2818852800 | 589230740000 | 2142246500 |
| 77 | 629760340000 | 3151044600 | 629604550000 | 2190019600 | 614091490000 | 2324624800 |
| 78 | 693253030000 | 3247925700 | 693085270000 | 2294298200 | 676127280000 | 2439954400 |
| 79 | 738758170000 | 3335226800 | 738578570000 | 2376148300 | 720652570000 | 2432865900 |
| 80 | 771976300000 | 3430928600 | 771785450000 | 2464750800 | 753518300000 | 2631788100 |

## Appendix II
# INFORMATION FOR WORK, LIVING AND ENTERTAINMENT:
## Classification Procedure for Mixed Media in the United States

Appendix II USES OF INFORMATION

### Radio Broadcasting

a. Radio was considered to supply no information for working.

b. Information for living includes news, public affairs, high culture programs, educational programs for persons over ten, commercials and other non-entertainment programs.

c. Entertainment includes entertainment shows, sports and shows for children ten and under.

### Television

a. Television was not considered to provide information directly related to working.

b. Information for living was defined to include news, public affairs, high culture programs, educational programs for persons over ten, commercials and other non-entertainment programs.

c. Entertainment includes entertainment programs, sports and programs for children ten and younger.

### Cable Television

a. Volume supplied by cable television, like those of radio and television was assumed to include only information for living and entertainment.

b. In the absence of adequate statistical breakdowns of cable television broadcasting by program types, the relevant time series for commercial television were used for the information for living vs. entertainment percents.

## Education

a. We viewed elementary and secondary school education as essentially socialization of the students, while higher education was considered to combine socialization and professional training.

b. Consequently volume supplied by elementary and secondary school education was typed completely as information for living. Volume supplied by higher education was typed as 50% information for living and 50% information for working.

## Newspapers

a. Newspapers with few exceptions, e.g., The Wall Street Journal, The Washington Post, Women's Wear Daily -- and then only for specific consumers like government officials, corporate executives -- supply only information for living and entertainment, not information for working. It was therefore necessary to estimate the percentage of an average daily newspaper's content which could be characterized as information living.

b. Information for living included: 1) news and editorial opinion concerning world, national and municipal affairs; 2) business news; 3) product advertisements, pre-printed inserts; 4) classified advertisements; 5) articles concerning food, health and consumer products; 6) reviews of high cultural events and letters.

c. Entertainment included: 1) human interest articles; 2) features, e.g., comics, movie reviews, horoscope; 3) sports; 4) entertainment advertising.

### Magazines

The original data collected on volume supplied by magazines were in the following magazine trade categories: general, trade, college, religious, agriculture, foreign language, other.

Trade and agriculture magazines can be characterized under this scheme as information for working. College and religious magazines can be judged information for living. The remaining categories, viz., general, foreign language and other, were more problematic. Magazines in the "other" category were primarily used to foster and maintain a community's or group's consciousness and thus could be characterized information for living. For general magazines an inspection of titles in a sample was used, resulting in a classification 10% for work, 56% for living and 34% for entertainment. None of the foreign language magazines could be principally information for working. The results of the title survey of general magazines were extended to the foreign language category by dividing the ten percent assigned to information for working evenly to information for living and entertainment.

## Books

a. The most frequent adequate disaggregation of yearly U.S. book sales lists units sold in the following categories: 1) Adult trade (hardbound and paperback; 2) Elementary and high school textbooks; 3) College textbooks; 4) Religious (hardbound and paperback); 5) Mail order publications and book clubs; 6) Juvenile (hardbound and paperback); 7) Professional; 8) University Press; 9) Subscription reference; 10) Others. Our strategy was to characterize each of these categories and to total the units sold yearly of books of each character. Thereby we could determine what percents of total units were information for working, information for living and entertainment respectively.

b. Information for working subsumes professional and university press books. Although the latter includes letters, art books, etc., the overwhelming bulk of university press books are for consumption by academics and other professionals in the course of their work. A similar case was made for subscription reference. In keeping with our view of U.S. higher education as part socialization process and part professional training, we considered 50% of college textbooks to be information for working. Finally, aware that much professional and other work related literature is distributed through books clubs and the mail, we estimated that one-third of book club, mail orders and other books were information for working.

c. Information for living subsumes religious books and elementary and high school textbooks. The characterization of the latter follows our stated view of primary and secondary education as essentially a socialization process. As suggested above, 50% of college textbooks was similarly characterized. In view of the high sales of cookbooks, health books, self-improvement literature, etc., one-half of the adult trade units were considered information for living and for purposes of consistency, one-third of book club, mail order and others were so estimated.

d. Entertainment included juvenile books, mass market paperbacks, one-half of adult trade and one-third book clubs, mail order and others. This procedure possibly over-estimates the word volume of entertainment supplied by the book medium since juvenile books, a sizeable component of that type, are presumably less word dense than are books in other categories.

### Mail

a. Data for first class (and domestic air) mail was originally collected in the following categories: 1) personal correspondence; 2) greeting cards; 3) business letters; 4) financial transactions; 5) government.

b. Business letters, financial transactions and government mail were characterized as information for working.

c. Personal correspondence and greeting cards were characterized as information for living.

### Telephone

a. We considered this medium as a transmitter of information for working and information for living only. All calls originating from a residence were considered information for living. Calls from a business were considered information for working.

### Telegrams

a. All international telegrams terminating in the U.S. were classified as carrying only information for working.
b. Domestic telegrams carry both work related information and more personal correspondence. It was divided half and half.

### Mailgrams

Mailgrams were treated like domestic telegrams.

### Unmixed Media

Records and Tapes and movies are considered to be all entertainment.
Direct mail is considered to be all information for living.
Telex, Facsimile, and data communications are considered to be all information for work.

Appendix II  USES OF INFORMATION

| unit yr | RADIO M vs.ln | M vs.le | TELEVISION M vs.ln | M vs.le | CABLE M vs.ln |
|---|---|---|---|---|---|
| 60 | 25144057000 | 89068768000 | 5420946200 | 17696953000 | 5035086 |
| 61 | 27824168000 | 98294452000 | 6434569300 | 20784253000 | 6286282 |
| 62 | 31259887000 | 110018230000 | 7520711200 | 24001250000 | 8184282 |
| 63 | 35743684000 | 125462240000 | 9004468600 | 28611165000 | 10319340 |
| 64 | 39890563000 | 139535070000 | 10399613000 | 32353658000 | 13228649 |
| 65 | 45005656000 | 157015500000 | 11787076000 | 35841840000 | 17225173 |
| 66 | 48767409000 | 169524060000 | 13546157000 | 40367410000 | 23770421 |
| 67 | 53828957000 | 186445840000 | 15720475000 | 46240612000 | 35535581 |
| 68 | 56550375000 | 195149010000 | 17576403000 | 50511693000 | 52466343 |
| 69 | 65609657000 | 225728530000 | 19037096000 | 53296252000 | 75094170 |
| 70 | 66473029000 | 227401560000 | 20661730000 | 57260627000 | 104934610 |
| 71 | 77596816000 | 263694800000 | 22783923000 | 62453601000 | 134132820 |
| 72 | 83874647000 | 283265630000 | 25776699000 | 70125687000 | 163702580 |
| 73 | 89362065000 | 299917340000 | 28362411000 | 75798749000 | 215447640 |
| 74. | 95225245000 | 316878420000 | 31524886000 | 83289039000 | 279062110 |
| 75 | 112800520000 | 318524840000 | 36688832000 | 85906218000 | 391992480 |
| 76 | 113539150000 | 336715980000 | 37540618000 | 90480968000 | 449510500 |
| 77 | 118755940000 | 351541440000 | 40339736000 | 97505384000 | 537354620 |
| 78 | 136068070000 | 382426900000 | 49689945000 | 105061760000 | 655757467 |
| 79 | 143086800000 | 396900910000 | 57555467000 | 119484720000 | 831683760 |
| 80 | 147836000000 | 407433590000 | 63460532000 | 131572610000 | 968677900 |

| unit yr | M vs.le | EDUCATION M vs.ln | M vs.wk | NEWSPAPERS M vs.ln | M vs.le |
|---|---|---|---|---|---|
| 60 | 17851669 | 176421250 | 5799600 | 4846414900 | 4651920500 |
| 61 | 22287725 | 181899040 | 6318000 | 5023851381 | 4818847719 |
| 62 | 29017001 | 189994030 | 6804000 | 5257118220 | 5039415780 |
| 63 | 36586751 | 199297260 | 7273800 | 5320880550 | 5097570450 |
| 64 | 46901574 | 206111220 | 8100000 | 5703128640 | 5461277360 |
| 65 | 61071069 | 210941910 | 8958600 | 5804196900 | 5554831100 |
| 66 | 84276949 | 214683400 | 9557999 | 5859522240 | 5604435760 |
| 67 | 125989790 | 219366490 | 10384200 | 5773889250 | 5519053750 |
| 68 | 186017040 | 225481860 | 11226600 | 5675197140 | 5420680860 |
| 69 | 266242970 | 228625680 | 12117600 | 5570812410 | 5316838590 |
| 70 | 372040900 | 231650590 | 12830400 | 5443271610 | 5194299390 |
| 71 | 475561810 | 232757020 | 13154400 | 5910702750 | 5634522250 |
| 72 | 580400060 | 231786400 | 13381200 | 6313903050 | 6017471950 |
| 73 | 763859830 | 231190520 | 13802400 | 6881378940 | 6558255050 |
| 74 | 989402040 | 232484040 | 14612400 | 6917981790 | 6575667210 |
| 75 | 1175977500 | 233871380 | 15762600 | 6486163771 | 6160783230 |
| 76 | 1423449900 | 233522220 | 16362000 | 6289239558 | 5966654442 |
| 77 | 1701623000 | 232170730 | 18289800 | 6288563771 | 5951996229 |
| 78 | 2076570300 | 207694050 | 18241200 | 7076757000 | 6531775000 |
| 79 | 2633951400 | 200036310 | 18743400 | 7548170000 | 6952775000 |
| 80 | 3067480000 | 195618570 | 19602000 | 7669657000 | 7065665000 |

FREQUENTLY USED VARIABLES

| | MAGAZINES | | | BOOKS | |
|---|---|---|---|---|---|
| unit | M | M | M | M | M |
| yr | vs.ln | vs.le | vs.wk | vs.ln | vs.le |
| 60 | 640063180 | 529029860 | 336990510 | 67899780 | 142857240 |
| 61 | 657995100 | 537205700 | 343437000 | 72339672 | 146443730 |
| 62 | 666191480 | 543556310 | 346191580 | 77114378 | 147748560 |
| 63 | 686940900 | 562729000 | 354666320 | 83124076 | 150864800 |
| 64 | 705668150 | 581306880 | 361791360 | 90574150 | 157358250 |
| 65 | 711535620 | 584813660 | 363466320 | 97279952 | 161833010 |
| 66 | 736673460 | 616598290 | 399464840 | 104798560 | 166983250 |
| 67 | 755043430 | 634717060 | 434230380 | 113002870 | 172495550 |
| 68 | 764175070 | 645107420 | 463488540 | 114365410 | 169220910 |
| 69 | 770377190 | 648983340 | 492290340 | 116124880 | 166512400 |
| 70 | 780771680 | 670272560 | 523436070 | 117922336 | 169808163 |
| 71 | 747875460 | 637780190 | 520853350 | 122188305 | 169705980 |
| 72 | 724632510 | 639596710 | 518329420 | 125482251 | 169570610 |
| 73 | 694752910 | 627744020 | 514910790 | 133571580 | 173994559 |
| 74 | 706154920 | 681974310 | 524428780 | 140048747 | 179698912 |
| 75 | 670104220 | 656571840 | 520578970 | 147272568 | 185034765 |
| 76 | 658971610 | 675839420 | 574707840 | 146214676 | 175457611 |
| 77 | 648181730 | 688632170 | 634338710 | 188762169 | 162767379 |
| 78 | 880476090 | 441626702 | 690104372 | 196184888 | 172077423 |
| 79 | 946365437 | 454328714 | 723664149 | 171763431 | 200531691 |
| 80 | 960314504 | 466109654 | 754037242 | 173052312 | 208439567 |

| | | MAIL | | TELEPHONE | |
|---|---|---|---|---|---|
| unit | M | M | M | M | M |
| yr | vs.wk | vs.wk | vs.ln | vs.wk | vs.ln |
| 60 | 32611364 | 9658369 | 3996590 | 24456767 | 24002255 |
| 61 | 33271208 | 9979777 | 4129587 | 25118091 | 24679934 |
| 62 | 34345060 | 10296919 | 4260819 | 26150674 | 25736819 |
| 63 | 35894488 | 10436919 | 4318750 | 27154488 | 26758108 |
| 64 | 38694653 | 10735380 | 4442252 | 28623772 | 28250566 |
| 65 | 41133808 | 11084203 | 4586594 | 30590653 | 30248182 |
| 66 | 43876505 | 11797023 | 4881556 | 32777537 | 32481492 |
| 67 | 46862954 | 12316099 | 5096347 | 34651268 | 34404783 |
| 68 | 48871265 | 12601678 | 5214518 | 36784364 | 36633695 |
| 69 | 51054903 | 13421608 | 5553801 | 39351948 | 39362628 |
| 70 | 49190460 | 14009435 | 5797042 | 41831944 | 41940160 |
| 71 | 47517674 | 14377920 | 5949519 | 44157018 | 44264503 |
| 72 | 44088358 | 14042802 | 5810849 | 46827053 | 47060490 |
| 73 | 43938020 | 14600766 | 6041732 | 49509596 | 49815395 |
| 74 | 44015320 | 14778889 | 6115438 | 52312395 | 52693035 |
| 75 | 45314636 | 14653981 | 6063752 | 54439972 | 55514326 |
| 76 | 43864402 | 14647752 | 6061174 | 57541229 | 59016610 |
| 77 | 48390301 | 14985030 | 6200739 | 61563010 | 63430917 |
| 78 | 50293156 | 15631086 | 6468074 | 65490630 | 67929600 |
| 79 | 50767516 | 17489582 | 6698547 | 69078700 | 72067300 |
| 80 | 50060020 | 18240194 | 6970759 | 71973800 | 75224800 |

Appendix II  USES OF INFORMATION

|      | TELEGRAMS | | MAILGRAMS | |
|------|-----------|-----------|-----------|-----------|
| unit | M | M | M | M |
| yr | vs.wk | vs.ln | vs.wk | vs.ln |
| 60 | 2969 | 2661 | 0 | 0 |
| 61 | 2795 | 2485 | 0 | 0 |
| 62 | 2658 | 2342 | 0 | 0 |
| 63 | 2414 | 2089 | 0 | 0 |
| 64 | 2227 | 1909 | 0 | 0 |
| 65 | 2126 | 1811 | 0 | 0 |
| 66 | 2062 | 1742 | 0 | 0 |
| 67 | 1958 | 1638 | 0 | 0 |
| 68 | 1797 | 1532 | 0 | 0 |
| 69 | 1570 | 1298 | 0 | 0 |
| 70 | 1335 | 1072 | 0 | 0 |
| 71 | 839 | 598 | 0 | 0 |
| 72 | 673 | 454 | 69 | 70 |
| 73 | 558 | 322 | 267 | 268 |
| 74 | 467 | 232 | 715 | 716 |
| 75 | 392 | 184 | 891 | 891 |
| 76 | 349 | 146 | 1047 | 1047 |
| 77 | 331 | 130 | 1217 | 1218 |
| 78 | 333 | 135 | 1430 | 1430 |
| 79 | 320 | 129 | 1673 | 1673 |
| 80 | 304 | 120 | 1740 | 1740 |

# Index

Note: Asterisks indicate that information on the topic is contained in a table or figure on the page or section (*) cited.

books   102–06(*)
CATV   85–88(*)
communications indices   2–5
computers. *See* data communications
costs:
    books   106*
    defined   7–8
    direct mail   106*
    education   94–96*
    general figures   17–20(*)
    magazines   106*
    mail and telephone   111*
    movies, records, tapes   92*
    newspapers   99*
    print media   106*
    radio   82, 87*
data collection and interpretation   8–13, 36–41, 46–50
data communications   27–34, 117*, 118–20
education   93–96(*)
electronic media   26*–27, 58–67(*).
    *See also* individual media names
facsimile use   43, 116–17*
information consumed:
    defined   5–6
    figures and trends   10–13, 16*, 19–24(*), 42–50(*), 79*, 80*
    uses of,   72–75

information flow    16*, 46–58(*), 60*, 75*
information overload    6, 20–24, 32
information supplied:
    defined    5–6
    figures and trends    16–19(*), 24–27(*), 42–50(*), 79–81(*)
magazines    101–02*, 104*, 106*
mail:
    direct (advertising)    105–07, 106*
    first class    66*, 67*, 107–11(*)
mailgrams    112–16(*)
mass media    50–60(*), 65–67(*), 104*
    *See also* individual media names
movies    91–93(*)
newspapers    25–26, 61–63, 96–101(*)
office communications    67–72
point-to-point media    50–60(*), 65–67(*), 81*
    *See also* individual media names
print media    24–27(*), 58–66(*), 104*
    *See also* individual media names
radio broadcasting    78–83, 86*, 87*
reading rates    46–48, 71–72
records and tapes    89–90*, 92*
telegraph use    43, 46, 112–16(*)
telephone use    28, 29, 70, 109–12(*)
television broadcasting    83–87(*)
telex use    43, 112–16(*)
words, as unit of information    5–6, 38–39